D1552821

Turmoil and Transition in Boston

To Paulette

Triplets at 48

The rest of life has

Been easy

Sunny

23 Oct 13

This is a photo of me with Quincy Market as a backdrop. I'm very proud of my role in bringing that dramatic change to Boston.

Turmoil and Transition in Boston

A Political Memoir from the Busing Era

Lawrence S. DiCara

With Chris Black

Hamilton Books

A member of
ROWMAN & LITTLEFIELD
Lanham • Boulder • New York • Toronto • Plymouth, UK

Copyright © 2013 by
Lawrence S. DiCara

Hamilton Books
4501 Forbes Boulevard
Suite 200
Lanham, Maryland 20706
Hamilton Books Acquisitions Department (301) 459-3366

10 Thornbury Road
Plymouth PL6 7PP
United Kingdom

All rights reserved
Printed in the United States of America
British Library Cataloging in Publication Information Available

Library of Congress Control Number: 2013944351
ISBN: 978-0-7618-6182-9 (paperback : alk. paper)
eISBN: 978-0-7618-6183-6

Photo Credits
Walter Bibikow: DiCara in front of Quincy Market, 1980
Mayor's Office of Public Service:
DiCara & Michael Dukakis;
DiCara as City Council President;
DiCara with Mayor Kevin White
Jay Callum: Teaching at Boston Latin School
"The Soiling of Old Glory," © Stanley J. Forman
Stanley J. Forman's Pulitzer Prize-winning photograph. Boston, April 5, 1976.
Melissa Garcia: photo of three DiCara daughters on graduation day

∞™ The paper used in this publication meets the minimum
requirements of American National Standard for Information
Sciences—Permanence of Paper for Printed Library Materials,
ANSI Z39.48-1992

To Mum and Dad,
who taught me to love Boston

Contents

"For time and the world do not stand still. Change is the law of life. And those who look only to the past or the present are certain to miss the future."

President John F. Kennedy (1917-1963)
Address in the Assembly Hall at Paulskirche in Frankfurt.
June 25, 1963

"There is an ethnic ballet, slow yet certain, in every big American city that I have reported, which underlies its politics. The ballet is different in each city . . ."

Theodore H. White (1915-1986 Dorchester native)
In Search of History: A Personal Adventure

Introduction

Friends have been encouraging me to write a book for decades. It was Jamie Bush, however, my Republican friend and former student and my insurance agent, who finally convinced me it was time to do it for the sake of my three daughters. Insurance agents have a great deal of credibility when they start musing about how one never knows how long one will be around or what memories children will retain of their parents.

At night, I often sit at my desk at home and do paperwork. Whenever I look up, I see formal photographs taken of my mother's parents, both Sicilian immigrants, around the time they married in Boston in 1911. When my grandparents came to the United States more than 100 years ago, they came because this country was the land of opportunity. Next to them are photographs taken of my parents in cap and gown when each graduated from college. My parents went through college during the worst economic depression in the nation's history. Because of their commitment, their hard work and savings, their children went to Harvard, Bowdoin and Simmons. Now my three daughters can look forward to marvelous opportunities that none of us could ever have imagined at their age. I think my parents and grandparents would be so proud.

While nearly 30 years have passed since I last ran for public office, I remember those days vividly, thanks to a good memory. When in doubt, I dug through the boxes of papers, diaries and speeches I saved from that time. Serendipity brought me a collaborator, my old friend, Chris Black, a longtime Boston journalist who spends much of her summer in Marion, Massachusetts, just as I do. Our conversations come easily, because we share so much in common. As we worked, the focus surprisingly shifted from a straightforward look back at my life and political career, to become as much a book about

Boston as one about me. It should not have been a total surprise. My history is embedded in the history of my home town. I like to think that in this book, history has prevailed over the narcissism that is endemic to anyone whose name has been on a ballot!

Acknowledgments

Books do not happen by accident. They require the assistance and coopera-
tion of many. In my case, I often use a Dictaphone to put words on paper.
That has required the tolerance of my longtime administrative assistant, Pa-
tricia Flanagan (we are so close that at one point she lived next door to me on
Burroughs Street), as well as Priscilla McDonald, Michelle Westhaver, and
Pam DiBella at Nixon Peabody.

Anyone who knows me realizes that I am always full of stories about our
three charming and opinionated young daughters. Catherine, Sophie and
Flora have heard many of the stories which will fill these pages many times.
I suspect they can each tell the tale of the Blizzard of '78 almost verbatim.

A word about my wife, Teresa Spillane: Teresa was an editor long before
she was a psychologist. Another author has acknowledged that it is necessary
that any introduction refer to thanking spouses and family "for putting up
with them through the grueling process of writing this book." How very true.
Ours has been an evolving relationship, now in the midst of its third decade.
I might have been able to write this book had I not been married to Teresa,
but I doubt it would have been as incisive or revealing.

I also called upon my brother, Vin; my old friends, Jim Dolan and Pat
Landers; as well as Tim Smith, my personal attorney, to review this text.
Peter Meade, a longtime friend who is now director of the Boston Redevelopment Authority, and the BRA's talented Director of Research, Alvaro Lima,
provided some demographic data which helped to make the case about the
remarkable changes that have taken place in Boston in recent years. I always
knew that my political fortunes were mirrored in the demographic changes
taking place in Boston in the 1970s. My daughter Sophie did the research to
show the ward by ward analysis of the votes I received in different elections
to demonstrate the correlation between my vote and the changes taking place

in the Electorate,as well as other valuable research. It was extremely helpful data and I was particularly delighted that one of my own daughters shares my affinity for raw political data. James Sutherland, a doctoral student at Northeastern University, was also very helpful in assembling data. JoAnne Deitch edited the text and got it ready for publication. She was very patient and supportive. I would also like to thank my partner, Mark Robins, for his legal guidance and thanks to the folks at Hamilton Books for their patience with a rookie. I deeply appreciate all their efforts.

Elected officials frequently do not realize when history is being made or when the old order is giving way to the new. Historians can also miss these seismic shifts, which only become apparent with the passage of time and the perspective of experience and age. I suspect this is true of most of us who lived through the tumultuous era in the history of Boston in the last third of the 20th century.

This book focuses on a time in Boston's history when I was in the room, at the table, in the trenches, present at the creation. You can pick your own phrase. My first election in 1971 and last election in 1983 are bookends to a remarkable transition in Boston's history. As I look back now with far more clarity than I had at the time, I can see that the political leadership and decisions made in that era contributed to the renaissance of a city that was once grouped with Detroit as a city past its prime. That time also saw the acceleration of the demographic trends that led to a more diverse, more affluent, more international Boston in a matter of decades. Change was often wrenching in Boston, but a stronger city emerged out of that pain and turmoil. Change is constant in great cities, and Boston is not an exception to that rule. I hope others can learn from our experiences.

Many professors, reporters and other authors have written extensively and well about Boston and this particular era. This book draws upon my first hand personal knowledge. I had little interest in revenge, but the passage of time and the passing of many of the important characters unquestionably give me the freedom to be more candid. Now I can tell, as the radio commentator says, "the rest of the story."

Lawrence S. DiCara
Boston, Massachusetts
2013

The Fight of My Life

To understand why I remember exactly where I was on the night of October 21, 1975, I need to explain a few things first. The Boston Red Sox played the Cincinnati Reds that night in Game 6 of the World Series. The Sox were playing at home at Fenway Park. The game was completely sold out, but I had two precious tickets. Red Sox fans are famous for their passion and loyalty, despite a painfully long stretch of losing seasons dating back to when the Sox owners sold the legendary Babe Ruth to the New York Yankees in 1919. Dan Shaughnessy, a great sports writer at The Boston Globe, wrote a book called *The Curse of the Bambino* that described the troubled history of the franchise after the Babe, the Bambino, left town. The relationship between the Boston Red Sox and its fans is like a longstanding but rocky love affair. We are committed to one another and nurse high hopes for the relationship, but for nearly one hundred years those hopes were never realized. Instead, the giddy promise born each spring shrivels and dies, usually in a devastating slump in August or September, year after year. The team truly seemed cursed. Yet the fans stuck around, suckers for punishment. Love cannot be denied. Every baseball season dawned with hope and ended in crushing disappointment. As a faithful fan, I ride that roller coaster every year.

I am blessed with an excellent memory and I can remember almost everything about the Red Sox dating back to my boyhood in the 1950s. The 1975 season was particularly exciting. Red Sox World Series aspirations ended the year before with a devastating swoon in August. But 1975 was different. The Sox actually made it to the Series. And Carlton Fisk hit a famous home run in the 12th inning of Game 6 to win the game 7-6 on the night of October 21. He and 35,205 out of their mind spectators willed it to stay fair. It did. That game went down as one of the greatest games ever played in baseball history . . . but I missed it.

I had given up my Red Sox tickets to work a small crowd of yuppies at a candidates' night sponsored by the Ellis Neighborhood Association in the South End of Boston. I was a candidate for reelection to the Boston City Council and I needed every single one of those votes. In the 19th century, the South End had been envisioned as a high fashion, high rent neighborhood—only a short walk from the downtown business district. However, the neighborhood hit hard times within decades of original construction and deteriorated into a slum: a district of shabby tenements and rooming houses, a few great jazz clubs, many aromatic sleazy bars, and a small but stalwart battalion of hookers who worked in the shadows of the ugly metal elevated rail tracks, the old "El," that ran down Washington Street to Forest Hills.

By the 1960s, a number of starry eyed urban pioneers, including a significant number of gay men, recognized the value and beauty of the elegant Victorian bow front houses and moved into the neighborhood. The so-called yuppies, young urban professionals, bought the red brick buildings and painstakingly restored to their original glory the lovely Renaissance Revival, Italianate and French Second Empire structures. By 1975, these new residents were changing the demographics and the voting patterns of Ward 4. I knew this because demographics and voting patterns were an important part of my business. The arcane specialty had fascinated me since my teenage years. Demographics is destiny in politics. More importantly, at this moment, these new voters were my supporters. They were well educated, affluent and politically liberal. If I was to win reelection, it would be on the strength of their support. So that is why I was mingling with a small group of young urban pioneers at a candidates' night in the South End and not watching the Red Sox at Fenway Park.

As the Red Sox struggled for glory in that autumn of 1975, I was in the political fight of my life in my second reelection campaign to the Boston City Council. I had finished in 7th place in the voting in the September preliminary election, exactly where I finished in my very first run for public office four years earlier. Boston municipal elections are "nonpartisan," because the overwhelming Democratic Party registration would assure victory to the Democratic candidate. To mix it up and provide some competition, everyone runs without a party label. The preliminary election cuts the field down to manageable size. Although not totally unexpected given the political climate that September, it was a crushing personal disappointment to finish 7th. I could only think that everything I had done in four relentlessly busy years in public office provided absolutely no benefit to my career and I was skidding very, very close to finishing out of the money, below 9th place in November. Moreover, I had leapfrogged ahead of many of my peers with my election to the Boston City Council in 1971. While many of my friends were still trying to figure out a career path, I had seemingly arrived. But four years and two citywide campaigns later, many of my friends had graduated from law school and were moving ahead of me in both their careers and their personal lives. I bought a lot of wedding gifts that year. My friends were finding love and success. I felt an overwhelming sense that I was losing ground, even as I worked harder and harder—so hard I had ended up secretly hospitalized from exhaustion two years earlier.

Let me step back for a moment to explain how this came about. In 1975, I should have been on top of the world. I was 26 years old, an at-large member of the Boston City Council. I had won the seat just months after I graduated from Harvard, that in itself a significant achievement for any boy from Dorchester. I was the youngest person ever elected to the Boston City Council at the age of 22, with more than 61,000 votes. I was the first Baby Boomer ever elected to the council. I was the first Italian to win a citywide slot, without having roots in one of the traditional Italo-American wards of the North End or East Boston. Two years later in my first reelection campaign, I came within 4,000 votes of topping the ticket in the city election. My first election triggered a spate of publicity describing me as a "new face" of politics in Boston, a real political whiz kid. I was being interviewed by the top reporters in Boston. Michael S. Dukakis, who later served three terms as governor and was the Democratic Presidential candidate in 1988, asked me to run for lieutenant governor before my 25th birthday. Mayor Kevin White tried to persuade me to join his administration as Commissioner of Parks and Recreation, and I had spent a few months running for Secretary of State, the job Kevin White used as a stepping stone to the mayoralty a decade earlier. I was single, "an eligible bachelor" by the standards of the time; well educated; and a member of the governing body for my hometown. I was a political success in an intensely political city where many residents still associated a political career and contacts with upward mobility and the ability to claim some small corner of the American Dream.

I should have been on top of the political world, at the top of my game, but that was hardly the case. The outward veneer of success proved to be a tinny cover for a young man who found himself whipsawed by forces far beyond his control. I still harbored high ambitions and hopes in 1975 and I ended up surviving that election. Only much later did I realize that I had been living on borrowed time that election season. My narrow victory in November just delayed the inevitable. I slogged on and kept working and trying and reaching; but eight years later my political career was over.

Looking back at that ambitious young man, it would be easy to see a political cliché: the grandson of immigrants who achieved success his forebears could not have imagined. I was a young man in a big hurry, brimming with the confidence of youth and plenty of hubris. However, the benefit of hindsight also shows me that my political career took place at a critical period in modern Boston history. Theodore White, the great historian who came of age in Boston, wrote eloquently of the urban ballet, the ever changing dance of ethnicities and races that takes place in American cities. It is a dance that literally never stops. Between 1971, when I won my first election, and 1981, when I left the Boston City Council voluntarily, and 1983, my final campaign—an unsuccessful campaign for mayor—the tempo of the dance accelerated.

My ten years on the Boston City Council proved to be the most challenging of my life. My political career coincided with a pivotal transitional time in Boston's storied history. While I held public office, Boston was ripped apart by racial turmoil and division. The famous "City on a Hill" envisioned by John Winthrop, the first governor of Massachusetts, as he sailed to the new world, turned into a seething sea of anger, resentment and violence. Transitions can be traumatic and this one certainly was. However, forces unleashed and decisions made in the 1970s set the city on a very different course to the future. The demographic changes speeded up by accelerated "white flight" in mid-decade and political leaders' responses to fiscal pressures transformed Boston into a more diverse, more affluent and more inclusive city. But the transformative process itself was not pretty and it helped to end my political dreams. My story is inexplicably part of the story of my hometown, Boston.

The 1960s and 1970s marked a time of enormous social change and political ferment in the United States. The anti-Vietnam war movement, the women's movement, the Civil Rights movement, and the fledgling gay rights movement, roiled American society. Traditional roles, behaviors and expectations on gender, in marriages, between races, among work colleagues and between neighbors were in flux and changed almost overnight. At Harvard, for example, when I enrolled as a freshman and moved into Pennypacker 45, dorm room visits by members of the opposite sex were tightly regulated. By the time we graduated four years later, the university janitors were doing a robust business selling full-sized mattresses to make it more comfortable for girl or boy friends to stay overnight.

At the same time, the United States economy had already begun to shift from one based upon brawn to one based upon brains, leaving behind the least educated and many in the working class. Much later, in 2008, Democratic presidential candidate Barack Obama took a lot of heat when he described working class voters as clinging to their guns and religion. He might have used more delicate language to characterize the reaction of the working poor to severe socioeconomic pressure, but he was essentially correct in his analysis. The economic transition in the United States badly hurt the workers who played by the traditional rules, stayed in the old neighborhood, graduated from the public high school and labored at a job at the telephone company or the electric light company or the post office for 40 years before retiring with a small but adequate pension. Their response to the tsunami of social and economic change was to hunker down and hang on to the familiar and demand that everything stay the same. This was futile. Nothing ever stays the same, particularly in urban America where change is as constant as the tides lapping Dorchester Bay.

When Federal Judge W. Arthur Garrity issued a busing order forcing poor white students to attend school in poor black neighborhoods and shifting poor black students from majority black schools in black neighborhoods to lousy white schools in white neighborhoods in 1974 and 1975, many of the white working class people and voters of Boston rebelled. An earthquake of social and economic change shifted the ground beneath and all around them and the white community struggled to make sense of any of it and retain control over their own lives. They looked for scapegoats to blame. Then as now, "others," minority group members, the unfamiliar people who lived across town, took the heat. It was no longer possible to drop out of high school and get a decent paying and steady job with benefits at Gillette or any of the smoke stack companies that once dominated Northeastern cities. They had to blame someone. After all, they had played by the rules that had governed their communities and families for generations. Working class black people also experienced tremendous anxiety and upheaval, though they attracted far less public notice at the time.

As the world and economy changed, the traditional lifestyle and traditional institutions in the old neighborhood became increasingly important to those left behind. They rose up to protect what they viewed as theirs and their way of life. I understood the impulse. I grew up in a traditional Boston neighborhood, too, and treasure to this day my boyhood experiences and memories. But my Ivy League education afforded me a broader perspective. As an undergraduate, I wrote an honors thesis on Hispanic students and bilingual education in the Boston Public Schools. I knew that the Boston School Committee had deliberately kept black students in black schools and white students in white schools. There was *de facto* segregation in Boston, a division by ethnic group and race that evolved over time because of the impulse among immigrants and racial minorities to live together in ethnic and racial conclaves—the same pattern seen in other older American cities. *De facto* segregation is not necessarily illegal because it evolves from neighborhood residential patterns. But the Boston School Department actively fostered segregation; this is known as *de jure* segregation. This was deliberate segregation. It was racist, illegal and wrong. It was also unnecessary. It was possible at many junctures to integrate the schools without the heartbreak that ensued. Men and women of good will could have done it. Anyone who was honest knew this, even at the time.

I grew up fairly straitlaced, the proverbial "good boy" who did as he was told and expected. There were plenty of racially tolerant people in Boston including my parents. One of my best friends at Boston Latin School was Arnie Waters, an African-American who lived at 144 Worcester Street in the South End. Arnie had only one arm because of a birth defect, but made up for his disability with a great mind and a gift for gab. He was my debate partner at Boston Latin School. It did not seem strange at all to me to have a black friend. Latin School drew the best and the brightest from every corner of the city. It was not only the oldest public school in the United States of America; it was the best public school in Boston, a prestigious exam school, where merit was everything. I have long realized that political leaders exacerbated the racial divisions in Boston because my experience at Latin School showed me that Bostonians of different backgrounds and races could be together, study together, and strive together without enmity or fear.

It was impossible for me to live with my conscience and play ball with the most rabid and powerful antibusing group, Restore Our Alienated Rights, better known by its aggressive acronym ROAR. Not embracing ROAR and its agenda nearly cost me my political career in 1975. The racial tensions rose so high in 1974 and 1975 that priests, including priests from St. Gregory's, my own parish, were participating in antibusing marches. People whom I had known my entire life refused for the first time to post one of my campaign signs in their front yards. Neighbors looked me in the eye and said they could not vote for me. The bad feelings from that campaign lingered so long that some old neighbors from the parish have not spoken to me for nearly 40 years. There is an old expression that the Irish forget everything except the grudge. I can attest to that. At the time, I was obsessed with the fear of losing my council seat and being deemed a failure.

1975 can only be described as an ugly year. Many agree with me that 1975 was the worst campaign, if not the worst year, in the modern history of Boston. It was ugly for many reasons. President Richard M. Nixon had resigned the previous summer, in August of 1974, after the Watergate deceit became exposed. Almost overnight, the United States seemed to lose faith in politics and government as a vehicle for positive change. The Arab Oil Embargo in 1973-74 sent shock waves through the economy. The price of a gallon of gasoline went from 30 cents to $1.20. Anyone would kill for $1.20 a gallon gasoline today, but back then it was the first indication that being dependent upon unreliable sources of foreign oil might not be such a great idea. Nixon banned gasoline sales on Sunday and lines of automobiles snaked for blocks around gasoline stations, waiting for rationed gas on the other six days of the week. Massachusetts members of Congress were so worried about the economic decline of the region they actually created a special Northeast-Midwest Coalition with colleagues from the Midwest who were also watching auto and steel jobs disappear, triggering severe economic dislocation in their districts.

The Vietnam War ended badly, leaving a sour taste behind. Returning soldiers, many draftees from the working class neighborhoods of Boston, many of them friends of mine, came home addicted to drugs and suffering from Post Traumatic Stress Disorder, which was little understood at the time. They often found themselves ostracized and jobless and unfairly blamed for the first war America had "lost." Many understandably self-medicated with alcohol and drugs. We understand this now, but back then they were treated unfairly by both their neighbors and the government which sent them to war.

Inflation was causing the price of everyday basics—food, milk, and bread—to soar. Property values in Boston sagged. In 1975, a suspicious series of fires took place that later was exposed as the devastating Symphony Road Arson ring responsible for more than 95 arson fires in the city. Landlords made more from insurance payoffs after a fire than from renting or selling their buildings. Upward mobility had seemingly stopped. Government payrolls were shrinking because of limited tax revenues, so the fallback jobs at the courthouse, at City Hall, at the local school dried up. The city was like a gas stove with a broken vent. Judge Garrity's busing order flicked a match into the stove. Boston blew up and I almost blew up with it.

The racial tension so visible in the antibusing protests was only one of the stresses on me that year. I was desperately unhappy. I was working full-time, campaigning non-stop, delivering speeches everywhere I could throughout Massachusetts, attending law school, and living in the attic of my parents' house in Dorchester. I was broke and worried incessantly about being able to pay my tuition bills and campaign expenses. Then, as now, I hated to ask anyone for money. Except for the six or so hours I slept each night and an hour or so I spent showering, shaving and dressing, I rushed from breakfast meeting to hearing to coffee klatches, lunches, appointments, events, times and parties. I never stopped. It may have sounded like fun. Yet I was lonely, exhausted and becoming more disillusioned by the day. The private reality of Larry DiCara in 1975 could not have been more different from the public image of the confident up and comer. Of course, I was still idealistic, ambitious and imbued with the blind self-confidence of youth. I still hoped to be elected Mayor of Boston some day and could not think of a single reason why that would not happen if I worked hard and played by the political rules that had governed Boston since long before my birth.

I had broken down politics to the nitty gritty of wards, precincts, ethnic groups, and votes. I could accurately predict the outcome of nearly any election in my hometown. However, that knowledge, hard work and ambition would not be enough. The rules were changing for me, too. My idealism and ambitions collided with the gritty reality of urban America during a decade of tumultuous and irreparable change. In the end, that transformation was about a lot more than me and my dreams. Some have suggested I may have been ahead of my time as a progressive Italian-American candidate. Perhaps, although to paraphrase the late George McGovern, the 1972 presidential candidate who lost in a landslide to Richard Nixon who was forced to resign two years later, I may have just had lousy timing. But as I look back, I can see that the social and economic trends that led to the prosperous Boston we see today began during that troubled time. Let me tell you what happened.

I grew up in Dorchester, a working class, heavily Irish-Catholic neighborhood that hugs the harbor and stretches south. Dorchester is a diverse and sprawling neighborhood. It is still identified by Catholic parishes, a vestige of the immigrant Catholic Church culture that dominated Boston from the late 19th century through much of the 20th century. The potato famine in Ireland set off an enormous diaspora as millions of poor starving Irish men and women left their homeland for the United States. Hundreds of thousands ended up in Boston. In 1847, the first big year of famine emigration, 37,000 Irish Catholics moved to Boston. At the time, the city population was only 115,000. Think about the impact those poor desperate people had on the city in a single year. The good Catholics reproduced at a steady clip changing the city from a WASP enclave to a heavily Irish city within decades. Political power followed demographic change. Hugh O'Brien, the first Irish born Mayor, was sworn into office in 1885. By the year of my birth, the Irish had been in control of the government in Boston for a solid 65 years.

St. Gregory's Parish is the oldest Catholic Church in Dorchester and one of the oldest Catholic parishes in Boston. It was built despite aggressive opposition from bigots, such as the Know Nothings, the anti-Catholic, anti-immigrant movement which actively opposed and loathed the hordes of immigrants moving into the city in the mid-19th century. These nativist bigots literally burned down one early parish church building and torched an Ursuline convent in Charlestown in another famous episode. But the immigrants had numbers and tenacity on their side.

The parish of St. Gregory's is so large that it includes many neighborhoods. It also enjoys an intensely political history and counts many successful politicians as parishioners. Boston has so changed in recent years that it is easy to forget how much the Irish still dominated Boston and its governing institutions then. I remember as a boy being impressed by the sight of Mayor John

B. Hynes alighting from a big black sedan in front of the church to attend Sunday Mass. Mayor Hynes lived a few doors away from Eddie McCormack, the state Attorney General, the son of "Knocko" McCormack, a well-known political figure, and the nephew of U.S. House Speaker John McCormack. McCormack lived two streets away from former state Attorney General, Francis "Sweepstakes" Kelly, the politician who first proposed the state lottery in Massachusetts. Later, Gerry O'Leary, my colleague on the City Council and later a member of the Boston School Committee, lived in the parish, as did Joe Timilty, scion of a political family whose uncle served as Police Commissioner, who became a state senator and ran unsuccessfully for mayor three times. Timilty then lived in the Mattapan section of the city, but St. Gregory's was so large, it encompassed part of that neighborhood, too. At one point we had two City Councilors and two State Senators living in our parish.

Politics was an integral part of the fabric of Dorchester. Every kid in the neighborhood distributed leaflets door to door, stuffed envelopes with flyers before elections, and gathered for Election Day rallies and parties. We grew up listening to our parents analyze candidates, elections and politics. Politics was part of our DNA. Politicians were people to be emulated.

For those of my generation there was another role model: John Fitzgerald Kennedy, the first Roman Catholic President—a young, charismatic, Irish Catholic from a big Boston family. We thought John Kennedy was a god. I took a cover photograph of John F. Kennedy from the *Saturday Evening Post*, clipped off the mailing label, and hung it on the wall in our attic. It hung there untouched like a religious icon until our family sold the house in 2001.

Boston was not only very Irish; it was very tribal back then. I remember one incident in July 1975. Kevin White had hired Bob diGrazia to be police commissioner several years earlier. It was a very unpopular choice. DiGrazia was not only professional and independent-minded but also from out of town, and he was most definitely not Irish. He had a mandate to reform the department and he went to town and instituted sweeping changes in the operation of the department including promotional exams. One day, Joseph V. Saia, a deputy police superintendent and a career police officer who had a very successful and long career in the department, inexplicably authorized a motorcycle police escort for the funeral of Giovannina Angiulo, the 82 year old mother of Gennaro "Jerry" Angiulo, head of the New England Mafia. The escort led the procession from the North End all the way through Somerville and Medford to Malden. DiGrazia ordered Saia removed from his position and demoted. To put it mildly, a police escort for the mother of the most notorious mob boss in the region was unacceptable. Italians across the city objected vigorously to the punishment. So the Boston City Council voted 7-1 with one abstention to demand that diGrazia appear before them and explain himself or else be fired. I was the lone negative vote. From my standpoint, diGrazia was doing his job and Deputy Superintendent Saia's conduct was unacceptable. It was also completely inappropriate for the City Council to second guess a personnel decision by the police commissioner. A few months later, I was campaigning in Roslindale and a couple aggressively confronted me and accused me of being "anti-Italian!" But Ian Menzies, a Boston Globe columnist, noticed I refused to go along with my colleagues. He wrote: "The City Council's harassment of diGrazia, Councilor DiCara being an exception, is predictable and reflective of that body's personal politics, vendettas and lack of class." My brother Vinny sent me a nice note from Maine saying at least one person on the Boston City Council had integrity!

Even the traditional feel good events soured in 1975. The tension in the city felt like a living thing. It was omnipresent, hanging like the morning fog over the entire city. There were certain expectations for politicians then as now. I was expected to show up at the wakes and funerals of constituents, for example. I will never forget the drizzly Friday, a day that the Irish grandmothers would describe as a day the heavens wept, at the end of June in 1972, when the city said goodbye to eight of the nine Boston firefighters killed in a tragic fire at the Vendome in Back Bay. The building collapsed when they were inside. It was a huge loss for the city. Watching those eight caskets, each one followed by a grieving family, come down the aisle at the Cathedral of the Holy Cross, the largest Roman Catholic Church in New England, one after the other after the other was simply wrenching. (The ninth firefighter was a Protestant who was buried separately.) The MBTA suspended service on the Orange Line for the three hours of the funeral service because the elevated was still running above Washington Street next to the cathedral.

I was also expected to march in parades. The Bunker Hill Day Parade on June 17 to commemorate the anniversary of the Siege of Boston in 1775 during the war for independence was one. The Dorchester Day Parade in June was essential. Other can't miss parades were the St. Patrick's Day Parade in March, when the weather can still be brutally cold, and the Columbus Day Parades in the North End or East Boston in October.

In 1975, the parades were particularly difficult. Busing sparked many threats against most of the authority figures of the day. I knew parade day could be problematic. In 1973 before the Bunker Hill Day parade, the Boston Police received a telephone threat that an Italian member of the Boston City Council was going to be shot in Charlestown. There were four Italians on the Boston City Council that year: Christopher Iannella, Fred Langone, Gabe Piemonte, and me.

Chris was born in 1913; a gentle soul and a true gentleman of the old school, and the threat absolutely terrified him. He went home. Fred was a tough old bird and shrugged it off. Gabe had announced his retirement and had skipped the parade. I was imbued by the sense of invincibility of the young and never really believed anything bad would happen to me so I forged ahead and walked with Freddy. An older overweight Boston cop was assigned to guard us through the parade route. He huffed, puffed and sweated up and down those hills in Charlestown and I'm quite sure was too exhausted to protect either one of us had an assassin suddenly leapt out of the crowd.

In retrospect, I have assumed the threat was aimed at Gabriel Piemonte. Gabe was another old school pol who served on the Boston City Council for 20 years between 1952 and 1972, with a couple of interruptions to run for other offices. His family operated a successful car wash called One Two Three Car Wash at 294 Causeway Street, an all-cash business that was clearly lucrative, until the city took the premises through an eminent domain proceeding in 1970. I presume the family did well by that transaction. When the Boston Redevelopment Authority advertised a parcel in Charlestown for development the following year, the Piemonte family submitted a proposal to build a car wash on the site. A group of activists led by Gus Charbonnier in Charlestown opposed the car wash. I supported Gus and his neighbors. Piemonte and I never did get along. He never forgave me for opposing his family's car wash.

Charlestown and South Boston were the centers of the most intense, most emotional and most violent antibusing activists.

During the 1975 campaign, our campaign workers were often confronted by antibusing groups, including "Powder Keg" in Charlestown. One day, two of my campaign workers, John H. Knowles, Jr., and Mark Roosevelt, both Harvard students and descendants of prominent nationally known families, were caught driving a foreign car with a DiCara bumper sticker and District of Columbia license plates in the middle of a Powder Keg demonstration. I am still amazed they got out alive.

East Boston, the traditionally Italian neighborhood linked to the city through a tunnel that ran underneath Boston Harbor, would have reacted like their fellow citizens across the water. The "Eastie" activists threatened to blow up the tunnel linking the city to Logan Airport. I'm not completely convinced that is what got East Boston exempted from the busing order, but I have to believe it was an element. There are many who are convinced the threat is precisely what got the neighborhood out of the busing loop. The Judge denied he was cowed by the threat. He claimed that he was committed to limiting bus rides to 15 minutes and East Boston was too far away to fall within the time limit.

South Boston had never been a strong area of support for me. It was heavily Irish and had few of the types of voters who tended to go for someone who was younger and more liberal, least of all Italian. I had some great individual supporters. The Burke brothers who lived on Logan Way, one of the public housing projects, distributed leaflets for me, but did it in the dead of night under cover of darkness so no one would see them. They were very matter of fact about that strategic approach. Who was I to argue; they had to live there.

People are invariably surprised to learn that St. Patrick's Day is an official holiday in Boston. The holiday actually marks Evacuation Day, the March day General George Washington and the Continental Army forced the British to end the occupation of Boston during the Revolutionary War. But for all intents and purposes, the Irish-Americans who settled in Boston had become so populous by the turn of the 20th century that they hijacked the holiday. St. Patrick is the patron saint of Ireland, the missionary who allegedly drove the snakes (symbolizing the devil) out of the island, and is also the patron saint of the Archdiocese of Boston. Of course, everything in Boston shut down for the holiday. The first Evacuation Day/St. Patrick's Day Parade was held in 1901 to mark the 125th anniversary of the military victory. The parade features the usual gamut of high school and college bands, floats, community organizations, and every politician in the city. John, Bobby and Ted Kennedy had marched in the St. Patrick's Day Parade. So did I. It was not so much a rite of passage as a necessity, particularly for candidates on the city ballot. I just could not blow off this parade.

By March of 1975, the antibusing sentiment had bubbled into an unprecedented level of violence and ugliness. Judge Garrity issued his ruling on June 21, 1974, and Phase I had begun the previous fall. Phase II was looming. School buses had been under attack. Police officers lined up to protect black students as they raced from the bus to the school buildings in Charlestown and South Boston. The Boston Globe installed bullet proof glass on the windows of its newsroom facing the Southeast Expressway after a disgruntled reader blasted out one of them with a shotgun. There were school boycotts and wild demonstrations. Many of those in the antibusing movement compared their cause to the civil rights movement. They were convinced that if they stuck together and made enough noise and demanded change, it would happen. Somehow, a federal judge would reverse himself or be overruled. There is something poignant about their implacable faith in the system all these years later.

So St. Patrick's Day in 1975 promised to be a particularly rowdy celebration because South Boston residents needed to let off some steam. The St. Patrick's Day holiday is an excuse to drink a great amount of alcohol. Drunken revelers can turn from friendly and jovial to hostile and threatening in a heartbeat. This makes it a tough parade for politicians, even when they like you. If they don't, it is far worse. The parade used to begin at Andrew

Square, named after John A. Andrew, the Massachusetts governor who served during the Civil War and is credited with the establishment of the 54th Regiment Massachusetts Volunteer Infantry, one of the legendary infantry units made up of free black soldiers. The parade makes its way down the length of South Boston to City Point, turns around and heads back down Broadway.

So while I was understandably uneasy about walking the parade route through Southie, it never occurred to me not to be there. Requesting police protection would make me look like a wimp. So Chip Daley, one of my friends, a tough street smart city guy, tucked a lead pipe up his right sleeve and hovered a few feet away from me every step of the way, ready for whatever came my way. Except for a couple of boos and shouts of "nigger lover," I got through the ordeal in one piece. Finally I reached Perkins Square, a corner at the intersection of Dorchester Street and Broadway named for Private First Class Michael Perkins, a Medal of Honor recipient from World War I. By Perkins Square the last stretch of the parade route included some of the most boisterous bar rooms in South Boston. I knew I could safely disappear at that point because I had the excellent example of Councilor John E. Kerrigan. Kerrigan served on the Boston City Council between 1933 and 1973. He was a bachelor who lived in Southie. He became Acting Mayor when Mayor Maurice Tobin was elected Governor in 1945. He then ran for Mayor himself, but lost to James Michael Curley. Kerrigan always wore a hat and when he got to Perkins Square, he would tip his fedora and say "See you tomorrow, boys," and drop out of the parade because he claimed the last stretch was dominated by drunks and nonvoters. I probably should have thanked Chip for the support, veered off and bolted for Dorchester and safety. But I did not follow Kerrigan's example. Perhaps foolishly, I walked down that stretch of South Boston which held the angriest white people in the city. In my defense, I was 25 years old and not as prudent as I would be years later.

Because I had refused to join my other eight colleagues in supporting the antibusing movement and ROAR, I became more politically isolated. ROAR had so much clout it held its meetings in the City Council Chamber and could count on the votes of 8 of the 9 city councilors and most of the state legislators from Boston. In the 1975 city campaign, ROAR purchased a full page advertisement on the back of a section of The Boston Globe and endorsed the reelection of every incumbent member of the Boston City Council, except for me. The isolation was ever present, like a cold wind blowing off Boston Harbor in the dead of winter. I was not completely without supporters and allies. The Boston Teacher's Union named me Legislator of the Year that spring and presented me with a beautiful Paul Revere silver bowl. It was entirely possible I received the award by a process of elimination. I treasure that bowl and keep it in a place of honor in my home.

The prospect of being defeated just scared me to death. I was slogging through the final classes needed for my law degree and felt I was not doing very well in my studies. It was hard to focus on my classes and impossible to find enough time to study. I worried about my ability to pass the Bar Exam and pay my last tuition bills. I was in a real funk.

This is all by way of explaining why I gave up those precious World Series tickets. Boston is a sports town with world class franchises, including the Boston Bruins hockey team, the Boston Celtics basketball team and the New England Patriots football team. But the Boston Red Sox are special. Boston is a maniacal baseball town. When I was a boy in the 1950s and 1960s, baseball was the playground game of choice. I played baseball with my pals at Walsh Park in Dorchester and collected baseball cards with the avidity of a fanatic. We all did, but my brother Vinny and I were unusual among our peers: we collected the cards of great African-American players, too. Most of the boys only wanted the cards of the white players. It is one of those telling details from my youth that set me apart. My parents were extremely good and tolerant people and raised me and my brother and sister to respect everyone regardless of gender, color or ethnicity. I suppose part of that was a survival instinct of being Italian-American in a heavily Irish-American city. We experienced a sense of being "other," not nearly as difficult as black people living in a white society, but Boston was still an overwhelmingly Irish city, and I had a tiny taste of what it is like to be different from the majority in Dorchester because I was of Italian descent and everyone else was Irish. All my friends could tell you their grandparents were born in County Mayo or Cork or Clare in the old country. "Which county?" was often the first question asked after introductions, meaning which Irish county did your parents or grandparents hail from. Little girls routinely signed up for Irish step dancing classes if their parents could afford the lessons.

When I was a Cub Scout leader, I discovered that many of the young scouts did not know how to swim. This was stunning, given they lived on the Atlantic Ocean, but not unusual among the urban working class. So I rented the pool at the local YMCA for $20 an hour and arranged for lessons for the boys. The scouts needed to be schooled in proper indoor pool etiquette so I instructed them to bring bathing suits, towels, soap and a change of clothes and told them all to shower before entering the pool, the established practice. I remember one day Patrick Joyce, who was probably 8 years old at the time, one of a large family of red heads, told me that his family used Irish Spring soap because they were Irish. His parents, Mike and Margie, wonderful and decent people, were from Ireland. He asked me if I was Irish. When I said I was not, he was totally perplexed. "What are you then?" he asked. That story reminds me of how insular the neighborhoods could be in those days.

So my brother Vinny and I assembled an impressive collection of Willie Mays, Hank Aaron, Larry Doby and Roy Campanella cards that are now worth a lot of money. My mother, bless her heart, saved every one.

To someone who had watched Ted Williams as a young man and who has jumped at nearly every opportunity to get to Fenway for more than 50 years, giving up World Series tickets was almost unthinkable. But I was so afraid that I might lose, with all the political lumber lining up against me, that I simply could not consider doing anything except campaigning. I campaigned as hard as I could and prayed to survive so I could fight again in a better time.

That election year is when I realized that politics was not about adulation, drinking up the respect and praise of the people the way I thought when I had seen John Fitzgerald Kennedy on television speaking to enormous adoring crowds. I finally understood that there were some situations that not even the brightest and most driven people can resolve. I could not read a book and find the answers. In my mid-20s, I now questioned this world of which I had so yearned to be a part. I heard the whispers about how cash in an envelope was the way to get your budget through the Council Ways and Means Committee. The political universe had survived, prospered and endured because things had stayed the same. But stopping change in a vibrant American city is as feasible as stopping the tide from washing onto Tenean Beach, that sandy patch in Dorchester. Even the U.S. Census, the head count of every American citizen taken every ten years, is described as a snapshot of a moving train. In fact, Boston has never stopped changing. Every neighborhood has undergone changes throughout the decades as new immigrants arrived and more established ethnic groups moved on to those greener pastures in the suburbs. Now, with the perspective gained by 30 more years, I see that my outsider status gave me an unusual perch from which to witness the beginning of a transformation that ultimately "saved" Boston. At the time, I certainly did not see it that way. I had hooked my hopes on a conventional political path of upward mobility. Now, everything was changing and so was I.

From Sicily to Dorchester

A child growing up in the 1950s breathed in hope and optimism along with oxygen. The very air seemed aspirational. The Second World War was over, the deep deprivation of the Great Depression lingered only in memory, and the postwar prosperity generated opportunity and a cornucopia of consumer goods that amazed our immigrant grandparents. Life was so much easier and more comfortable for us than it had been for them and for our parents. We had nowhere to go but up and the future looked as limitless as the clear blue sky over Dorchester Bay.

I grew up in a very different Boston from the city most of us know today. Boston was then a very blue-collar city, and it was a very Catholic city. Churches were packed. It was a city of neighborhood institutions. There were many American Legion posts and Knights of Columbus halls. My neighborhood was fairly typical. The U.S. Census conducted in 1950, the year after my birth, shows South Dorchester was very working class, family-oriented and white. (Boston's population was 94.7 percent white in 1950.) Of the 77,242 people recorded as living in South Dorchester in 1950, only 201 were nonwhite. Most of the residents were married couples with children. The median school years completed was 11.9 years. In other words, half of the adults in my neighborhood had not even graduated from high school. The foreign born white population was 16,310, or one out of every five residents. The city had not yet fully emerged from the Great Depression or the stringent limitations of the war years. It was a very different place. It is hard to believe now but in those years just after World War II, there were still Boston law firms that refused to hire Jews or Catholics.

The birth of my generation, the baby boom generation, represented an explosion of pent up demand. The war years took many men far away to the war fronts in Europe and the Pacific. For those who stayed behind, wartime shortages put lives on hold for the duration. My father had been exempt from military service because he was the sole support of his aging mother. Once armistice was declared, it was no holds barred. Millions of wedding bells sounded in a clamor and millions of children were born into a world that offered more upward mobility, more educational opportunity and far more prosperity. Family automobiles became the norm, giving many families unprecedented physical mobility and freedom. My mother brought her 1937 Plymouth, an automobile she had bought on her own which was unusual at the time, into her marriage. We bought our first television set in 1954 when I was five years old. Today, at a time of smart phones, flat screen TV's, iPads and other technological marvels, it is hard to imagine how revolutionary the television was. It was a noteworthy occasion when a Dorchester neighbor acquired a television set. Those televisions brought the world into the family living room. The flicker of images on the black and white television sets entertained us and enticed us with evidence of accomplishment just beyond the borders of our neighborhood.

As the first born of three, I suspect that I unconsciously absorbed the hopes of my parents and grandparents even more than my siblings did. My grandparents on both sides were Sicilian. Sicily is the largest island in the Mediterranean Sea, a triangle of land at the tip of the boot of Italy. Although the island is less than two miles from the mainland at the narrowest divide, it has always had a separate and distinct culture and identity. Throughout the ages, its location made it the site of frequent invasions as well as many friendlier visits. The Greeks, the Romans, Vandals, Ostrogoths, Byzantines, Arabs and Normans all left a bit of DNA in the populace and fingerprints on the culture. Geography turned Sicily into a melting pot of ethnicities. The island was a regular resting spot for pilgrims heading to the Holy Land and at one point had a substantial Jewish population. Sicily spent nearly 700 years as a separate kingdom until it became part of Italy when the country unified in 1860. Not long after, the economy collapsed and a series of cataclysmic natural disasters took place, nudging my ancestors off the island and to the United States.

My mother's parents, Lorenzo Alibrandi and Josephine DiBella, were born in the village of Annuziata near Messina in northeastern Sicily, the city closest to the mainland. They knew one another as children and married after settling in Boston. My grandmother Josephine, my Nonna Peppina, who was born on June 25, 1889, came to the United States with her older sister, Agatha, who was known as Concetta. My grandfather, my Nonno, Lorenzo was born on February 10, 1891. He anglicized his name to Lawrence and I was named after him. He remarkably came to the United States in 1904 at the age of 13, all by himself. He may have accompanied others from his village which was not unusual at the time; but he did not come with family. Lorenzo and Josephine were married on March 27, 1911. He was 20; she was 22. They had one child, my mother, Concetta C. Alibrandi, who was born four years later on September 27, 1915.

My father's father was Carmelo DiCara. He was born in Villa Rosa, Sicily to the west of Catania in 1891. He worked as a coachman to a wealthy family and met my grandmother, Virginia Vegnani in Catania. I called her Nonna Virginia. She was born on March 10, 1884. Her father, Vincent Vegnani, was a composer and concert master. He died young and her widowed mother sold his music to put food on the table when Virginia was growing up. In September 1919, Virginia came to the United States with a baby in her arms, my father, Salvatore, who had been born just a year earlier on August 17, 1918. My father was their only surviving child. Three others, brothers Anthony and Vincent, and a sister, Maria, who were born in Italy, all died in infancy. This high infant mortality rate was tragically quite normal at the time. Virginia passed along her love of music to my father, who grew up playing the violin. Little is known about her husband Carmelo who came to the United States separately soon after. This was not unusual. Ship fares, even the lowest fares, were expensive and families often immigrated one by one as money allowed. My father rarely spoke of his own father who effectively abandoned him and his mother. Any questions I may have had about why I had two Nonnas but only one Nonno would cause the conversation to change abruptly. I could tell my Nonna Virginia felt the shame of being abandoned by her husband.

I do know that Grandfather DiCara was listed as a cobbler on some U.S. Census forms and he obtained a patent for a submarine rescue suit on June 27, 1933, when my Dad would have been almost 15. He was living in California at the time. In those years, California might as well have been a foreign country. Long distance telephone calls were expensive and rare. A letter from someone who could not write English and had limited writing skills in Italian was difficult. So even if Carmelo had wanted to keep in touch with his wife and child, circumstances would have conspired to defeat him. Growing up, I could sense my Nonna Virginia was an angry woman, a victim of downward mobility caused by conditions completely out of her control. My father was devoted to her.

Virginia came to the United States more than a year after World War I ended in 1918. We believe Carmelo served in the war as a draftee. Italy had a checkered history in World War I. It hung back initially to see which side would win and eventually threw its support to the winning side. The war took a devastating toll; more than 600,000 dead, 950,000 wounded and another 250,000 disabled for life. A 27 year old uneducated ex-soldier with a wife and child would also have little opportunity to make a living after the war. The poverty of rural Sicily was extreme. There were no paved roads, no running water, no electricity, street lights or central heating. None of my grandparents got past the fourth grade of school. The end of war triggered high unemployment and inflation. This encouraged those with the energy and means to pack up and head to America, the land of opportunity. From their perspective, any place else had to be better.

Without natural disasters and economic deprivation, my ancestors doubtless would have stayed on the lovely Mediterranean island but Mount Etna, the largest volcano in Europe, sputtered ominously throughout the 19th century, erupting with striking regularity every five years or so and continued to do so in the 20th century. In 1908, just before Christmas, a combination earthquake and volcanic eruption wiped out two cities, Messina and Reggio. On December 28, a tsunami, set off by the earthquake, hit the island. The Italian government records say more than 96,000 people died. In 1910, Mount Etna erupted again in March and smothered entire villages in ash. The home of my mother's paternal grandparents was destroyed in the 1910 eruption. The phrase "terra modo," meaning the earth moves, had real meaning to those folks. Our family legend holds that Lorenzo Alibrandi, my grandfather, promptly sent for the other members of his family after the 1910 disaster. He was only 19 at the time. I often wonder what my political career would have been like if he had lived a few years longer.

In the late 19th and early 20th centuries, Italian and Irish immigrants in Boston routinely worked in low paying back-breaking service jobs, lived in little more than hovels without running hot water or central heat, and saved their pennies so they could bring over younger brothers and sisters and other relatives, one at a time. As each new immigrant arrived, he or she moved in with or nearby those who had come before creating ethnic enclaves and sometimes entire neighborhoods of families from the old country. Our family fit snugly into that pattern. Although they never lived in the Boston neighborhoods that were predominantly Italian, they did live in communities populated by immigrants who came to America as they did—in search of a better life.

Most Americans are descended from immigrants who fled something. The Puritans of New England fled religious persecution in England at the beginning of the 16th century, just as the Jews of Russia fled the czar's pogroms in the 19th. The Irish fled desperate poverty caused by phytophthora infestans (or potato blight) which destroyed the potato crop, the main source of nutrition for the tenant farmers. The good produce went overseas while the Irish starved, a grudge the Boston Irish still hold against their English overseers more than 150 years later. For my ancestors, volcanic eruptions and earthquakes destroyed homes and life as they knew it in their tiny villages. Mount Etna is the key variable in the migration patterns of many Sicilians. Each time it erupted, more people left. With homes and livelihoods destroyed, these peasants had little choice but to leave for a foreign country where they did not even speak the language. They came with literally nothing but their hearts, hands and their hopes for a better life.

My grandfather was known in Roxbury as "Lawrence the barber." He was the proud proprietor of a two-seat barber shop on Blue Hill Avenue, the graceful boulevard that stretches from Dudley Square in Roxbury to Mattapan Square. I keep his barber scissors on my desk at home to remind me of my roots. At the turn of the 20th century, the area teemed with immigrants from all over Europe. Few people had personal telephones in their homes in those days. Indeed, his barber shop never had a telephone. Customers exchanged news and discussed politics face to face as grandfather provided an expert shave and a haircut. The barber shop was a gathering spot for the neighborhood, a center of community news and gossip. My grandfather's natural warmth made it a popular neighborhood hangout. My Nonno never fully mastered English, but his example provided me with a North Star of dignity and decency for my entire life. My grandfather was an outgoing, social, and kind man. He was instinctively entrepreneurial, a natural organizer and businessman, and a true survivor in every sense. He bought his own home in Roxbury within years of coming to Boston, a remarkable achievement for a boy who was barely a teenager when he arrived on his own. He took great pride in his heritage. He was one of the founders of the Sons of Italy Lodge in Roxbury, which is now in Roslindale, and he was an officer in the Italian American Citizens Club of Roxbury. When he neared death, confined to bed, he insisted my father drive to the clubhouse with his dues to maintain his active membership in the Sons of Italy Lodge 1606.

Nonno rented storefront space from Kasanof's Bakery at the corner of Edgewood Street and Blue Hill Avenue. I can still remember the intoxicating smell of hot bread that enveloped the building in a delicious haze. Family lore has it that he never charged a priest, a minister or a rabbi for a haircut or a shave. That practice did nothing for his bottom line, but it clearly brought him great blessings. When I was young, my grandfather rented the second chair in his shop to Simon Hadley, a Greek Jew who escaped the Nazis. His son later went to Boston Latin School as I did. In Italian neighborhoods like the North End, it was not unusual for immigrants to speak only Italian and never learn English, but Roxbury was not predominantly Italian. To survive, my grandfather needed to learn to speak English. Ward 12 was then mostly Irish and Jewish, with perhaps 20 percent everyone else, including Italians. The Italians had already begun a long history as a key swing vote in city elections.

My parents were under tremendous pressure to become Americans and to assimilate. This was typical for immigrants and the children of immigrants.

My father, Salvatore DiCara, did not speak a word of English until dropped off at the steps of a public school when he was age 6. Because of his father's absence, his mother supported them by working at a garment factory, where swift fingers and a solid work ethic mattered far more than language skills. They lived in a cold water flat in a very tough section of Dorchester, a mixed industrial area near what is sometimes called Glover's Corner, with Virginia's older sister and her husband, and their elderly mother. A cold water flat was exactly as it sounds. There was no hot running water. Water would have to be heated for bathing and cooking. The five of them shared that apartment for many years. Nonna Virginia's mother was born in 1850 and I'm told could thread a needle without the need of eye glasses until she died in her early 80s. My father was the only person in the apartment who could speak English, so he acted as the family interpreter, even for visits to the Boston City Hospital, which must have been a bit embarrassing. On Saturday afternoons when the work week was done, they all went to the Opera House. Music and opera remained an intrinsic part of their lives in the new country.

My father worked his way through Northeastern University in Boston on the Cooperative Education program and became an accountant. Northeastern was a street car school on Huntington Avenue at that time and the Co-Op program was the ticket to the middle class for many working class students who earned their tuition while working in a job related to their field of study. Dad maintained a lifelong loyalty to Northeastern University and served as secretary-treasurer of his class. He died shortly before his sixtieth college reunion. When I read at home in Jamaica Plain, I sit in Dad's Northeastern University chair.

Dad worked as a student Co-Op at the old Boston Herald, then the "Re-publican" newspaper in Boston, a handsome and staid broadsheet paper that bears no resemblance to the current tabloid of the same name. When he graduated, the newspaper offered him a full time job. He worked there for more than 30 years as an accountant in the circulation department. He was laid off when the owners sold the company to the Hearst Corporation in 1972, an early victim of an unfortunate transition in the economy that put profits ahead of loyalty to employees. He was 53 years old. It was a terrible blow for my father to lose his job and his anticipated pension with little chance at his age of getting another comparable position. He handled the transition with dignity, however, eventually securing a job with the help of a family friend at the Bank of Boston. He rode the subway downtown each day in a suit for the next ten years to finish out his working life. The only difference was that he stopped bringing his lunch to work. He and my mother realized that the bank subsidized the cafeteria so deeply that it was actually cheaper to eat in the cafeteria. Moreover, Mrs. Favale, one of the cafeteria workers, always gave him an extra helping because I helped her son Joe get a job when he returned from Vietnam. Joe Favale went on to become a Boston Police officer and served with distinction until his retirement.

When Dad graduated from college, he became the family breadwinner and moved with his mother to their own apartment on Roche Street, one street over from the cold water flat on Greenmount Street, and later to Gibson Street in Fields' Corner, the first family apartment with hot water. Dad no longer had to go to the Y for a shower!

My mother was born on Warren Street in Roxbury. There was a large Italian immigrant population in the South End of Boston at that time which spilled across the neighborhood line to Roxbury. The South End was largely an immigrant ghetto. Mother attended Roxbury Memorial High School and graduated in 1933 in a class that included Jews, Irish, Italians and African Americans, a reflection of the diversity of the neighborhood. She was a musician and played the piano, so, like my father who played the violin, she had many Jewish friends. Music and education were two pillars of the culture for the Jewish immigrants from Eastern Europe and Russia. A prominent Bostonian from her era was Leonard Bernstein, who graduated from Boston Latin School in 1935. Mother's dearest friend was Mildred Spiegel, later Zucker, who studied piano with Bernstein. Anti-Semitism unfortunately followed the Jews to the new world, but in my parents' day, the Jews—with their love of education and culture—were people who were admired and respected by families like mine who shared their appreciation and interest in upward mobility.

Despite their own lack of education, my grandparents sent their daughter to college at a time very few girls received a higher education. Looking back, this was radical. It was one thing to send a son, but Grandpa decided to send his daughter perhaps because he had no sons. He doted on his only child. My mother studied at Boston Teachers' College, a forerunner of UMass Boston, in the midst of the Depression. Then it churned out young first generation American school teachers. After earning her degree, my mother became one of the first Italian-Americans to be hired as a teacher in the Boston public school system. The Boston School System was initially a Yankee enclave and then overwhelmingly Irish-American. She first taught at the Sherwin School in Roxbury and later taught at the Gavin School, an all female junior high in South Boston. Still later in her career, she taught music to the children who lived at Columbia Point, one of the most violent public housing projects in the city. She was an excellent and beloved teacher.

She had to give up her job when she married. The law did not allow married women to teach in the Boston public schools in 1948. It also did not require the school system to pay male and female teachers the same. Men were paid more than women to do the exact same job. She often told the story of handing her bridesmaid her letter of resignation and warning her not to put it in the mailbox until after the wedding reception. She knew of a female colleague who resigned just days before her own wedding only to be left in the lurch at the altar. The school system refused to reinstate her colleague to her old job. My mother took no chances! When the rules loosened up and her three children reached school age, mother returned to teaching. She topped the teacher's exam, even though her competitors were recent college graduates half her age, and continued to teach and inspire generations of students for many years.

My parents were considered "older" when they married at St. John's Church in Roxbury on May 31, 1948. Dad was nearly 30 years old at the time of their marriage and mother was almost 33. The marriage of my mother was a painful moment for her father, who left their home at 29 Maywood Street in Roxbury early on the morning of the wedding to shave and dress in his barber shop so he would not have to say goodbye to his daughter in the home that must have seemed quite empty without their only child.

My parents' wedding was a cause of great celebration in the Italian community. Their eclectic and diverse circle of friends came to celebrate the nuptials. It was a huge wedding with more than 250 guests at the Copley Plaza Hotel. Photographs of their wedding show people of all ethnicities and races. Indeed, mother had to secure permission from the Archdiocese of Boston so her Jewish friends, Victor and Dorothy Alpert, could play the viola and violin in the balcony of St. John's Church for the wedding ceremony. The Catholic Church rules were very rigid in those days: Catholics were not allowed to set foot in non-Catholic houses of worship and non-Catholics were not welcome in Catholic Churches. Decades would pass before the hierarchy recognized the folly of its exclusivity and things loosened up after the Second Vatican Council in the 1960s.

After World War II, in the late 1940s and early 1950s, over two million returning GI's went to college on the GI Bill, but attending a university or college was hardly typical. My parents were unusual because both had graduated from college. In 1950, only 6.2 percent of the adults in Boston had earned a bachelor's degree; only 4.8 percent of the women had a college degree. (In contrast, fifty years later, nearly 40 percent of the adults in Boston had earned a bachelor's degree.)

When my parents married, my mother moved into the Gibson Street apartment. Dad came as a package deal with his mother. My mother never questioned that she would live with her mother-in-law. It was simply the way things were, even though it was unquestionably difficult. My grandmother never learned English and the apartment was small; two bedrooms, a living

room and dining room, a bathroom and kitchen. Grandmother wanted to accompany them on their honeymoon but they convinced her it would be a bad
idea. I arrived about 11 months later on April 30, 1949, a second wave Baby
Boomer.

Although my parents belonged to a generation that truly became American
in every way, they still retained Italian values. So for them, family was everything. Edward C. Banfield, the famous sociologist, noted the importance
of family in the culture of Italian families in his 1958 book *The Moral Basis
of a Backward Society*, which was based upon his observations of a poor Italian village in southern Italy. He wrote that there were two kinds of people to
these poor peasants: family and everyone else. I grew up hearing other members of my own family talk about the strani or strangers and the 'mericani,
a universal term that meant anyone who was not Italian. Banfield has been
controversial, but other sociologists agree that family was the only institution
that remained consistent and reliable for Italian peasants. The peasants, the
great majority in Italy, were the largest class of people and the class with the
least. Most families, including mothers, fathers, grandmothers, grandfathers
and children, lived in humble one room houses. They had little hope of things
ever getting better because there was virtually no upward mobility in Italy.
The peasant children could not even go to school because their labor was
needed to support the family. Italian peasants grew up believing that only
family could be trusted. They relied upon the family for sustenance, survival,
and succor. My parents' first step towards upward mobility took place when
they learned not to fear—and eventually to trust—people who were different.
It is a lesson that I absorbed from them and from my own experience. At the
same time, they valued family. Our family was particularly close because
my parents had no siblings so I had no aunts, uncles or cousins. Our entire
family, all surviving three generations, eventually lived under the same roof
in Dorchester.

By 1956 when I was 6, the apartment at 63 Gibson Street was overcrowded
with three adults and three children, which included my younger brother
Vinny (born 21 months after my birth on January 29, 1951,) and my sister,
Ginny (three years later on February 24, 1954). For the last two years that we
lived on Gibson Street, I slept on a cot in the dining room, which made sleep-
ing problematic when family or friends visited. By the standards of the day,
our family was considered unusually small. The Irish neighbors had 5, 6, or 7
children or more. Family planning was not only forbidden by the Church but
unreliable at the time. The U.S. Food and Drug Administration approved the
first birth control pill in 1960. Within four years, the pill was the most popular form of birth control in the United States and on its way to transforming
the professional lives of women, including Catholic women, who used birth

control in the same percentages as non-Catholics, despite the Vatican stand against any means of artificial family planning.

I attended the Rochambeau School, directly across the street from our apartment, for kindergarten and first grade. My kindergarten teacher, Miss Glover, taught us how to make butter. I believe she was from Vermont and had firsthand experience in all things dairy. My teachers told my parents that I had a speech impediment. There was nothing wrong with my speech, I was simply bilingual! I spoke Italian at home and sometimes spoke a mixture of English and Italian at school. We all spoke Italian at home because my Nonna Virginia spoke no English. The school beat the Italian out of me with speech therapy. Unfortunately, I gradually lost my facility with Italian as I grew up and began to speak English exclusively. That early experience, quite typical for the time, sparked a lifelong interest in bilingual education. My experience at school also hinted at a future in politics. In the spring of 1955, the school sponsored an event and parents were invited. I was assigned the job of greeter and I performed with great aplomb. Talking to strangers and adults came easily to me even at the age of 6.

We moved in February 1956 from Fields Corner. The two bedroom apartment had become overcrowded with my grandmother, my parents and three children. I remember the move vividly because I left my old school just before Valentine's Day on February 14. My mother, aware of the importance of the tradition of exchanging greeting cards among classmates, drove back to my old school with a batch of valentines so I would not feel left out. We moved to a two-family home which my grandfather bought at 86 Codman Hill Avenue in the section of Dorchester known as Lower Mills in St. Gregory's Parish. The house was part of a development that John Driscoll, a developer and father of John T. Driscoll, a politician who became well known in Massachusetts as State Treasurer and chairman of the Massachusetts Turnpike Authority, had built. The development was built in the 1920s on the site of an old farm. The house cost $18,500 and my grandfather, being self employed, could not get a conventional mortgage from a bank. He borrowed money from Prince Carbone, an insurance man and fellow Italian, to cover the difference between his proceeds from the sale of his house on Maywood Street in Roxbury and the cost of the new two family house. Such financial arrangements were quite common in the immigrant community. My grandfather was well known and respected in the Italian community at this time and clearly viewed as trustworthy.

My mother's parents moved into the first floor apartment on Codman Hill Avenue soon after we moved into the second floor. Nonna Virginia still lived with us upstairs. I eventually moved up to my own room in the attic midway through high school in order to have space to do my school work. Being the oldest had its prerogatives. I lived in that room until 1981. It was difficult for my grandparents to give up their own house on Maywood Street. But they were getting older. In the 1950s, Social Security payments were paltry and there was not yet a Medicare program of health insurance for seniors. Living together also was better for the family. My grandfather could take the bus to his barber shop and my two grandmothers could watch the grandchildren while my mother returned to teaching. Soon after we moved, we switched from coal to oil heat, regulated with a thermostat, and the old black stove in the kitchen was replaced by modern appliances.

On Codman Hill Avenue, everyone on the street seemed to be related to someone else. Many families had relatives upstairs and down, as we did. Others lived next door to relatives. It was a heavily Irish neighborhood with lots of kids, a perfect place to grow up. The house was near the Baker Chocolate Factory, so the scent of chocolate was always in the air. It was heavenly. In addition, our house always smelled of tomato sauce, that magical concoction of tomatoes, onions, garlic, salt, pepper, peppers and love that is the lifeblood of every Italian family. Nonna Peppina often had a pot of sauce on her stove.

There was a special reason we moved into that house, however. As a teacher, my mother had an insider's perspective on the Boston Public School system. While some homebuyers might have been concerned about the number of bedrooms or a back yard or updated plumbing, my mother plotted real estate based upon the locations of the best public schools. She did not mess around. She knew how many students from each elementary school gained admission to Boston Latin School, the gem of Boston's public schools. She wanted her children to go to the best schools and strategized like a military general to maximize our chances.

Her target was the Charles H. Taylor School, named after the Civil War general and early publisher of The Boston Globe. The school was only a short four minute walk away; it had small classes and it was one of the best elementary schools in the city. My mother always said it was superior because of the mixture of students: some Irish, some Jewish, a few Greeks, at least one WASP, and a handful of Italians. I met the first Protestant I ever knew in life at that school, Richard Alan Clarke, a classmate of my brother Vinny. Richard later became my debate partner at Boston Latin School. As an adult, he became an internationally regarded counter terrorism expert who worked at the White House under several Presidents. In those days, the Boston Public Schools still had inkwells. We dipped our pens in the ink to learn how to write cursive style until ballpoint pens arrived later in the 1950s.

In those years, we were also introduced to the wondrous institution known as the Boston Public Library (BPL). Mrs. Crowley, the children's librarian at the Dorchester Lower Mills branch, became a great friend. She later facilitated my first appearance on the radio with Gus Saunders, a popular radio personality in Boston. That early exposure to those wonderful books made me a lifelong supporter of the BPL.

Then disaster struck. My grandfather suffered a massive stroke on January 27, 1958. I remember it vividly. With the benefit of hindsight, I understand now why he got sick. He was overweight, smoked heavily and kept smoking, even though he had suffered a heart attack a few years earlier. In the 1950s, medical doctors appeared in advertisements touting the benefits of smoking. This was before the U.S. Surgeon General issued the warning on the health hazards of smoking. His stroke left him seriously disabled. He could barely speak. He could barely move his legs. A group of nuns, still the most reliable safety net for immigrants at that time, taught my grandmother how to lift him out of bed, bathe him and care for him at home. There was never any other option. Families took care of their elderly in those years. Very few went into nursing homes. He lived like that, helpless and sadly diminished, for six more years until he died in 1964. I would stay with him when my grandmother left the house to buy groceries. He rarely left the house in those years; though I do remember he somehow got to church in the spring of 1961 to celebrate his fiftieth wedding anniversary. He shuffled down the center aisle with a cane to renew his vows to his bride. I still treasure that cane and anticipate I will use it myself someday, just as Senator Edward M. Kennedy relied upon the cane of his own father during his final illness.

Nonno had a remarkable memory despite the stroke. He dictated to me the names of the people whom he had invited to my mother's wedding more than a decade earlier in order to invite them to his fiftieth anniversary party which was a singular event. Very few couples survived long enough to mark that golden anniversary in those days. I went back to St. Gregory's 50 years later and had a special Mass celebrated to mark the one hundreth anniversary of their wedding.

His widow, my Nonna Peppina, lived downstairs until her death in 1978. She could sew almost anything. She made many of my clothes, including the pants and blue blazer I wore to Boston Latin School, and most of my mother's work clothes. Her physical strength was remarkable. She scrubbed her floors on her hands and knees until her final brief illness. Until six weeks before her death, at the age of 88, she had never spent a night in a hospital. There are many advantages to being the descendent of hardy Italian peasants. I have enjoyed robust good health throughout most of my life as well.

Roxbury today is known as an African-American community because of the influx of black Americans who moved up from the South after World War II in the Great Migration. In 1948, when my parents married, it was a glorious melting pot of ethnicity and race. While the North End of Boston and

East Boston became known as Italian neighborhoods, neither of my parents grew up or lived in an "Italian" neighborhood and neither did I. I grew up in Dorchester, the city's largest neighborhood, which throughout the years has remained varied and diverse—although the ethnic groups have shifted and changed with the years. Dorchester has a rich and long history. The first settlers of Boston landed at Columbia Point and settled at Columbia Road and Massachusetts Avenue in 1630. Waves of immigrants followed for hundreds of years. The diversity of the neighborhood later contributed to my success in city political elections and unquestionably helped form my outlook and views. My Dorchester roots gave me an extremely solid foundation for a political career, because the neighborhood's size and political tradition produced a huge number of votes.

My parents had a firm grip on the emerging middle class. Our family eventually owned our house. They earned enough money to keep us fed and clothed. They saved for the future. We were hardly wealthy, but we never considered ourselves poor. Yet my parents, like most people, often lived paycheck to paycheck. I remember waiting for my Dad and his weekly paycheck at the subway stop at Fields Corner so we could shop for groceries at the Capital Market on Friday night. And mother often tucked a note into my silver piggy bank: "Mommy owes Larry $5," after borrowing a few bucks to tide us over until the next paycheck. She always paid me back. My parents, as part of the generation of children who grew up during the Great Depression years, never lost that sense of foreboding that economic disaster could be right around the corner. I don't think they ever bought a single thing on credit. They paid cash or they did not buy it. I inherited that sensitivity to debt and to this day I am instinctively frugal in a way my own children find comical.

Growing up in the 1950s and 1960s in Dorchester, Massachusetts was close to idyllic. There were many reasons I probably should have been an unhappy child. I was a physically small but chubby Italian boy with eyeglasses and no discernible athletic ability in an aggressively and overwhelmingly Irish city, where men and boys were still judged by physical prowess and athletes were neighborhood heroes. Yet I had a wonderful time. I was a very happy kid. I loved school, and hung out with my friends at the local park where I played energetic, if barely serviceable, baseball. We lived in the city but the threats that keep parents sleepless at night now simply did not exist. We walked from Codman Hill Avenue to Franklin Field for Little League games routinely. We rode public transportation by ourselves; we played in the parks and streets; we explored the neighborhood without many constraints. It was a very different, simpler and safer time. Most mothers were at home and kept a close eye out on all the neighborhood children. But most important, I was cushioned like a precious jewel by the love of my parents and grandparents. That great love gave me the self-confidence that served me so well in my own life.

There were cultural touchstones that I still remember vividly, such as my first Red Sox game at Fenway Park. Nonno put on his straw hat and took me and Vinny to watch the Red Sox play the Tigers on July 31, 1957. The Red Sox lost that day to the Tigers 5-3. Thunderstorms interrupted the game but we sat in the covered grandstand and stayed dry. I remember eating lots and lots of ice cream. The loss meant nothing to me. It was simply a thrill to sit in that ballpark watching the great players of the day: Ted Williams, Jimmy Piersall and Jackie Jensen. It was the first of many visits to Fenway Park, which is as meaningful to Boston Red Sox fans as a great Cathedral is to the denizens of European cities. Our mother was a big baseball fan, too, because her father had taken her to games when she was a child. When Vinny and I were small, she helped us practice by pitching to us. I am sure she was the only college-educated, dress-wearing, left-handed pitcher in Dorchester in those years. She took me and Vinny and our sister Ginny to Sox games on what were then called "Ladies Days." Women were admitted on those days for 50 cents. She got me and Vinny tickets to the All-Star game in Boston in 1961, ostensibly for helping her get our house ready for our grandparents' fiftieth wedding anniversary. Neither Vinny nor I can remember that we did much to prepare for the party but our mother was glad to do something nice for us. Today I bring my own children and still enjoy each game as if it were the first, and go to Spring Training in March.

Vinny and I played baseball, near our house at Walsh Park and joined the Little League based at Franklin Field. In the early 1960s, the Franklin Field location of Little League meant that our friends were even more diverse because they were drawn from several neighborhoods and included black kids. I pitched my first game and walked nine batters before hitting a young black boy named Willie. I thought he would certainly head out to the mound to wreak revenge bat in hand. He fortunately did not. I gave up one hit and struck out one batter. After that game, I played second base.

I grew up with friends from all types of families. They represented the rich ethnic tapestry of the city and different socio-economic groups that ranged from very poor to middle class. Few people were truly wealthy back then, and if they were, they did not live in Dorchester. Most of my friends' parents held jobs as MBTA bus drivers, or firefighters, or worked for Edison or the telephone company. The telephone company was a highly desirable employer in those years. An employee could spend an entire career there and then retire with a pension. The immigrants and children of immigrants put a high value on Civil Service jobs and those at major employers, like insurance companies. Few things were more important than job security. Spending an entire career at a single employer was not unusual.

My grandfather dealt with the public as a barber, so he was comfortable with people who were "different" or non-Italian. My parents had grown up in diverse neighborhoods and attended college so they, too, had a high degree of tolerance and respect for people from different backgrounds, religions and races. Bigotry was not something tolerated at our house.

Then one day at the L Street bathhouse, I experienced an early brush with hate and bias. Our mother drove us over to South Boston to the L Street Beach for swimming lessons. My mother always handed me a single dime for a telephone call in the event of an emergency. This was long before cell phones and it only cost ten cents to make a call from a pay phone. (This led to the expression "getting dimed," or exposed, in political circles.) After my lesson, I retrieved my clothes and found the dime was missing. A much bigger kid swaggered up to me to ask what was wrong. When I told him I had lost a dime, he sneered, "we don't like Jews here." When I told him I was Italian, not Jewish, he barked: "we don't like Wops either." I was incredulous that someone would even think that way. I found the experience remarkable and it stayed with me.

We never spent a night away from home because of our elderly grandparents. My first night away was in 1965 when I went to Germany on a troop ship with the Explorer Scouts. I joined the Cub Scouts when I was in the third grade. It was my very first affiliation. I also served as an altar boy at St. Gregory's Church, our enormous parish that spread from Dorchester, Mattapan and a tiny piece of Milton, and included the Carney Hospital, the Catholic hospital in Dorchester where the priests said special Masses for the patients and "shut-ins." My parents were good Catholics. We never missed Mass and the Catholic Church and its teachings were another pillar of respectability and authority in the community.

Our lives revolved around the Church. St. Gregory's was not only the place for worship, it was the epicenter of our social lives. We buried three grandparents and my parents from St. Gregory's. It is where my parents and maternal grandparents celebrated their fiftieth wedding anniversaries; where my sister Ginny was married; and where I used to sell newspapers on Sunday for Mr. Connolly. It seemed as though everyone went to church on Sunday and everyone bought one or more Sunday newspapers. All those mornings selling newspapers in front of St. Gregory's or St. Mary of the Angels in Egleston Square left me with an abiding dislike of getting caught in the rain. Sunday was a true day of rest, reserved for family. All the stores were closed.

I had my first date at an Explorer Dance (with Mr. Connolly's daughter, Peggy) at St. Gregory's. The Explorers, like the Boy and Cub Scouts, were centered at the church. I wrote an Op-Ed for The Boston Globe many years ago about midnight Mass at Christmas at St. Gregory's. The DiCara children were different in one respect: we attended public school, not parochial school. I benefitted from having friends from Church-affiliated activities, as well as friends who never stopped into a Catholic Church. I think I am the better for it.

I do remember being terrified by the local pastor at St. Gregory's. Monsignor Bernard J. McNulty presided over St. Gregory's with a firm hand from 1952 until his retirement in 1970. He was rumored to be close to Cardinal Richard Cushing who ran the archdiocese with remarkable political skill and became nationally known through his friendship with President John F. Kennedy. Cushing presided over John Kennedy's wedding to Jacqueline Bouvier, prayed at Kennedy's Inauguration and then, sadly, presided over the funeral Mass after his assassination. Monsignor McNulty was not exactly a poet. He tended to speak in clichés: "Hitch your wagon to a star," was a favorite punctuation point in his sermons.

The election of Massachusetts Senator John F. Kennedy to the Presidency in 1960 electrified us. I idolized Kennedy and identified with him. He was from Boston; so was I. His father went to Latin School and I intended to go there. His mother Rose, the daughter of Mayor John F. "Honey Fitz" Fitzgerald, grew up in Dorchester (on Ashmont Hill close to where I eventually bought a home), just like me. He was Catholic, just like me. Politics was followed as avidly as sports in Dorchester in those years and having a son of Boston in the White House inspired an entire generation to a career in politics. I was no exception.

Our teachers at the Taylor School arranged for a television set to be brought to school so we could watch his inauguration on January 20, 1961. But it snowed in New England just as it did in Washington, D.C. and school was cancelled so I ended up watching it at home. I was rapt. During the summer of 1960 I had watched both national nominating conventions. John Kennedy was the first U. S. president to be elected who was born in the 20th century, and his election represented generational change in national leadership and an enormous turning point for the country. The torch indeed had been passed to a new generation and when he spoke those words in his inaugural address it felt as though he was speaking directly to all of us.

The priorities in my family were very clear. My parents and grandparents were far more interested in where I might go to college than whether I had a good fast ball. The subway line ran directly from Ashmont in Dorchester through Park Street on Beacon Hill and across the Charles River to Cambridge right to the doors of MIT and Harvard, two of the most prestigious universities in the world. Grandpa said over and over: "Lorenzo, you go to

Harvard or MIT." The three DiCara children reflected this mindset and became good students. In my six years at the Taylor School, I earned all A's
and B's with only one C. Mr. Martin, the woodworking teacher, gave me a C
in woodworking in 1960. I could never cut a straight line with a saw, an early
lesson in how one needs to recognize one's inherent talents and develop them.

My parents welcomed all my friends at home so I often brought friends
home from school. My grandmothers were always around. Having elderly
Italian grandmothers in the house gave me an interesting perspective on
American culture. Nonna Virginia, for example, had been born in 1884 and
never spoke English and American customs left her befuddled. Football, for
example, utterly confused her. Bostonians would watch the New York Giants on television on Sundays in those years, before New England acquired
its own professional football team, and one of the players was an end named
Andy Robustelli who wore Number 81 for the Giants. She knew a family
named Robustelli back in the old country so she always perked up at the
sound of his name. She thought the jersey numbers, however, signified the
age of the player and marveled that an eighty-one year old would be allowed
to play professional football. Nonna never did get it.

Nonna Peppina, a great cook and optimist, always thought my Harvard
friends were much, much too thin and assumed they were sickly and not getting enough to eat. Explaining that long lean bodies were essential for sports
like track and light weight crew never seemed to satisfy her desire to feed
them.

Mother's plotting was successful in terms of my education. I was accepted
into Boston Latin School. Boston Latin is the oldest school in the United
States, more than a year older than Harvard. It was founded by the town of
Boston on April 23, 1635. An early leader of the colony, Rev. John Cotton,
wanted to create a school similar to the Free Grammar School in Boston, England, which taught its students Greek and Latin. Five of the 56 signers of the
Declaration of Independence attended Boston Latin School, including John
Hancock, Samuel Adams and Benjamin Franklin. The distinguished alumni
include four Governors of Massachusetts, four Presidents of Harvard and
Ralph Waldo Emerson, as well as countless leaders of commerce, law and
medicine in Boston. Education has always been the surest ticket to upward
mobility in the United States, but never more so than during my lifetime.
Boston Latin School would improve my odds of getting into an excellent college and winning academic scholarships. It also helped me begin the process
of using and creating social networks to run for political office.

I entered Boston Latin School in the seventh grade on September 10, 1961.
When I attended, Latin was an all-boys school. It did not admit girls until
1972. My wife Teresa Spillane attended after the school became coed, but has

never shared my affection for the place. Boston Latin is located in the middle of a sea of hospitals and colleges at 78 Avenue Louis Pasteur. Nearly all of us took the subway from our neighborhoods to the school. The headmaster, John Doyle, a member of the class of 1912, was a dour, older man who was overweight and chain smoked. He served as headmaster from 1954 until 1964, when Wilfred L. O'Leary, Class of 1925, a World War II veteran who remained active in the state National Guard and wore his uniform to school every Memorial Day, took over the job. Dr. O'Leary earned his doctorate in education at Calvin Coolidge College of Liberty Arts, a tiny school in downtown Boston established in the 1940s in response to a Massachusetts Supreme Court ruling that required all students taking the bar examination have at least two years of college. Calvin Coolidge College never won accreditation and closed down in 1968. I learned much later that his doctoral thesis in 1954 was titled "The Responsibility of the Principal in the Problems of Discipline and Juvenile Delinquency." It said everything that needs to be remembered about "Doctor" O'Leary.

In retrospect, Doyle and O'Leary were products of a sclerotic system. They advanced in the Boston Public Schools because of who they knew, rather than what they knew, and because they were unimaginative protectors of the status quo. They feared change, like most bureaucrats, and resisted changes to the curriculum. Boston Latin School did not teach biology until the mid-1960s. Wilfred O'Leary eliminated the teaching of Russian as an elective, perhaps because he had read too many books warning of the Communist menace. I credit the rank and file teachers for the fact that so many of us did so well. I remind my conservative friends that the teachers were children of immigrants, public employees and union members. We succeeded because of them, despite the shortcomings of the system.

On my first day at Latin School, Headmaster Doyle gave the classic "look to the right of you, look to the left of you" speech letting us know that only one of the three of us would be there for graduation. He was right.

Latin School was a formative growing experience. I met students from all over the city, including West Roxbury, which we considered an affluent neighborhood because many of the houses were single family, and East Boston, which was Italian . . . but in such a remote spot across the Boston Harbor that it might as well have been Europe. Most of the Chinese students lived in Chinatown, right downtown. I shared a locker with a heavy set boy from East Boston named Gaeta. Another classmate, Charles "Chaz" Willoughby, lived on the same street my mother had grown up on in Roxbury. The school demographics were about one-third Irish; one-third Jewish and one-third "other." I was among the "other" along with the Greeks, the Poles, the Chinese, and the African-Americans. The school was disciplined, classic and tough. I studied

Latin, Greek, mathematics, English, history, and German. My feeble efforts to participate in sports foundered at Latin School. I ran cross-country as a sophomore. I did finish every race, but invariably trailed the other runners.

I did learn that the best muscle in my body was in my head. I found my talents and set the course for my future at Latin School. My brother Vinny says Boston Latin School is where I first learned to be a leader. My first English teacher, John Hughes, convinced me to try out for public declamation or speech making. The first speech I ever delivered (from memory) was Franklin D. Roosevelt's Third Inaugural Address on February 12, 1962. Roosevelt delivered the speech on January 20, 1941 as the world teetered on the verge on a Second World War. I am not sure why I picked that speech but something in those stirring words spoke to me. The speech includes a riff on democracy that lifts my spirit to this day:

> *Democracy is not dying.*
>   *We know it because we have seen it revive—and grow.*
>   *We know it cannot die—because it is built on the unhampered initiative of individual men and women joined together in a common enterprise—an enterprise undertaken and carried through by the free expression of a free majority.*
>   *We know it because democracy alone, of all forms of government, enlists the full force of men's enlightened will.*
>   *We know it because, if we look below the surface, we sense it still spreading on every continent—for it is the most humane, the most advanced, and in the end the most unconquerable of all forms of human society.*

Declamation taught me the power of persuasion through words. It also gave me a formal speaking style that seems a bit old fashioned today. At that time, speaking was still essential to success in politics. The legendary James Michael Curley had built his career upon rhetorical flourish in Boston. In Dorchester, where dropping leaflets in the fall was as normal an activity as raking leaves was in the suburbs, the ability to communicate through rhetoric and words was a useful skill.

I also figured out how to build networks of friends and supporters. My classmates and I bonded over our shared experiences at a very challenging school. We were in the academic foxholes together and many of us have remained friends for life. Although I was a dreadful athlete, I was involved in sports as manager of the football and basketball teams. I wore a purple beret to the football games and acted as a cheerleader, an early indication of a willingness to do whatever it took to secure the approbation of others.

I set my goal on being elected senior class president in my sophomore year. I had already memorized the names and faces of my classmates. I had a voter identification system that was so accurate I was only four or five votes off. At the age of 15, I was organizing, cajoling, encouraging and bringing diverse people together. I won the class presidency, 141 to 102, and defeated an Irishman from South Boston, a Greek from Hyde Park, a black from the South End and an Armenian from Jamaica Plain. It is worth noting that all five of us went on to Harvard.

My networking skills took a leap forward when I was chosen to attend Boys State in the spring of my junior year. Boys State was created by the American Legion in 1935 to encourage good citizenship and leadership skills. Representatives came from all across the state and we held mock elections at the city, county and state levels. Two boys from each state would go to Washington, D.C. for Boys Nation and organize themselves into national offices. A high school boy from Hope, Arkansas was photographed shaking the hand of President John F. Kennedy in the Rose Garden at the 1963 Boys State summer program. That boy, Bill Clinton, was elected President of the United States fewer than 30 years later.

Boys State became an important part of my life. I quickly learned the slogan that was so effective at Latin School: Fly high with LSD, did not work in this context. But I was chosen to go to Boys Nation in Washington. For those who did not grow up at that time, I should note that my initials were also the acronym for Lysergic acid diethylamide, an illegal but popular hallucinogenic drug. I remember a young man named Steve Botts from Tennessee was elected president pro tempore of the Boys Nation Senate. He declared "The South will rise again!" and I was shocked to realize he meant it. Eight of my Boys Nation classmates that year went to Harvard.

Dr. O'Leary physically blocked me from delivering a speech at my Latin School commencement. I find it hard to believe that anything I would have said would have been that controversial, but 1967 was a year of great turmoil in politics, culture and society. The civil rights movement, anti-Vietnam war movement, women's movement and environmental movement were all moving forward simultaneously. To strait laced people like O'Leary, it must have seemed as though the old order was collapsing. At such times, people in authority tend to hold the reins a bit tighter, an invariably bad idea.

Not being able to deliver my speech really did not matter. I had been accepted at Harvard as my grandfather had always wanted. The legendary Jack Reardon, a career administrator at Harvard who has subsequently headed the alumni association, interviewed me as a prospective candidate at Latin School. We discussed Boston politics. Almost 50 years later, he told me it was the only interview he ever conducted where he could not get a single word in edgewise. I was on my way.

Ashmont to Harvard

The distance between Ashmont Station in Dorchester and Harvard Square in Cambridge is less than ten miles. The subway runs straight to downtown Boston then makes a graceful arc over the Charles River on the leg that links Boston and Cambridge. The subway ride takes about 25 minutes depending upon the time of day. But when I enrolled at Harvard as an ambitious 18 year old freshman, the distance could not be measured in mere miles. Harvard was simply a different world with a culture completely alien to the multiethnic, working class environment of Dorchester. The subway line now known as the Red Line was to me the longest subway line in the world.

I mistakenly assumed that I would do at Harvard what I had done at Boston Latin School. I was accustomed to holding a leadership position and being "a big man on campus." In my naïve view, why would Harvard be any different from Latin School? I was in for a shock—a true culture shock. The physical environment, the history, and the people were different from anything in my experience.

Harvard is the oldest university in the United States and one of the best in the world. It has produced eight United States Presidents, 75 Nobel Laureates and more billionaires than any other institution of higher education in the country. Thanks to James Bryant Conant, the legendary Harvard President who served between 1933 and 1953, it is also a meritocracy. A bright well rounded student from humble beginnings and a public high school has a shot at an Ivy League education on Harvard's not inconsiderable dime, because Harvard also has the largest university endowment in the world.

A wise assistant football coach took me aside not long after my arrival and explained to me the facts of life, Harvard-style. I assumed that I would be a student manager of the football team at Harvard just as I was at Boston Latin School. I was not the only Harvard freshman to exhibit this type of hubris.

This wise man explained that every year 1,200 young men arrived at Harvard Yard as I had. (At that time, Harvard was all male. Several hundred women attended the sister college, Radcliffe.) Each was convinced that he was the smartest, most talented, most accomplished young man Harvard had ever seen based upon his own narrow life experience. That class of 1,200 probably included 300 or 400 senior class Presidents, 500 Valedictorians and Salutatorians, 50 star quarterbacks, and hundreds of others who been enormously successful as high school students, as well as the inevitable cadre of "legacy" students, whose ancestors had walked the hallowed halls of Harvard before them. At Harvard, he explained, each discovered for the first time that he was not the best. My days as a big fish in a small pond were over.

Of course, I was prepared to make an impact. Long before Mark Zuckerberg dropped out of Harvard to create Facebook, there was The Facebook, a book containing the names and photographs of each incoming freshman. Each freshman received one during the summer, prior to classes starting. I used the same mind-skills which helped me memorize baseball card statistics and the catalogue at Boston Latin School and later the wards and precincts in Boston to learn the names and faces of my classmates in The Facebook. I can still pull the correct name from the recesses of my memory at class reunions.

In September of 1967, Harvard was still very traditional with customs and practices as time honored as the ivy climbing the brick masonry. My classmates and I wore jackets and ties to every meal. Women were not allowed in the freshman dorms except during very limited hours and were restricted in upper class dorm rooms as well. Life for freshmen was governed by the same rules followed by the fathers and grandfathers of the legacy students.

I headed to college full of excitement and anticipation. I borrowed the family car, a '63 Buick Special, to check into my room at Pennypacker Hall, one of the freshman dormitory buildings. Pennypacker was a former apartment building constructed in 1927 and acquired by Harvard in 1958 to house freshmen. All freshmen live in dormitories, while upper classmen live in the famous Harvard Houses. I was assigned a triple with two roommates on the fourth floor. There were two bedrooms in the suite; one with two beds, the other with one. I was the first to arrive so I took the single room for myself. I moved in quickly because I only brought a few clothes and a manual typewriter. In those days, students did not head off to college with laptop computers and all the other electronic paraphernalia of modern life.

My two roommates were radically different from anyone I had ever met. They smoked Gauloises, nasty, short, unfiltered French cigarettes with a pungent acrid odor favored by those who considered themselves bohemian. The room reeked of tobacco. With the benefit of hindsight, I now realize my roommates were an Ivy League version of what became known in that era as hippies, the iconic long haired, pot smoking, anti-establishment cultural rebels of the day. They did not appreciate my old pals from Dorchester showing up at 8 a.m. with a case of beer. In many respects, I was much too traditional for them, so I sought friends in other places at the university. Several of my Latin School classmates joined me in that class along with eight of the young men I had met at Boys Nation the previous summer in Washington. I also discovered I was more comfortable among the prep school graduates, perhaps because their experience in high school had been more like my own at Latin School, but also because they seemed a bit more mature. They had already been living away from home for four or six years before beginning college and felt less need to be openly rebellious. From the start, I was someone who was most comfortable working within the system and making change from the inside out.

I quickly discovered kindred spirits at the Institute of Politics (IOP) at the John F. Kennedy School of Government. The school was originally Harvard's Graduate School of Public Administration and renamed in 1966 for John Kennedy. Richard Neustadt, the legendary political scientist and specialist in the presidency, was the founding director of the IOP where I was chosen to serve on the Student Advisory Council. I was also elected by my classmates to serve on the Student Faculty Advisory Committee (SFAC). I faced the first tough vote of my life on the SFAC. The Committee had to take a position on whether there should be a Reserve Officers' Training Corps (ROTC) program on campus. ROTC trained commissioned officers for the U.S. military services on college campuses. The program provided scholarship help to participants in return for a mandatory term of military service after graduation. It was a standard offering on most campuses until the war in Vietnam, which triggered massive anti-military sentiment in many quarters in the United States. On some campuses, though not Harvard, the program was compulsory. Antiwar sentiment turned the program from a compulsory to a voluntary one on many campuses and got it expelled from others. The push at Harvard was to abolish the program. I voted to keep ROTC on campus. It was a grievously unpopular position and I was the only under-graduate on the SFAC to vote in favor of the program. But I felt that a Harvard education would be beneficial to the military and that the academy and military should not be so sharply divided. I was on the losing side and ROTC was expelled from Harvard and not reinstated until March 4, 2011, after repeal of the Don't Ask Don't Tell policy which finally allowed gay military service members to serve openly. I like to think I was right about the policy, although at the time it was very hard to be diametrically opposed to my classmates.

As I look back, I see I was moving inexorably towards a career in elective office, though another year would pass before I made a deliberate and firm choice to run for office. The predisposition was already in place. The assassination of John F. Kennedy in 1963 had hit me hard. I was a 14 year old freshman at Boston Latin School on that tragic November day. One of my responsibilities at Latin School that year was acting as an escort for a blind boy, Donald Dawes. He had been blind since birth and provided me with an early lesson in how determination and drive can overcome any obstacle. He was taken to and from school in a taxi cab. On that Friday afternoon, November 22, 1963, I walked Donald out to Johnny Miller's cab. The cab driver told us that the President had been shot and was believed to be dead. The cabbie wept openly as he told us the terrible news. I had never seen a grown man crying like that. That and the horrific news of the death of my hero shook me to my core. I put Donald in the cab and headed downtown and watched the black bunting being draped on Boston City Hall. The entire country was grieving, but Boston was staggered. Boston had lost a favorite son. As I walked down Tremont Street to Park Street station to catch the subway home to Dorchester, I noticed no one was talking. Everyone looked preoccupied and sad, lost in his or her own thoughts. It was utterly tragic and stunning to me to see how the death of one person could affect everyone so profoundly.

Of course, I was deeply upset as well. John Kennedy had been my boyhood hero. John Kennedy inspired many in my generation to public service. Some served in the Peace Corps which he created by executive order. Others ran for public office. He appealed to the idealism of my generation, as well as to our sense of destiny. When he spoke of how every man could make a difference and every man should try, I felt the call. I was not the only teenager who cried himself to sleep that evening and vowed to dedicate his life to public service as a way to honor a dead hero. I watched every minute of the funeral and can still recreate those sad scenes in my mind, particularly the parade of world leaders walking quietly behind the caisson, all humbled in the face of the untimely murder of a young leader. I can still hear that sad funeral music in my head.

A Harvard education was not cheap, but it was not nearly as expensive as it is today and my parents had saved diligently for the education of their three children. I also received scholarships from Harvard and Boston Latin School. My parents agreed to pay my book bills at the Harvard Coop. The Coop, run by the Harvard Cooperative Society since 1882, serves the Harvard and MIT communities and is one of the largest college bookstores in the country. I eventually became a member of its board of directors.

I picked up all sorts of odd jobs to make pocket money to buy clothing, cover any social activities and pay for personal items. I rented out refrigerators, a wildly popular amenity in the dorms and Houses. The refrigerators were available through the Harvard Student Agencies, which paid me 10 percent to peddle two sizes: $35 or $50 for the entire academic year. The sales pitch was helped by the fact I had memorized the names and faces of my fellow freshmen. Many years later, fellow students remembered how I extolled the virtues of a personal refrigerator to them. My mother had sent me off to the Boston Public Library to borrow a book on typing when I was younger, so I had already taught myself to type. I made a few dollars typing the papers of students whose mothers had not shown the same foresight. I also sold shirts at Kennedy's Department Store, a clothing store that specialized in well-made, but moderately priced, tailored preppy clothes, at the busy shopping times of Christmas and Easter. The employee discount came in handy.

I never ever lost touch with my family and neighborhood. It was inconceivable that I would not go home every Sunday. I rode the MBTA back to Ashmont and walked to St. Gregory's Church where I was lector, or the reader of Scripture, for the 9:45 a.m. Mass. I then went home, read the newspapers, opened my mail, visited with my family, and enjoyed a huge Italian meal. As I headed out the door, my Nonna Peppina would always hand me some of her biscotti. She baked the biscotti, a wonderful twice baked almond flavored Italian biscuit in the shape of a log, and then cut it up into serving pieces. I can still close my eyes and see her arthritic hands carefully cutting the biscotti with her old kitchen knife. She was sturdy, stern and never used a recipe. She put the treats in a plastic bag, hugged me and sent me back to school. Those biscotti never lasted longer than Sunday evening on campus. My father always drove me back to Cambridge with a bag of clean, pressed laundry. We walked upstairs and I gave him a bag full of dirty laundry. Mother belonged to the generation of women who pressed everything, including underwear. At the time, I did not appreciate what a luxurious service that was.

During my last two years at Harvard, Quincy House became a second home. Bill McCue, Henry Kettell and Warren Knowlton were three great roommates who understood that my priorities were different from those of many of my classmates. My college friends became lifelong friends, whom I value as much today as I did then. Tom Stemberg and I are godfather to one of each others' children; to this day, Ben Beach continues to preside at our tailgate party each time Harvard plays Yale. It is the only day of the year when I drink beer and eat hamburgers well before noon. When we get together it is as if we were still young men in Quincy House in the 1960s.

I would love to say that I excelled academically at Harvard, but it would not be true. I was a middling student. I was simply much more interested in things other than class work. I did the minimum required. Frankly, no one could flunk out of Harvard in those years even if he tried. The war in Vietnam was raging. The military draft was in force and college students were deferred from military service. Anyone who flunked out of college could literally be on the next train to Army boot camp. The university did not want to turn Harvard men into cannon fodder for what was an almost universally unpopular war and therefore overlooked academic shortcomings. The lottery, based upon birth date, was introduced and those whose numbers came up would be called up first. I had a high number so the likelihood of being drafted after graduating from college in 1971 was slight. This allowed me to think more broadly than my classmates with low numbers, who needed to enroll in graduate school if they wanted to avoid military service after graduation.

My favorite activities increasingly involved politics. I grew up steeped in politics as a Dorchester kid. I stood at the polls and distributed leaflets and marked up voter lists during puberty. It was second nature to me—just like my ability to talk to virtually anyone about anything and my ability to recall names, faces and facts. Indeed, I quickly discovered that those innate characteristics contributed to my success as a student leader at Boston Latin School, at Boys State and Boys Nation and at Harvard.

Sophomore year I moved into Quincy House, where I had a more compatible roommate. Quincy House is one of the upper class Houses. It is located on Plympton Street between Harvard Yard and the Charles River and named after Josiah Quincy III, a former President of Harvard, Mayor of Boston and member of Congress. My sophomore roommate was Alan J. Weisbard, a very bright student from Miami Beach. He later went to Yale Law School and became a professor at the University of Wisconsin Law School. Alan was one of the first people I ever met who could legitimately be called a computer nerd. Computers were just beginning to emerge as the powerful technological tool that has transformed modern life. With Alan's encouragement, I signed up for a course called Natural Sciences 110, taught by Professor William H. Bossert. It was one of the first computer science classes ever offered at Harvard. As part of the course, each student had to create a computer program. At the time, computer code was punched by hand on punch cards which were then fed into a code reader and run through a mainframe IBM computer. Personal computers, laptops and tablets were nonexistent. I was intrigued by the potential of computers.

I decided to create a program analyzing the 1967 election results in Boston. The year 1967 was a mayoral election year when Kevin H. White, then the Secretary of State, beat Louise Day Hicks, a member of the Boston School Committee, to win his first term as Mayor of Boston. I was looking for a way to run successfully for public office. I hoped to find the clues in the most recent City Election by analyzing the ward and precinct totals of certain candidates.

In those days, all candidates for the nine member City Council and the five member Boston School Committee ran citywide. This gave an inherent advantage to candidates with name recognition, to incumbents and to members of the dominant ethnic groups. Women, African-Americans, people of French or Polish or Asian ancestry would have a difficult, if not impossible, time winning election in a citywide contest. The advantage went to white men of Irish or Italian ancestry. The nine candidates who won election to the Boston City Council in the 1967 municipal election were all men: eight were white. The lone minority group member was Thomas I. Atkins, a distinguished African-American and Harvard Law School graduate who later held several senior positions with the NAACP. Six of the nine were Irish-Catholic: William J. Foley Jr., John E. Kerrigan, Gerald F. O'Leary, Jr., Garrett M. Byrne, Patrick F. McDonough and Joseph F. Timilty. Frederick C. Langone was the only Italian-American. The ninth member was John L. Saltonstall Jr. More than half of the victorious candidates came from either South Boston or Dorchester. Joe Timilty had a Mattapan address but he was from Lower Mills and a St. Gregory's boy. Pat McDonough was born in Ireland and lived in Dorchester and Foley, Kerrigan and O'Leary lived in South Boston. That ethnic and neighborhood mix: six Irish, one Italian, one Yankee and one African-American, explained a lot about the demographics and voting patterns of Boston in 1967.

I found a roadmap for my own eventual run for public office in those election returns. The analysis drew my attention to three names: John L. Saltonstall Jr., John F. Fitzgerald and Velia DiCesare. Although Saltonstall was the only one of the three to actually win election and finish in the top nine in November, the results of the two losers were just as enlightening.

John L. Saltonstall was a Boston lawyer and denizen of a famous old Massachusetts political family. He was a graduate of Harvard and Yale Law School and a progressive civil libertarian. He defended a Harvard professor charged with contempt of Congress for refusing to disclose the names of Communist Party members during the Army-McCarthy red baiting hearings in the 1950s and went to Mississippi to defend black civil rights workers against bogus libel charges in the 1960s. His votes showed me the location of progressive voters in the city who would always be inclined to vote for a liberal and a reformer.

John F. Fitzgerald was from Dorchester. His most distinguishing characteristic was he carried the exact same name as John "Honey Fitz" Fitzgerald, the grandfather of John F. Kennedy. His brother Richie was also my classmate at Boston Latin School. I noticed that this John Fitzgerald pulled a good vote, but only in Dorchester. This portended good things for me, another Dorchester native, because Dorchester is the mother lode of votes in the city of Boston, as the largest and most populous neighborhood in the city.

Velia DiCesare, a candidate for the Boston School Committee, came from Readville, a section of Hyde Park in the southern tier of the city and a poor base for a citywide candidate. However, she pulled votes from the North End and East Boston, the two dominant Italian neighborhoods which were miles away, as well as from precincts with large numbers of Italian-American voters in the southern tier of the city. Her votes showed me where a candidate named DiCara could find fellow paisans. As a side note, I was recently delighted to see that Velia was commended by the U.S. Department of Labor for being the longest serving tenured unemployment compensation worker in the nation a few years ago. Velia started working when she was 19 years old and 74 years later, in 2010, was still working at the age of 92. She was an active labor union member and reformer when politically active in the 1960s.

I looked for three candidates who had something in common with me. Jock Saltonstall was an Ivy Leaguer. John F. Fitzgerald was a young guy with a Dorchester address. Velia DiCesare was an Italian, not originally from the North End, and also a reformer. The analysis I conducted to comply with the course requirements for my computer class convinced me I could run city-wide and cobble together a coalition of liberals, Italians and Dorchester residents . . . and win, despite my youth and relative lack of political experience. I began to talk about running for office someday and, needless to say, my friends and relatives were extremely skeptical. I suppose they had good reason: I was 19 years old; I did not have money; I was not a well-known name; nor did I have much life experience. But I was brimming with self-confidence. So I began two years of plotting. I kept boxes and boxes of conventional 3 X 5 inch index cards, each one holding a name, address and telephone number of a potential campaign worker, financial supporter or voter. The days of computerized voter lists were far in the future. My focus increasingly shifted to my future rather than my present. I was truly a young man in a hurry.

In the spring of 1970, my father won $1,500 at a Dorchester Lower Mills Council Knights of Columbus #180 raffle held to benefit the K of C youth hockey team. My father insisted upon paying taxes on his windfall even though the money came to him in cash and the IRS would never had known about it. He was truly a man of integrity. I persuaded him to buy a second car with the balance and was able to take it to school with me the next September. Parking at the Harvard Business School campus just across the Charles River only cost $100 a semester back then. The used car gave me mobility and I spent as much time in Boston as I did in Cambridge. I used money from a summer job to buy a mimeograph machine. Before Xerox machines, there were mimeos, a messy process of making copies involving a stencil. I think it is fair to say that I was probably the only Harvard undergraduate to own a mimeo instead of a stereo. When I turned 21 that April 30, I got up early, showered, put on a suit coat and tie, and took the subway to Boston City Hall to register to vote. For me, this ritual signaled that I had grown up and my political career could begin.

My summer jobs were opportunities for me to learn and further my political ambition. During the summer of 1967, I worked as a playground instructor for $56 a week at 'The Prairie," which was located in Roxbury across from the Old Mr. Boston plant at 1010 Massachusetts Avenue (which subsequently became a city office building). The distillery produced its own label of gin, bourbon, rum and brandies from 1933 until it was closed in 1986. You could smell the booze from the distillery. I was told that the Prairie was a "white field," even though the location was at the intersection of Dorchester, Roxbury and the South End. I insisted upon integrating the playground, a grievously unpopular position in some quarters, and got beat up as a consequence. For that same reason, the field house got torched that summer. Although that section of Roxbury was already integrated, some of the white residents felt they were being crowded out of their longtime neighborhood. I was told quite emphatically: "This is a white people's park." That experience taught me a great deal about the fears of working class white ethnics, which later played out during the busing years.

In 1968, I worked on the congressional campaign for $50 a week for Chandler Harrison Stevens, an Independent candidate who challenged Rep. Philip J. Philbin for the 3rd Congressional District. Philbin, a Democrat, served for two more years before losing the Democratic primary to Robert F. Drinan in 1970. Drinan, a Jesuit priest, then dean of Boston College Law School, and an antiwar candidate, served with distinction until Pope John Paul II announced in 1980 that no priest could hold elective office. The Pope reportedly was trying to shut down the radical priests who espoused liberation theology and worked with the desperately poor in Central and South America, who found great appeal in the Communist Parties. Father Drinan turned out to be collateral damage in that policy decision. But the 1968 election and Stevens' candidacy showed that Philbin, a longtime incumbent who served for 28 years, was vulnerable. Harry Stevens served as the John the Baptist for Father Drinan. I learned a lot about practical politics on that campaign.

During the summer of 1969, I worked for the Town Manager in the small town of Saugus, which is located on the North Shore of Massachusetts and is the site of the first integrated iron works in the United States, an historic site that dates back to the 17th century. A friend rented his Mustang to me. I was able to dispense with the duties of the position fairly quickly and discovered that I had free time. I used it to sit in the Saugus Public Library and draft legislation, which I filed at the Great and General Court, the formal name for the Massachusetts State Legislature. Two of the bills became law. One expanded the right of citizens to put non-binding questions on a local ballot and the other allowed for the creation of student advisory committees to local school boards. I learned a lot about the legislative process that summer.

I went to work in the summer of 1970 for Philip Johnston, who ran the Robert F. Kennedy Action Corps, for $100 a week. Phil later became a state representative and chairman of the Massachusetts Democratic Party. The Robert F. Kennedy Action Corps is a private non-profit child welfare agency that provides care, counseling, treatment, education and rehabilitative services for at-risk children in Massachusetts. I wanted to be able to say I was employed when I ran for public office in 1971, so I continued to work part time during my senior year of college. I earned enough money to buy a couple of suits on sale at the Harvard COOP. I favored striped rep ties. My grandmother altered all my shirt sleeves for me. Old photographs of me show a very formally dressed young man, rarely without a suit jacket and tie. I desperately wanted to look like a grown up.

By my senior year at Harvard, I was fixated on the 1971 city election. Mayor White would be running for reelection and I knew that a mayoral contest would increase turnout, bringing out more young people and more casual voters than in an off year election. This always is a good political environment for a newcomer. In another stroke of luck that promised to boost the turnout of younger votes, the 26th amendment to the U.S. Constitution won approval on July 5, 1971, lowering the voting age to 18. The war in Vietnam contributed to its passage. Young men could be drafted into the military and killed for their country at the age of 18 but not vote until age 21. It just struck almost everyone as fundamentally unfair.

I felt confident that I could mix together the exact right combination of voters to win citywide and build upon the network I began to consciously develop as a high school student at Boston Latin School. My Boston Latin School classmates came from all over the city. They and their families proved to be an enormously helpful entrée to new people and places. A political campaign is a viral enterprise. When all goes well, one person leads to another, one network generates another and one connection or link creates yet another one. One contact, a Latin School classmate, for example, would lead to a house party hosted by the classmate's mother and an introduction to her friends and neighbors, who in turn would mention me to their relatives, friends and neighbors. I had many networks to work: the Knights of Columbus and its almost 1,000 members in Lower Mills; the parish of St. Gregory's; and the Boston Latin School alumni. I even found people in Roxbury who remembered my grandfather and his barber shop fondly and won their support because of that old familial connection.

I announced my intent to seek office in 1971 to my parents in the autumn of my senior year of college in 1970. I deliberately chose to break the news at a time I had to leave the house right away for another appointment, because I did not want to get into a debate with them. I knew they would be concerned. In fact, they were hesitant. They worried about my youth and feared I would be hurt in the rough political environment of Boston. My mother said, "Son, everyone will say you are too young." My parents were not naïve. They knew there were some questionable characters and practices still in force in Boston politics. The cash laden envelope or a patronage no-show job was still an effective way to secure the vote of certain city councilors. My parents appreciated my enthusiasm and idealism but worried I would be crushed by corruption and cynicism. As I look back, my parents had a better sense of what I would face than I did. But they were wonderful parents. They stifled their fears and supported me without reservation in literally everything I ever did. My father served as treasurer of that first campaign and every subsequent campaign of my career. Having Dad in charge of the money was better than an insurance policy because of his impeccable sense of integrity and honor. My mother fed me and Chip Moore and whoever else I was campaigning with most every day that summer. She, like my Nonna, fretted endlessly about my eating. One night she, my sister Ginny and my campaign manager, Bill Guenther, stayed up all night to finish a mailing because the price of postage was going up two cents the following day. They saved the campaign a few hundred dollars in postage. I was so lucky.

Every campaign is an adventure, a frenetic, often chaotic adventure full of bigger than life characters. In 1971, most of them were young, very young, but we had our share of eccentric contributors, old friends who did not de-liver, people I barely knew who did deliver, and sensible young mothers wearing sensible shoes, who were intrigued by the whole political exercise.

In political campaigns, the first challenge is to develop a message and then to anticipate all liabilities and turn any potential liability into an asset. There are two time honored pitches for political candidates and the approach depends upon age. The grizzled old timer campaigns on his "experience" and ability to deliver for his constituency. The newcomer argues "It's time for change." I was going to be a change candidate. I waited until after my birthday in April when I turned 22, and three days before my graduation from college, to announce my candidacy so I could be described as age 22 and a Harvard graduate. I announced my candidacy on June 14, Flag Day. My slogan was "A New Face in a Tired Crowd." It was a derivative of the 1965 slogan used by John Lindsay in New York City. I was young, not Irish, not a conventional Italian candidate and, indeed, not the typical council candidate. So I ran as an outsider and as a reformer.

Although I felt certain I could find the right combination and quantity of votes to win citywide, it still troubled me that anyone else, say a black candidate from Roxbury or a female candidate from Jamaica Plain or Brighton or a Chinese candidate, could never hope to replicate my strategy. Tom Atkins won in 1967, probably because of the higher turnout of blacks and liberals who wanted to make certain Louise Day Hicks did not become mayor. Indeed, John Saltonstall topped the ticket in his very first run for the City Council, which speaks volumes about the composition of that 1967 turnout. It just seemed unfair to me that the deck was stacked against "other" in a Boston City Council election. I had written my undergraduate thesis at Harvard on bilingual education in Boston, a personal interest since my first teachers had dubbed me defective because of my facility with Italian, and concluded that the Boston School Committee, also elected citywide, failed to represent the diversity of the public school student body. I proposed district representation—a system whereby a majority of the members of the School Committee would be elected from specific districts to make it easier for minority group members to win and serve, allowing the governing board to better reflect its constituency. I dusted that off and used it as the basis of a proposal for charter change in Boston—to also allow a majority of city councilors to also be elected from districts rather than citywide.

Needless to say, the incumbent Boston City Councilors thought this was a terrible idea. Anything that changed the existing system and challenged the status quo represented a huge threat to them personally. I am pleased to say that by 1983 Boston had adopted charter change and a hybrid system of some candidates who ran citywide and a majority elected from districts. This led to the election, the very first time, of Thomas M. Menino from Hyde Park as a district councilor. His colleagues eventually elected him President of the City Council and when Mayor Raymond L. Flynn became Ambassador to the Vatican during the administration of Bill Clinton in 1993, Tom became the first Italian-American acting Mayor of Boston. His performance got him elected in his own right repeatedly and he served with distinction for decades. I suspect Tom would agree with me that he never would have been elected mayor under the old system. The new system gave him the opportunity to serve and show voters what he could do.

In that first campaign I also opposed expansion of Logan Airport into the East Boston neighborhood and opposed an extension of Interstate 95 through Jamaica Plain into downtown Boston. The highway construction boom of the 1950s had gone into overdrive and suburban residents liked the idea of zipping straight from their suburban homes (accessible via interstate highways) into the heart of the city. The families and businesses in the path of those proposed extensions were wildly opposed, so these populist positions helped solidify my standing as an outsider—not afraid to take on the powerful interests and stand up for city residents.

A grand total of 67 candidates pulled papers to run for the Boston City Council in 1971 and 41 names ended up on the ballot. For a just turned 22-year-old who had never held public office, the challenge of finishing in the top 18 for the preliminary and then the top 9 for the final was daunting.

The campaign passed in a blur. I literally campaigned from dawn until well after dark and never stopped moving. I had a cadre of volunteers: family members, classmates from Boston Latin School and Harvard, and other old friends. My candidacy attracted many young people who volunteered their services. In those days, professional campaign staffs were nonexistent. I lived on the money my relatives gave to me as graduation presents that spring. I had very little money. Indeed, the campaign ran on fumes most of the time and had no paid staff. My campaign began in my sixth floor room at Quincy House at Harvard and the headquarters was an abandoned storefront at 154 State Street that the landlord agreed to rent to me for $1 if we cleaned it out. I had to open up a bank account for the campaign before holding my first event so I went to the State Street Bank in downtown Boston and set up the DiCara for City Council account. When Tim Cooney, the banker, asked me how much I wanted to deposit, I had nothing but a single dollar bill and a single subway token to get me back to Cambridge. That kind man took pity on me, pulled out his own wallet, and drew out a $5 bill. That $5 became my first campaign donation. I never warmed up to the task of asking others for help or money. I was so grateful for that $5. I have never forgotten his generosity.

We held two announcement parties to reflect my different worlds: one at the Cambridge Boat Club and the other at the John McKeon AmVets Post 146 in Dorchester. The entrée fee was $8 for men and $4 for women at the boat club and everyone paid in cash. We raised $1,000 in cash and I promptly ordered buttons and stationery. The McKeon Post was not as big as Florian Hall, the big union hall in Dorchester, but big enough to hold a couple of hundred people and raise a few thousand dollars in $5 and $10 increments. Bill Guenther, a Harvard student from New York City who was a year behind me, was campaign manager. Harvard looked the other way while he lived at Quincy House over the summer.

I loved to campaign. I had always enjoyed meeting new people and talking to them. Soon after Labor Day, we dreamed up a publicity stunt: a walk from one end of the city to the other. I started in Charlestown early in the day and ended at the Dedham line as the sun was setting. Walking down Washington Street showed that I was young and vigorous. I am convinced my weak ankles are the result of wearing loafers on those campaign jaunts. On that day, I stopped at the Cardinal Cushing Center for the Spanish Speaking across from the Cathedral in the South End. I handed them a copy of my Harvard thesis: *The Failure of the Boston Public Schools to Educate Spanish*

Speaking Children. I have doubts whether that symbolic visit helped advance my candidacy.

The campaign was not without incident. I was making my way through the North End, the neighborhood on the Waterfront just by downtown that had been heavily Italian for several generations. I worked my way through its tiny crowded streets, stopping at each café and coffee shop, walking up creaky old stairs to reach apartments tucked above the store fronts when I was urged to go upstairs to "The Club," where a card game was underway. Ever eager to shake every hand and ask for every vote, I marched right upstairs. An older gentleman sipping a glass of red wine at the card table wished me luck. "I've heard about you, kid," he said. "Good luck." It was Jerry Angiulo, the most infamous mafia don in Boston. For once in my life, I was speechless. I must have stammered some sort of response but I was in shock and I ran out the door and down the stairs. The very idea of being caught in the company of a mob boss was clearly a career killer. In one of those only in Boston coincidences, Angiulo and my father had been classmates at Boston English High School.

One campaign worker, Charlie Perkins, who came to Boston for the summer to avoid his parent's divorce in Philadelphia, went door to door for me at High Point Village, a subsidized housing development in Roslindale. Charlie was young, skinny and preppy looking and had the accent of a Main Line patrician. A woman accosted him suggesting he was "One of the rich Kennedy kids . . . you know what you are, you are pretty!" Charlie replied: "You know what you are: you are fat!" She did call the campaign headquarters to complain.

On another day, one of my volunteers, a high school student, was going door to door on Moss Hill, an affluent enclave in Jamaica Plain. He rang one bell to be greeted by a buck naked woman. "Oh," she said, "I thought it was the mailman!"

The template for my door to door campaigning was the analysis I had conducted of the 1967 election results. If Willie Sutton robbed banks because there was where the money was, I campaigned in precincts where I knew I was most likely to get a positive response and a vote. Chris Iannella, the fatherly City Councilor who befriended me, once told me that he did his own version of targeting by sending campaign literature to Italian-American families with three or more registered voters.

On Labor Day, I fell asleep on Tenean Beach, the tiny beach in Dorchester that can be seen from the northbound lane of the Southeast Expressway. I was utterly exhausted and took a few hours off. I was able for the next few weeks to brag about my "Tenean Beach tan" with total honesty. Towards the end of the preliminary campaign, Jerry Williams, the most popular talk show host on Boston radio, invited Jack Casey, another young candidate, on his radio show. During that broadcast, Jack was described as the youngest candidate on the ballot. I knew that was wrong. I was younger by several months so I asked my friend Mike Keating, a lawyer, to call Jerry Williams' radio show and demand equal time for me to correct this grievous error. Williams was a good sport and he invited me on his show. Naturally, I never stopped talking and after the first hour, he asked me to stay around for the second hour. So I had two full hours of time on the most popular radio show in the city at a critical time in the campaign when voters were starting to pay attention. In those days, everyone listened to Jerry Williams. He literally defined talk radio in Boston. I cannot know for certain how it helped me, but I'm certain it did not hurt and that extra exposure separated me from the other newcomers on the ballot, including the other young candidates. Only one of us was likely to be successful given the odds and I was determined that I would be the young candidate who broke through the pack. After the preliminary election, I also won the endorsements of The Boston Globe and the Boston Herald. My Harvard degree helped me with the newspaper endorsements. An Ivy League degree was a credential that newspaper editors respected. Those newspaper endorsements helped enormously.

I had one more stroke of sheer luck. Joseph "Jo Jo" Langone III, the state representative who was the brother of Freddy Langone, an incumbent member of the City Council, was convicted of assaulting a federal drug investigator parked outside the family funeral parlor and sent off to prison just days before the election. (The agent reportedly had Jo Jo's son under surveillance.) The newspaper headlines blared "Langone Goes to Jail." That it was Jo Jo and not Freddy mattered little in a contest where voters so casually tossed one vote to the Italian candidate and another to the neighborhood candidate. Langone lost and I won.

There is no way to explain the adrenaline rush of a first election. In our case, we did not know I had won until after midnight, when Richie Serino rushed into St. Mark's VFW Post with the news after hearing the final results on his car radio. I have a photograph that shows me standing next to my parents that night, all of us up on chairs so the crowd could see us. I was so proud to be their son and they were so proud of their son, the newly elected City Councilor.

Early the next day, telegrams began to arrive in great numbers. The first one came from Richard A. Clarke, then a senior at the University of Pennsylvania, who had been a boyhood friend and debate partner at Boston Latin School.

An analysis of the 1971 results conducted by my daughter Sophie shows that my victory came about precisely as I had guessed. I put together a coalition of votes from the Italian wards of East Boston and the North End in Wards 1 and 3; of Dorchester residents in Wards 16 and my home ward of 17; of liberal voters in Ward 5—the Back Bay and Beacon Hill. I ranked in the top six of vote getters in those wards. Although every voter can vote for as many as 9 candidates, most vote for six or fewer. In a practice called "bulleting," some politically savvy voters would only vote for one or two candidates to maximize the impact of their vote.

Six incumbents ran for reelection that year. Five won reelection The incumbents who won reelection were: Chris Iannella, a genteel older lawyer, who acted as a surrogate parent to me on the council; John E. Kerrigan, "Silent John," a bachelor from South Boston who served 15 terms on the Boston City Council beginning in 1933. (He served as acting mayor in 1945, when Maurice J. Tobin was elected governor but was beaten by James Michael Curley in the mayoral election that year); Gerald F. O'Leary, who later served on the School Committee and spent 13 months in federal prison for extorting a bus company hired to implement the busing order; Gabe Piemonte, the first Italian-American politician elected citywide, who loathed me because he felt I was not sufficiently respectful of him; and Albert "Dapper" O'Neil, a crass Irish-American hack, who could be counted upon to denigrate women, gays, minorities and anyone else he decided to hate that day. I think it is safe to say that Dapper didn't like me much, but then he hated everyone.

Four new faces joined the Council: me; J. Joseph Moakley; Joseph Tierney (who was helped by the candidacy of the ticket topper in the School Committee race, Paul Tierney, even though they were not related. Joe's talented daughter Maura later became a famous Hollywood actress.); and Pat McDonough. Pat had been on the Council before, and 1971 was one of the times he made a comeback. Pat always barely held on. Moakley was angling to run for Congress the following year seeking a rematch against Louise Day Hicks.

I was the youngest person and the first member of the Baby Boomer Generation ever elected to the Boston City Council. I was the first Italian elected citywide without a political base in the North End, the traditional Italian neighborhood. Gabe and Chris no longer lived in the North End, but had been raised there. Although I was a bit of an old soul at the age of 22, I definitely felt different from my colleagues. From the start, I was an outsider because I was younger. I was also far more liberal than most of the other Councilors and I was full of ideas and ambitious to cut a swath through city government.

My election was an upset. I had seemingly come out of nowhere. No one outside of my personal circle of friends really knew who I was. When John Henning, a tall good looking television journalist who became a broadcast legend in Boston over the course of a long career, came to our house and interviewed me on the steps after the election, he kindly stood on a lower step to minimize the extraordinary discrepancy in our heights. From a distance, we looked to be the same height. My grandmother, who measured about 4 feet 10 inches high, stood on the porch to watch. Nonna always kept her house immaculately clean, as if guests were expected at any moment. I was thrilled to be interviewed by such an august journalist. I felt I had arrived.

With the benefit of hindsight, I do not believe my election was an accident. There is a cyclical and generational pattern to politics and I was part of a first wave of Baby Boomers beginning to take a seat at the electoral dinner table. In the 1946 election, the first after the end of World War II, John Kennedy, Richard Nixon and many other prominent leaders of the postwar period won their first elections. In 1971, many Baby Boomers were just beginning to emerge. For example, Gail Dunfey, a friend from CYO, the Catholic Youth Organization, had won election to the Lowell City Council that same day. The Dunfey family was well known in Lowell and beyond. Her relatives managed the Parker House, a downtown Boston hotel near the State House, for years. In fact, when they opened the bar called The Last Hurrah in the basement of the hotel soon after the election, Gail and I were the toast of the town. The bar was named after the barely fictitious novel of the same name based upon the colorful career of Boston Mayor James Michael Curley, a roguish politician of the old school who served some time in federal prison for taking an examination for a pal and a second stint for mail fraud.

Gail's political career was cut short when she married Ronald Sinicki two years later and refused to change her maiden name to Sinicki. She had good reasons politically. She won election as a Dunfey and professional women were just beginning to retain their maiden names as a feminist statement. She was seen as flouting convention. The Lowell City Clerk kept calling out the name Gail Sinicki each time he called the roll of the City Council and got no response (The first time he did that, Gail was on her honeymoon and out of town so it was not really fair. The powers that be in Lowell were making a point about this young whippersnapper.) She went to court to get legal authority to keep her maiden name but the legal victory proved hollow in 1973 when she finished more than 200 votes out of the running.

Generational change happens in politics, as well as in other sectors of life. Kevin White was a game changer in Boston and generational leader just as John Kennedy had been nationally. White brought extraordinary diversity to the leadership of the city. He had black men and white and Hispanic women as deputy mayors and introduced a generation of young people to politics, giving many of them leadership roles in the city when they were very young. Many later became prominent leaders in Boston and nationally.

They included Kirk O'Donnell, a top aide to Speaker Thomas P. O'Neill, Jr.; Congressman Barney Frank; trusted advisor Lowell Richards; and Ira Jackson, who had distinguished academic, government and business careers. I had taught a seminar at the Institute of Politics on local and state government and felt I understood how things worked. But there is no text book for being on the Boston City Council. And back then, there was absolutely no orientation. I had to figure it out for myself and, boy was I in for a surprise.

Before the Storm

When I took office at the beginning of 1972, Boston was in tough shape. The city had been rocked back on its heels like a lot of other older cities in the Northeast and Midwest. The economy was changing in a way that would ultimately prove to be beneficial for brainy Boston. But the traditional manufacturing and industrial jobs that had allowed generations of Bostonians to raise families in relative comfort were disappearing and the transition deeply hurt blue collar workers and their families. It was not only jobs that were disappearing like a pedestrian strolling into the morning fog on Malibu Beach; it was a way of life. The decades of the 1960s and 1970s represented a time of extraordinary social and cultural change and all sorts of people were being helplessly shaken out of their comfort zones. Everything was changing. Widespread availability of the first reliable method of birth control, the pill, gave an entire generation of women new opportunities in the workplace. This one change alone utterly changed the social order of the time. For many, change was wrenching. Working class men lost their primacy in their families and the workplace. Those unable to support their families because of the loss of jobs also felt emasculated and threatened by the social and economic changes taking place all around them.

The demographics of the city were also changing. Since the end of World War II, many city residents abandoned Dorchester, South Boston, Hyde Park and Jamaica Plain for Burlington, Tewksbury, Quincy, Braintree, Needham and other suburbs to claim the split level ranch house and plot of green grass, that postwar incarnation of the American Dream. Public policy put afterburners on this trend. Federal veterans' benefits gave returning military veterans access to higher education and low cost mortgages, the two policies that contributed to the biggest explosion in the size of the middle class in American history. One of the great achievements of the Eisenhower Administration was the creation of the interstate highway system. In Massachusetts, the construction of Routes 3, 128 and later Routes 93 and 95 carried thousands of families away from Jamaica Plain, Dorchester and Hyde Park to the fresher, newer, subdivisions of suburbia. Those long stretches of highway literally transformed an American way of life. The Southeast Expressway made South Boston and Dorchester an easy drive to the towns south of Boston that had once been known for their affordable summer cottages. If you could live in Burlington, a town north of Boston, where you could own your own single family house with a nice big yard and decent public schools, and drive to Boston in 20 or 25 minutes (in those days before bumper to bumper traffic), why wouldn't you do just that?

It cannot be denied that as the 1960s progressed, white flight was taking place in the city. You had to be deaf, dumb and blind not to know about the court cases percolating up through the legal system on racial segregation in the public schools. The Supreme Court struck down Jim Crow and the notion of separate but equal with Brown v. Board of Education of Topeka in 1954. Massachusetts adopted its own Racial Imbalance Act in 1965, which ordered public schools to desegregate or else lose state funding. Of course, that state law only affected two places: Boston and Springfield, the only two cities with any significant minority population. The case that led to busing in Boston, Morgan v. Hennigan, was filed in 1972, just a year after a Supreme Court case Swann v. Charlotte-Mecklenburg ruled that busing could be used as a remedy to rectify *de jure* or deliberate segregation in public schools.

As the population shifted from the cities to the suburbs, following the trail of jobs, opportunity and those literally greener pastures, the city population shrunk. Those left behind tended to be the older, poorer and less educated. They were also more likely to be a member of a minority racial group. After the war, the white population of Boston dropped by one-third as the black population grew to more than 100,000 people, or about 16 percent of the city. Boston had always had a small black population. But the black slice of Boston grew in the 1950s and 1960s as the white population declined. The Great Migration of black Americans fleeing Jim Crow in the South brought dramatic change in many northern cities. As a result, African-Americans and Hispanic residents slowly were becoming a bigger segment of the total population.

Banking policies denied mortgages to black people in the suburbs and certain "white" Boston neighborhoods and steered minority loans to certain "black" sections. The traditional neighborhoods shifted along with the racial composition of the city. Those exclusionary banking policies exacerbated the migration of Jewish residents from Roxbury, Dorchester and Mattapan in Boston to the suburbs of Sharon, Randolph, Brookline and Newton. African-Americans took their place. Within a remarkably short period of time, the

Jewish population of the city almost disappeared. Banking policies also exaggerated the natural tendency of newcomers to live near friends and relatives and people who were like them. Segregation of neighborhoods by race became more pronounced. By the time federal law outlawed redlining, it was too little too late. The practices of decades took an enormous toll on the social fabric of the old and exhausted cities of America.

As a result, Boston and many other older urban areas were effectively left in the dust. The cities came to be associated with the words old, tired, and broke and it did not help that an air of seedy corruption clung to some of the more visible politicians of the era. In the 1970 gubernatorial race, a WASP Republican named Frank Sargent from the tiny town of Dover not only decisively defeated Boston Mayor Kevin H. White statewide, but he also beat him in the city of Boston and in West Roxbury where Kevin's family had lived for some time. Sargent labeled Kevin "a Boston politician." The term became an epithet as deadly as if he had been labeled a terrorist. I did not know it at the time but the energy and key to political success in Massachusetts had already moved to the suburbs. The "reformers" and progressive politicians like Michael S. Dukakis, the Swarthmore and Harvard educated son of Greek immigrants from the town of Brookline, came to dominate state politics. On paper, Michael and I were not terribly different, though he was older than I. We shared ethnic backgrounds, progressive views, and a great education. With the benefit of hindsight, I see now that a guy from Dorchester, whose role models were older city politicians, did not have a prayer in this new climate.

At the time I was profoundly different from my colleagues on the City Council. It was not only an age discrepancy that separated us. It is fair to say that few of the other City Councilors viewed themselves as law makers or policy wonks. Quite the contrary. The Mayor set the policy agenda and the Council, more or less depending upon the issue and state of relations with the Mayor, rubber stamped it. When I stopped by City Hall after the election, I was told I would get an office and could hire two staff people. One was paid $165 a week and other $135 a week. The practice at the time was to hire a secretary to do typing and answer the phone for the lower paid position and an aide de camp, who was also a constituent service coordinator and political aide, for the higher paid job. I searched in vain for a secretary who was smart, spoke some Spanish and could take dictation. Jim Dolan, an old friend from Boston Latin School agreed to be my administrative assistant. I had to cross a picket line of Boston police officers to attend my own inauguration at Faneuil Hall (they were protesting a contract dispute) and until I actually took office, I did not know that my office had its own bathroom and the job came with a 24 hour accessible parking spot—in the City Hall Garage—which even then was a huge amenity in downtown Boston.

After my election, I received a call at home from the office of Mayor Kevin White. He wanted to see me. I had shaken hands with him once before, but did not know him at all so I put on my best dark suit and a crisp white shirt and responded to the summons. When I walked into the Mayor's office, the Mayor was standing at the window staring out, the classic Kevin White pensive pose that was played up in the campaign slogan "A loner in love with the city," and endlessly parodied. The Mayor's office overlooks what is now Quincy Market and Boston Harbor. Then, the marketplace was a rundown eyesore and the ugly elevated portion of the Central Artery divided downtown from the waterfront and blocked the view of the ocean. I walked up next to him, joined him in looking at the scene and said, "Nice view" for lack of anything else to say. The view at that time would only appeal to a true visionary. He replied, "Don't get any funny ideas, kid!"

While I was ambitious and eager to be mayor some day, Kevin White, who was twenty years my senior, never viewed me as a rival. In 1973, when I ran for reelection, I bragged about the fact that my mother had baked 328 delicious chocolate brownies as refreshments for a political event. The next day I received a box containing 329 brownies and a note from Mayor White. I still have the hand written note from him. It read: "Larry, I love you as much as your mother. Thanks, Kevin" Politics was friendlier and gentler in many respects in those days.

Mayor White was one of a number of progressive mayors holding office at that time. I called them the Great White Hope Mayors and they included John Lindsay of New York, Joseph Alioto of San Francisco, and Carl Stokes of Cleveland. (I did not use "Great White Hope" in a racial context. Even though Carl Stokes was African-American, I viewed him as very much a member of this class of mayors.) These men served as mayors at a time of riots and protests; they inherited cities badly in need of overhaul and an infusion of capital. In Boston, for example, the infrastructure was so old that fresh water gushed through dirt where the old wooden water pipes had simply rotted away. Raw sewage poured into Boston Harbor. The schools were literally crumbling. Much of the housing stock was falling down. Kevin had ambitious plans, but absolutely no money to implement them. This was a typical urban problem at the time. New York City defaulted on its general obligation bonds in 1975 and Cleveland followed three years later. When New York City nearly went bankrupt in 1975 and President Ford refused to provide a federal bailout, the New York Daily News published the famous headline, Ford to City: Drop Dead! The oil shocks of 1973 and 1979 contributed to the worst economic performance for the United States since the 1930s. Inflation was so high that President Gerald R. Ford launched a Whip Inflation Now campaign (WIN) to encourage personal savings and other steps to bring it under control—to little avail. With political power already shifting to the suburbs, this was an understandable, if short sighted, response from the short term Republican President.

Boston, like most Northeastern cities, relied upon property tax revenues for most of its revenue. The property tax base was shrinking as tens of thousands of residents and many businesses headed down the Expressway to suburbia. The city was so broke that the beautiful, large indoor heated swimming pools it opened in the early 1970s stayed idle. While the city paid off debt service on the pools, it did not have enough money to keep the pools operational. Of course, Boston did not help itself. The city had never conducted a comprehensive reevaluation of its real estate and most property was seriously undervalued. The only time an assessment might go up was when a house was sold and the new sale price became the new assessed value and that was not necessarily a given. The city went after business property with some aggressiveness, but that made the city a more expensive place to do business and effectively drove many businesses to the suburbs, an obvious if unintended consequence. High taxes, regulation, congestion, union wages and work rules conspired in a lavish mix to push big businesses with large work forces to the Sunbelt states, where low taxes, no regulation, wide open spaces and right to work laws would guarantee lower overhead and more profits. Eventually those same factors led business to outsource jobs overseas.

There were some practical reasons for avoiding reevaluation in the neighborhoods. To suddenly put the real market value on a family home owned by an elderly woman on a fixed income who had lived there for 40 years would probably raise the taxes so high she would lose her house. No one wanted to even think about that. Property values were all over the map. For example, my grandfather paid $18,500 for the two family house where I lived in Dorchester but the assessment was just over $8,000, the same assessment levied when Mr. Driscoll built the house in the late 1920s. I knew of a family friend in Hyde Park, Mrs. Yolanda Mazzarella, who lived in a much bigger two family house in a nicer neighborhood. (She was the sister of the wife of my father's godfather and my Dad was her son Vincent's godfather.) Her house had an assessment of $4,000, because her house had been built around 1880 and the assessment had never been increased. I remember speaking one day with Diggory Venn, whose son Tim was a Harvard classmate. They lived in a townhouse in the Back Bay where elegantly restored buildings were fast becoming among the most valuable real estate in the city. He paid lower property taxes than my grandmother. The assessment on his house was less than the assessment on our home. It made no sense until I learned that his house was a companion to an adjacent house built by a city assessor and, as a result, neither house had been reassessed in decades.

If property taxes were a third rail of politics in Boston, so was racial seg-regation of the Boston Public Schools. You had to be willingly ignorant not to know there was a problem that was building up a head of steam which would blow the city apart when the first busing order was implemented. In an opinion piece I wrote for The Boston Globe, published on April 10, 1975, I bemoaned the attitude of "procrastination and escapism."

"It grows from the feeling that it is better to postpone problems until tomorrow rather than confront them today," I wrote, "The trouble with this attitude is that today's problems will not go away. Instead, they will grow and persist."

I had an acute awareness from the beginning that busing would be deadly for me politically. I knew that elected public officials would be expected to take sides and I was going to be on the side of law and order, civil rights, and fairness. Judge Garrity's 1974 decision on desegregation was flawless from a legal standpoint. Of course, I will go to my grave convinced his remedy was wrong and unnecessarily divisive and I believe time has proven I was right about that. But such distinctions would never be heard in the cacophony that followed his decision. You would be seen as either a friend or enemy. To paraphrase Louise Day Hicks' famous slogan, there was never any doubt about where I would stand. I had a premonition that my position would cost me votes and it did. I wondered at the time whether my conviction would also cost me my fledgling political career.

So I was aware of these two ticking time bombs. While most of my coun-cil colleagues were more concerned with constituent services than policy, I had a much more ambitious notion of my job. From the start, I had so many interns and research assistants and policy advisers—all unpaid—that we ran out of space and chairs. I found I had more in common with the young policy experts in the White Administration than I did with the patronage-focused Councilors. It would have been political suicide to confront the issue of prop-erty taxes and school segregation in a straightforward way. So I focused on broader municipal financial issues, including the interest rates being paid by municipalities on borrowed money; the need for civil service reform; and the system of financing the pensions of city workers.

My new "job" would not officially begin until January. By November of 1971, my graduation money had been spent and I had to borrow $200 from my parents for pocket money and subway fare. I was a bit of a celebrity but I was also a broke 22 year old recent college graduate, living with his parents. There was already a gap between the public perception of Larry DiCara and the reality.

Those first days on the Boston City Council were heady. I discovered I had some power. There were only nine of us and five needed to be in agreement at any given time for anything to pass. My vote counted. The first significant vote was the vote for Council President. Gerry O'Leary asked me to vote for Gabe Piemonte, but I declined. I voted for Chris Iannella. The other Italian members of the Boston City Council simply hated one another. The rivalries dated back decades and were intensely personal. Bob Hannan, a Boston political reporter, called it the "war of the pizzas." Chris Iannella and Gabe Piemonte had been feuding since Gabe beat Chris for a state legislative seat in 1948. Chris claimed Gabe stole the election. Of course, the existing system encouraged rivalry because all nine members of the Council ran against one another every two years. One person's gain was likely another's loss. There was very little ideology to these rivalries. It was all personal. When Joe Moakley ran for Congress in 1972, for example, Freddie Langone slaved away for him in the North End because Joe's election to Congress would clear the way for Fred to return to the City Council. Fred had finished tenth, just one place out of the money in the previous city election, so Joe's resignation would put him back on the Council.

Over time, I have come to appreciate the unpredictable vagaries of election wins and losses. The most unexpected things could and would happen. Chris Iannella died at the age of 79 on September 12, 1992, while serving as President of the Boston City Council. He had been in ill health for some time but his family kept his death a secret to protect the political interests of his son who had the same name. Christopher A. Iannella, Jr., was running for reelection to the Governor's Council, a throwback to colonial times which approves all judicial nominations, and the Democratic primary election was just days away. So the family stashed Chris' body at the Robert J. Lawler Funeral Home on Centre Street in West Roxbury and told anyone who asked about Chris' physical condition that he was "about the same." That was true; Chris was quite literally on ice at Lawler's. Chris, Jr. won his race.

I picked my side and never regretted voting for my friend Chris Iannella for Council President, but Gabe had the votes to win the presidency and retaliated by denying me every one of the committee assignments I requested. He did put me on the Ways and Means Committee, which was chaired by Joe Moakley—to whom I became very close. Joe Moakley and I had offices on the same corridor. His administrative assistant, John Burke, was a neighbor from Dorchester. Joe and I became fast friends. He acted like a big brother to me. Joe had little interest on being on the City Council. He had been a State Senator and ran for Congress when Speaker John W. McCormack retired in 1970 but lost to Louise Day Hicks in the Democratic primary. He was plotting a rematch in 1972 and ran for the Council to have a platform for that challenge. In fact, Joe became the fifth vote I needed to pass legislation which created the community schools councils, which would give neighborhood residents a say in how the schools were used. The White Administration built five beautiful big community schools with amenities like gyms and swimming pools and located them in spots that straddled neighborhood lines. These magnet schools were built in response to the Racial Imbalance Law, but opened too late for them to make any difference in the racial mix of the school system. The school custodians wanted the schools shut down at 2 p.m. for their convenience; the communities wanted the schools open for after school and weekend activities. The proponents were stuck on getting that fifth vote so I approached Moakley. He told me that he was confident he would win election to Congress in November and then would not care about the powerful school custodians. So he told me to keep quiet but promised to vote for the bill after the election and before he left the council. He kept his word and the bill passed giving the people in the neighborhoods a voice in the management of their schools.

I was glad to quietly help Joe beat Louise Day Hicks and calculated that he would beat her by winning the suburban town of Needham. Joe ran as an Independent so he would benefit from the bigger turnout of voters in the presidential election in November. He bested Louise by 3,400 votes and won the race by carrying Needham—just as I predicted. Our friendship lasted nearly 30 years until his death in 2001. I got back at Gabe a year later by putting together five votes to oust him from the Council Presidency in 1973. In a larger legislative body, no freshman could ever have had that kind of power.

My colleagues provided a compelling example to me. I decided two things: I would never ever be so desperate for the job that I would grovel for votes, favors or anything else, and I would never be financially dependent upon a public pay check. The notion of being beholden or being so powerless that I would need to beg or be a supplicant in any way was repugnant to me. I did not want to ever have to go hat in hand to the Mayor and beg for a job for a constituent. I did not want to be dependent upon a public office for my livelihood. I had seen my father lose his job through no fault of his own and find himself with few options for employment, after a career working for a single company, simply because of his age. I wanted to avoid that at all costs so I decided to become a lawyer. I knew I would always be able to make a living, even as a sole practitioner. There is a time honored tradition of a politician/lawyer hanging out a shingle. Law was my insurance policy for future independence.

Suffolk Law School in Boston, then and now, is a favored law school for elected public officials. It is located within an easy walk of the State House and City Hall. Generations of state representatives and senators and their aides have walked down the street to class and earned law degrees there. Convenience means a lot to busy public officials. I could walk to class from

City Hall and be back at my office within seven minutes for a meeting or hearing. I decided to attend Suffolk Law School in the fall of 1972. Although Suffolk then ran the only decent night school for law in Boston, I made a fatal error; I enrolled as a full time student. At that age, I thought I was invincible. I was young, energetic and believed I could do anything. But full time legal studies, combined with full time City Council service, combined with my own frenzied speaking schedule throughout the city and state, and a relentless schedule of meetings, hearings and events eventually proved to be too much, even for me.

The year 1972 was a presidential election year and I was asked to do some public speaking throughout the state for George McGovern, the antiwar candidate and Democratic Presidential nominee. McGovern famously lost that election in a landslide. Massachusetts was the only state to vote for him over Richard Nixon. Even then, Massachusetts had antipathy towards Richard Nixon dating back to when he had the temerity to run against favorite son John F. Kennedy in 1960. It is fair to say that Nixon was obsessed with the Kennedys and Massachusetts, and not in a good way. The White House tapes showed as much. Nixon shut down the Boston Navy Yard in 1974 in retaliation. The Boston Navy Yard was first established in 1801 and was one of the Navy's oldest shipbuilding facilities. The loss of those jobs devastated the city. I remember riding the subway to Charlestown and shaking hands as thousands of men (they were all men then) were pouring in and out at shift change. Those federal jobs not only paid a good and steady hourly wage, but provided benefits that allowed a single wage earner to raise a family and enjoy financial security.

I quickly fell behind in my law school work. I still have nightmares, 40 years later, of lagging behind my classmates and struggling to catch up. But I pressed on. The Boston City Council may have been the crowning achievement in the political careers of many of my colleagues, but I did not want to end up being a 25 year member of this club. I wanted to run for Mayor someday. I wanted to be able to run the city and implement all the policy changes and innovations described in those white papers being churned out by my young volunteers.

I was determined to improve my standing in the 1973 city election results. My first citywide network was based upon my Boston Latin School network. Not every neighborhood had Latin School students in equal numbers. There were not many black students at Boston Latin School, for example, and my closest black friend from BLS was from the South End, not Roxbury. But I saw opportunity in black neighborhoods like Roxbury because most voters from those wards only cast an average of three votes in the City Council race. Few voters cast all nine of their votes. That meant they could toss a vote my way if they were so inclined. Given they were highly unlikely to vote for someone like Dapper O'Neil, I worked hard to expand my support in the black community. For years, I was one of the few white politicians to visit black churches on Sunday. I was always warmly received and acquired a great appreciation of black culture and music. The choir music was always dazzling. Rev. Michael Haynes served for decades as the Pastor of the Twelfth Baptist Church. I would often visit. Jeep Jones, one of the lay leaders of the church, would usually escort me to the front of the church, where I would join in singing the hymns. Rev. Haynes once commented that he was going to call Cardinal Medeiros and trade me for two or three of his men, given I sang the hymns better than they did!

I also made a practice of just showing up for community events in Roxbury. Woody Allen once said that showing up is 80 percent of life. In politics, it is probably worth more than that. My 1971 vote in Charlestown had been low. Then I joined with Charlestown residents to oppose the relocation of Gabe Piemonte's car wash in their neighborhood in the spring of 1973. Beyond the obvious merits of their case was the chance to make some friends there. I scheduled office hours at Kevin White's Little City Halls, the small all purpose constituent service offices he set up in every neighborhood. People came in and talked to me and were often amazed that a City Councilor was sitting there all by himself without an entourage or a police escort. I made new friends in neighborhoods like Allston and Mattapan.

I was becoming very aware of a double standard at work among my colleagues. Some neighborhoods were way more equal than others. The high voting wards in places like West Roxbury or South Boston or Dorchester always got the most attention. If a hearing was held in one of those neighborhoods, all my colleagues showed up. The minority wards and the lower voting neighborhoods of Allston, Brighton or the Fenway were virtually ignored. I spent a lot of time in those ignored neighborhoods and scored political points just by showing interest. It also underscored to me the need for charter change, to change the method of election of the School Committee and City Council. The existing system perpetuated a two-tiered discriminatory system of representation.

All that work took a toll. I ran like a hamster on an exercise wheel from dawn until late at night every day, including weekends. I was never still. I was not taking care of myself: I ate heavy calorie-laden meals late at night, or just grabbed junk food; I never needed a lot of sleep, but was getting the bare minimum in those years; I tried to run on the beach in South Boston for exercise, but rarely got a chance to break a sweat before someone stopped me to talk. I was spending a lot of time in smoke filled rooms. Many people smoked in those days and alcohol was the most common lubricant in public life. It was almost impossible to walk into any event and not be offered a drink. The combination of bad food, booze, smoke exposure, too much work and stress and too little exercise proved to be toxic. My body finally just gave out. I collapsed.

My physical collapse embarrassed me. I was 24 years old and did not want anyone to know I was sick. Exhaustion did not fit with the public image of the young vigorous reformer. So with the help of discrete friends, on the Fourth of July weekend when it seemed half the city was on Cape Cod, I quietly checked into the Carney Hospital in Dorchester, a small community hospital that was the first Catholic hospital in New England. There was no name plate on my door. I was given a number of tests, treated for exhaustion, and told to take better care of myself. I would love to say that hospitalization taught me a lesson, but I worked myself into collapse a second time in the spring of 1974.

I was fascinated by the cityscape and the potential for revitalization and renewal of Boston. Like many Bostonians, I am an unabashed fan of the city. I was born in Boston, have always lived in Boston, and expect to die in the city. I love Boston. It's my home. By the 1970s, the urban renewal strategies of the 1950s to bulldoze away unsightly older buildings and entire neighborhoods were considered a failure. By the 1970s, policymakers were waking up to the merits of historic preservation and the charm inherent in what is still one of the most European cities in the United States. Boston was old . . . but old could be turned into an asset. The streets of downtown Boston are small and twisty because they had once been cow paths. Faneuil Hall, the small elegant building just outside Kevin White's window, was a national treasure. Peter Faneuil, once the wealthiest merchant in Boston, had built it and presented it to Boston as a gift in 1742. It was the scene of the first protest against the British Sugar Act in 1764 and establishment of the doctrine of "no taxation without representation." To this day, it is the scene of pivotal political debates and major public announcements and celebrations. After construction of Faneuil Hall, three other long buildings were constructed: Quincy Market, North Market and South Market. For more than 100 years, these buildings were the central marketplace for the city, where vendors and farmers sold their wares. Kevin White's father-in-law, a former President of the Boston City Council, William J. "Mother" Galvin of Charlestown, ran Quincy Market for years.

By the 1960s, the three buildings had been virtually abandoned. Homeless people slept in them in the winter and set fires to stay warm creating a huge fire hazard. The historic buildings had become an eyesore of open stalls and ratty warehouses. Some people thought the whole thing ought to be demolished.

Kevin White had a different idea. The White Administration teamed up with a visionary developer, James Wilson Rouse, to turn the old market place into a new urban center. The notion was controversial. The city would have to spend millions of dollars to fix up the exteriors of the three market buildings to keep them from falling down. The few merchants still working in the center market building would be displaced at least temporarily during construction and had no guarantee of being able to return because an out of town vendor would hold the master lease. The City Council needed to approve a 99 year master lease to make it worthwhile for the developer to proceed and to give the Mayor authority to borrow the renovation money. It was not a hard vote for me because I was familiar with the Rouse family. I had known Jim Rouse's niece, Ellen, a short, smart redhead, at Harvard and had read about the pioneering work her uncle had done. Jim Rouse created the first enclosed shopping mall in America. He had also created an entire planned community, Columbia, Maryland out of farm land in Howard County. It was a precursor of what came to be known as New Urbanism. I knew of his reputation as a visionary urban planner and a creative pioneer.

We needed six of the nine votes and the merchants from the center market building lobbied hard against any change. I had some sympathy for them. They were worried about their livelihoods. However, I could see that this disruptive change would be transformative for downtown Boston. The demolition of Scollay Square and construction of Government Center and of the new City Hall had been phase one of the revitalization of downtown Boston. This represented phase two. I led the floor fight for the bill giving the city permission to borrow the renovation money and to sign the long term lease and we won. The vote showed I was prepared to stand up to special interests and take a leap of faith on a new direction for the city. Quincy Market opened in 1976 and was a smash hit from day one. Quincy Market now draws more than 18 million visitors a year. This wildly successful marketplace has been copied, but never equaled, all across the country. It is one of the best things I ever did. I still display on my office desk, with great pride, the scissors I used to cut the ribbon for the third market building opening. I am convinced that the success of Quincy Market contributed to the successful effort to depress the Central Artery and reopen the waterfront to the rest of the city.

All my hard work paid off in the election of 1973. I improved my showing from the 1971 election. I finished 4th in the preliminary election in 1973, so well that I thought I might top the ticket in the general election. But an off year election draws a smaller and more conservative electorate and I finished third in the general election in November. Louise Day Hicks topped the ticket. Louise had decided to run for the Council again after losing her congressional seat to Joe Moakley the previous year. It was no surprise. She had little interest in Washington and national issues. When she returned to the City Council, she sat next to me and a surprising friendship evolved. Louise was then at the apex of her power, the symbol of resistance to busing, a tremendous political force. She was the daughter of a judge and a lady in every way. She dressed modestly and carefully, sometimes with white gloves and a hat. She spoke in a high pitched voice with precise elocution and sounded like a school marm from another century. She never once lied to me. She took an almost maternal interest in me. Although we disagreed on many issues, we developed an enduring friendship.

I was disappointed that I had not topped the ticket, but felt my position was solid enough to begin actively planning my next career step. Moreover, I was emotionally exhausted after the 1973 election and began to look around for a way to speed up my plan to become mayor someday. I took note that no City Councilor had been elected mayor since James Michael Curley's election in 1913. To me, 1913 might as well have been the Middle Ages. John Collins served as Register of Probate when he was elected Mayor. Kevin White ran successfully for Mayor as Secretary of State. Kevin's career path seemed very achievable, to me so I began exploring the possibility of running for Secretary of State. The Secretary of State is the chief Elections Officer for the state and the keeper of records. All births, deaths and marriages, for example, are on file at the office. It is not a particularly powerful position but the statewide platform held great political appeal and Kevin had been able to create a public image as a reformer with that job.

There were a few inklings that the 1974 state election would be something of a bellwether in Massachusetts. The incumbent Secretary of State was John Francis Xavier Davoren, an old style pol from Milford, who had been Speaker of the Massachusetts House. By 1974, Davoren looked like a sitting duck. Kevin White resigned as Secretary of State after his election as Mayor in 1967. The Legislature appointed their leader and friend, Jack Davoren, to fill the vacancy. While Kevin used the position as a stepping stone, it represented what some called "Irish retirement" for Davoren. He was an affable guy but he did not do much and took a lot of heat for running a patronage operation. The Boston Globe reporters trailed after him and found that he rarely came to the State House and spent most of his time in his little hometown of Milford. The day when voters would accept such behavior was long gone and conventional wisdom suggested he was vulnerable.

At about this time, I received a phone call and a request for a meeting from Michael Dukakis, a former state representative from Brookline, who had been the Democratic nominee for lieutenant governor in 1970. Mike Dukakis intended to run for governor in 1974 and he asked if I would run for lieutenant governor. This was before Thomas P. O'Neill 3rd, the son of Congressman and later House Speaker Tip O'Neill, got into the race. Tommy O'Neill eventually won the race. I decided to stick with the Secretary of State race because another candidate from Dorchester, Robert Quinn, intended to run for governor, too, and I thought two Dorchester candidates on the same ticket was a bad idea. In Massachusetts, the governor and lieutenant governor run separately in the primary election, but are co-joined in November on the same ticket.

My campaign for Secretary of State lasted all of three months and cost about $7,000. It ended at a voluntary Democratic Party caucus on March 23. I had once again worked myself sick and was in bed utterly exhausted a week before the caucus in March. At about that time, Kevin White called and asked if I would like to be the Boston Parks Commissioner. I could not see myself working for anyone else and declined. Kevin may have seen some merit in the appointment but it is also safe to assume that Kevin may have wanted me out of the way.

State legislators are always a powerhouse at any Massachusetts political gathering and they all rallied behind their colleague, Paul Guzzi, a state representative from Newton, who graduated from Harvard about 7 years before I did. Even Mel King, an African-American state representative from Boston, was trying to get some of my people to switch to Guzzi. Mel was convinced every member of the Boston City Council was a racist. I withdrew after the second ballot. I hated to lose, but I realized Guzzi had the votes and two Italian-Americans running against Davoren would only help the incumbent and split any anti-Davoren vote. I could have lost the endorsement of the caucus and still run in the primary, but as a 24 year old law student it made sense to end my candidacy and endorse Paul, who went on to victory in November. As disappointed as I was, I knew there would be another day for me.

I worked hard for Mike Dukakis' election as governor that fall of 1974. It was not an easy position to take. Mike had beaten Bob Quinn, the Attorney General and a Dorchester native, in the September primary for the gubernatorial nomination. I was the only Dorchester public official to back Dukakis. I was beginning to feel somewhat alienated. Law school was a hard, frustrating slog. I could never catch up. I was also woefully out of step with my peers. Wanting desperately to appear to be grown up enough for the job, I missed a lot of the fun and perhaps formative aspects of college and young adulthood. I always wore a coat and tie in public, for example, while most people my age were wearing blue jeans and growing their hair long. I was scrupulous about my public conduct in every way, including in the choice of the young women whom I dated. One memorable date that encapsulates my romantic life in those days took place around St. Patrick's Day in 1975. The Irish Social Club of Boston, a social club created in 1945 having 15,000 members at its height, invited me and the other city councilors to their annual St. Patrick's

Day dinner in an old Protestant Church on Stanton Street in Dorchester near St. Matthew's Church. In those days, the custom was to assemble the officials who would sit at the head table in a separate room and then march them into the hall to music provided by a local band. I went to so many of these events that I became great friends with most of the waitresses at Hart Caterers, the favored caterer for such events. I was still in law school and invited one of my classmates as a date. She was a bright young woman, just over 5 feet tall and quite genteel. Her parents lived in Chestnut Hill, a wealthy village just six miles west of Boston. She had been educated by the Madams of the Sacred Heart. We arrived on time and were escorted to the holding room where a waiter asked her if she would like a drink. She asked for a gin and tonic. The waiter replied: "Lady, we got whiskey and we got beer. Take your pick." Then things got worse. No one wanted to begin until the founder of the club, Mary Concannon, arrived. She was missing. After a long wait of two hours, the head table was finally marched into the hall and seated. Shortly afterwards, the MC announced, "Mary Concannon was found dead on the floor of her house in West Roxbury. God rest her soul." The party paused momentarily to consider the demise of the dear departed and then resumed apace. I don't think my genteel friend and I ever had another date.

I also have to admit I was not exactly a typical guy in his 20s. I no longer had time to share a Cape cottage with my pals in the summer time, for example, and when I visited, I either carefully restricted my alcohol intake or simply walked out if anyone pulled out a joint of marijuana to smoke. Such circumspection was the downside of being a whiz kid. I knew any infraction, no matter how innocent, would result in politically devastating headlines. I do not regret the investment of time and work in my political career. It provided a foundation for the rest of my life. But I did miss out. For much of my 20s, I simply had no private life. I went to law school year round, including the summers of 1974 and 1975, in order to complete my class work as soon as possible.

At about this time I began to get the feeling I was out of step with my generation. I had leap frogged ahead of my classmates upon graduation from Harvard, but now they seemed to be moving ahead of me. Friends were graduating from law school and business school. Many were announcing engagements and getting married. I went to five weddings one October. I was still taking dates to political chicken dinners, still living in the attic of my parent's house and discovering that my $12,500 City Council salary which had seemed so generous in theory barely covered my law school tuition and basic living expenses. I decided to pay for law school out of pocket because of the uncertainty of elective office. I would routinely borrow $200 from my Shawmut Bank Master Card and then deposit the cash at the First National

Bank of Boston to write a tuition check and drop it off at the bursar's office on the day it was due. I had a real aversion to borrowing money; the juggling was stressful and I worried constantly about running short.

Just before the Democratic caucus in the spring of 1974, I got sick again. I was campaigning in Fitchburg and began to sweat profusely. I was violently ill and so exhausted I could barely stand. I got out of bed to attend a Jaycee dinner the night before the caucus, where I was to be honored as one of Ten Outstanding Young Leaders. I was so sick I went to Framingham, the location of the caucus, the night before to preserve my limited strength for what I thought would be a big day.

Two physical collapses in less than a year at the age of 24 finally woke me up. I realized I had to take better care of myself. Ira Jackson, a top aide to Kevin White, who subsequently became Tax Commissioner for the state under Governor Dukakis and held a number of high ranking positions in academia, played the role of the Archangel Gabriel in my life. At several key junctures, Ira, who was a year or two ahead of me at Harvard, gave me a reality check with a message and piece of advice which proved to be pivotal in my life.

I ran into him outside City Hall on a lovely spring day just after the caucus. We were both outside to enjoy the sunshine and buy a hotdog from a food vendor. I told him about my recent illness. Ira gave me a gentle lecture on the importance of maintaining my health. He told me to make time in my schedule for regular aerobic exercise. Exercise is a great remedy for all sorts of ailments. In my case, it addressed my poor physical condition, provided an outlet for stress, and gave me a badly needed mental health break from my 19 and 20 hour days of study and work. He recommended I learn how to play squash and volunteered Tom Weber, another young White administration policy maven, as my instructor. I began playing squash at the Harvard Club. I was never very athletic and did not play well at first, but I stuck with it and eventually got better. I still play squash and since that time exercise has been fixed part of my life: a way to keep my weight stable, my heart and lungs strong, and my mood high. Since that time I believe I may have gotten sick two or three times. I learned an important lesson about taking care of my body.

This advice came at an opportune time because I was about to face the most challenging time in my career in public office: the busing crisis.

I was well aware that the Boston public schools were segregated by race. Everyone knew that. By 1971, two thirds of the black students enrolled in the Boston public schools attended schools that were more than 70 percent black, while 80 percent of the white students were in schools that were more than 80 percent white. Public schools in Roxbury and adjacent Dorchester, where most African-American Bostonians lived, were so overcrowded that the school administration proposed double sessions. This did not happen by accident. I had done my own analysis of the racial composition of the city when working on my Harvard thesis on bilingual education in the Boston public schools. As a law school student, I was reading the legal decisions building up to Morgan v. Hennigan. I knew what the 14th amendment meant concerning equality before the law and I knew that black parents' complaints about a dual standard—resulting in overcrowded and underfunded schools— were correct.

Of course, the schools where poor white students attended class were not much better. I had made a practice of offering to teach government classes at public high schools and went to a variety of schools. My personal experience confirmed that the poor white kids were as bad off as the poor black kids. There were exceptions, of course. Boston Latin School always stood out for its excellence and there were many neighborhood elementary schools that provided a superb education. But an enormous number of public schools were doing a bad job for both black and white students.

There were some explanations for this: The Boston School Committee was, plain and simple, a patronage driven operation. The committee members did not receive salaries, but they could and did accept money, often cash, from corporations, wealthy individuals and businesses, school department employees, and those who wanted to be school department employees at "times." A "time" was like a fundraiser with no rules. Anything went in those days. The incumbent could accept money so long as he or she was not actually a declared candidate for public office. As long as the income was declared to the IRS, they were home free.

The school custodians were a powerhouse back then. They donated money and did extraordinary amounts of campaign work for free. They were paid back in the form of salaries that were higher than those received by school teachers. The school nurses actually earned more money than the nurses working shifts at Boston City Hospital. To get a job, you needed to know someone. Custodians were appointed in groups of five so that the five members of the School Committee could each name one favored candidate.

When the entire public school system is a patronage haven and "who you know" and "how much you gave" is more important than where you earned your academic degree or how good a teacher you are, quality education becomes an afterthought.

The School Committee, like the Boston City Council, knew where the votes were located. Black voters did not vote for white candidates with few exceptions. Moreover, black voters did not hold a majority in the city. As a result, the School Committee members played to the high voting wards and made sure that the school district lines and school assignments conformed to the racial composition of the highest voting white neighborhoods.

Here is one example. The Columbia Point Housing Project was the largest and eventually the worst in the city. The high rise buildings for 1,500 families were built on a peninsula jutting into the harbor with a spectacular water view, but the site had been the city dump. At one point, the area was used as a prisoner of war camp. From the day it opened in 1954, Columbia Point was troubled. Putting the poorest people in the city into high rise buildings with no grocery store, no playground, no amenities whatsoever, was a disaster. My mother taught at the William E. Russell School on Columbia Road, just a short walk away, and she told me about children who came to school with rat bites and how there were towers without a single adult male in residence.

South Boston High School can be seen from Columbia Point. As the housing project became increasingly black, none of the teenagers who lived at Columbia Point were assigned to South Boston High School. They were all assigned to English High School, which was located a walk and then two subway rides away on Avenue Louis Pasteur in the Fenway. White teenagers who lived in Savin Hill in Dorchester, a neighborhood visible from Columbia Point, were assigned to South Boston High School, because South Boston is where the white students were assigned. South Boston High became so overcrowded that the city created a school annex at the L Street bathhouse for classroom space.

This was a clear and blatant violation of the 14th amendment, not unlike the ruling made in Brown v. Board of Education. In that case, a class action suit was brought in 1951 on behalf of a group of African-American parents and their children in Topeka, Kansas. The named claimant was Oliver Brown, the father of Linda Brown, a third grader who had to walk six blocks to catch a bus to attend a black public school one mile away from her home, while the white elementary school was located just seven blocks from her house. The parallels were very clear and Tallulah Morgan and the other African-American parents of school children in Boston were making the exact same arguments. This was not *de facto* but *de jure* segregation. In other words, this was deliberate.

Not every voter in Boston was insensitive to the situation. Citizens for Boston Public Schools ran reform slates for the Boston School Committee a good 10 years before the busing ruling, warning of forced busing if nothing were done to rectify the situation. The majority dug in and elected people like Louise Day Hicks, Pixie Palladino and John J. Kerrigan, who was not related to my old colleague, John E. Kerrigan, but benefited from the similarity in names. They played to the lowest common denominator and did not take the steps that could have been taken to avert Garrity's ruling or at least lessen the severity of the remedy. I remain convinced that a majority of Bostonians would have accepted modifications in school district lines and some moderate busing to achieve racial integration in the schools. The extremists would never accept any busing, but most people were just not that extreme.

Federal District Judge W. Arthur Garrity handed down his ruling on June 21, 1974. The School Committee appealed and lost the appeal. By that time, there was little time left to prepare for the opening of school in September, so Garrity had his two consultants, two professors from Boston University with no connection to Boston, come up with a busing plan which pitted the poorest white neighborhoods against the poorest black neighborhoods. The teenagers in Charlestown and South Boston were bused to Roxbury and the Roxbury kids were bused to South Boston and Charlestown. The remedy ignored the reality of the neighborhoods. It was based on geocodes, but Boston is not a city of geocodes. It was ill-conceived, incendiary and counterproductive. I argued for a metropolitan solution and eventually co-authored a law review article making the case for such a solution. It made no sense to me that the lily white suburbs, whose state lawmakers had approved the state racial balance law, not be part of an answer if the goal was quality education for every child in the state. Apart from the METCO program, which bused some black children to a handful of tony suburbs to attend school, no regional solution was ever proposed. It was Boston's problem. When school started in the fall of 1974, Boston blew up.

As I looked towards another reelection campaign in 1975, I was standing on the wrong side of a volatile issue. I was a weary, discouraged, rather lonely young guy whose first foray into statewide politics had been unsuccessful. I had to wonder if my precocious political success was about to come to an ignominious and premature end.

Busing

The start of school in September of 1974 was far worse than anyone could have anticipated. The rage, frustration and fear exploded into street violence. The local and national news showed angry white mobs tossing rocks at school buses filled with black children. Contributing to the tension were a series of horrible street crimes in the preceding years and months: a white woman assaulted and burned to death in Roxbury; a 17-year-old black teenager killed by a sniper outside his apartment in a South Boston housing project; a Haitian man yanked from his car at a stop light and nearly beaten to death; a 20-year-old college student, driving a cab for tuition money, pulled out of his cab and stabbed to death. Those incidents put everyone on edge and contributed to a climate of suspicion and fear. The City of Boston, the alleged bastion of progressive politics, overnight became a symbol of racism and northern resistance to integration. It was disastrous and tragic and signaled the beginning of the end of "old" Boston. There was a real fear that the city was unraveling. I was afraid that the unraveling would also bring about a premature end to my political career.

I knew these people. Some were neighbors. Many had been supporters. While I do not dispute that some opponents of the busing order were racist, not every opponent was racist. For some people, racism had nothing to do with it at all. There were good people who opposed busing. Having your own children reassigned to a different school every September and bused miles and miles from home when there was a perfectly good public school a block or two away would make any parent a little nuts. To say that education became an afterthought in the first years of busing would be an understatement. Teachers and school administrators labored mightily just to maintain order in school corridors. No one was parsing Latin verbs or diagramming sentences or studying American history and literature in those days.

For many Bostonians, particularly lower income residents who had few options, busing represented a final indignity. They felt desperate. The first busing plan took children from South Boston and bused them into the heart of the black ghetto. It took black children from Roxbury and bused them into working class white neighborhoods in South Boston and Charlestown, where they were greeted by angry mobs. The herky jerky reassignments to new schools every year caused serious disruption in education. Black parents did not feel any better about this than white parents. It was their kids sitting on those buses being subjected to the most vile racial insults and facing risk of real harm from these white mobs. Their kids were not getting much of an education either, except for a first hand schooling in hate and bigotry. Parents, regardless of race, felt they could not protect their own children and had absolutely no say or control over where their kids went to school.

The antibusing forces ironically took a cue from the Civil Rights movement. In the 1960s major news events were playing out on the evening television news for the first time. The people of South Boston, Charlestown and East Boston had seen black people in the South standing up for their rights, defying Bull Connor and other symbols of oppression in the American South, and taking to the streets to rectify a grievous wrong. They had watched antiwar demonstrators challenge the President of the United States and his policy on the Vietnam War on the 6 o'clock news. They reasoned that they were entitled to do the exact same thing. For the most ardent antibusing activists, there was no difference between the Civil Rights and antiwar movements and their cause.

Of course there were profound differences, but few would pay a bit of attention to the legal niceties or reasoned arguments about the rule of law in those days. These folks felt that THEY were the ones who had been denied the right to keep their kids in schools within walking distance of the three-decker family home. And they were not completely wrong about that. The busing remedy as implemented was harsh and extreme.

It did not need to be so. For the first year of busing, Judge Garrity used a boilerplate plan developed by the state Board of Education to balance the schools. The state had been feuding with the Boston School Committee for almost ten years over school segregation. The School Committee, naturally, just ignored the state bureaucrats, who only became angrier as time passed. Needless to say, that initial remedy was a crude instrument which pitted the most racially segregated and poorest neighborhoods against one another. I always felt it was grievously unfair to make the most disadvantaged people in the city, who had so little, shoulder the burden of busing. Judge Garrity used that plan for Phase 1 and appointed a series of "Masters" to develop Phase II. We all hoped that Phase II would be more reasoned and there was cause for the hope. Eddie McCormack, the former Attorney General, a politically savvy lawyer and Boston native, was one of the most prominent of these "Masters." He and his colleagues worked hard on a remedy that minimized busing and recognized the realities of the city neighborhoods but still addressed the underlying issue of racial segregation in a far more sensible manner.

McCormack had an impeccable Boston political pedigree. His father was Edward J. "Knocko" McCormack, Sr., a well known political insider, James Michael Curley coat holder and bartender from South Boston, and his uncle was House Speaker John W. McCormack. Eddie had served on the Boston City Council, so he knew the city well. As Attorney General between 1958 and 1963, he earned a strong record on civil rights. He was a life member of the NAACP. He ran for the U.S. Senate in 1962 against Edward M. Kennedy in the special election held to fill the vacancy created after John F. Kennedy won the presidency. That is the election where he famously said: "If his name was Edward Moore, and not Edward Moore Kennedy, his candidacy would be a joke." In that race, the joke was on Eddie and Ted won in a landslide. Voters were evidently persuaded by a slogan Kennedy recycled from one of his brother's campaigns: He can do more for Massachusetts. Sadly, Judge Garrity found fault with the Masters' recommendation and went with a plan developed by two Boston University professors who knew nothing about the city or its people and to the best of my knowledge never consulted with a single elected official. That was a mistake. I wrote Eddie a note commending him for his work and he replied: "We think it is a plan that will desegregate and defuse – but it will only work if it is supported and believed." How true.

Political leadership is important and never more so than at difficult times, such as war, or economic recession, or, in this case, a busing order to achieve racial integration. It is an historic fact that many of the elected "leaders" of Boston pandered to the lowest common denominator. Some of my colleagues knew better. They understood the law. They knew that public school assignments had been determined by race for years. Yet instead of trying to help people cope with the disruption and confusion of the busing order, they inflamed them with reckless rhetoric that gave opponents hope that the court order could be rescinded or reversed.

I had a choice. I had to figure out how to survive in this hostile political environment. The prospect of being washed up at the age of 26 was real. I knew no one would listen to an academic explanation of the 14th amendment rights of the black school children of Boston. Yet I could not live with myself and my own internal code and come out against a judicial order that was reasoned soundly and according to legal precedent and the law. The only way to overturn Garrity's order would be on appeal to a higher court and I knew enough about the law and Supreme Court precedents to know that would never happen. I agonized about what I should do. I knew that one relatively young City Councilor standing by himself had as much potential of success as a toddler capturing the incoming tide at Tenean Beach in his plastic toy bucket. So I decided to try to steer a middle course, to never say anything I did not believe, but not to taunt the opposition or court their hostility. I did a lot of public speaking and delivered serious speeches on the nature of civil disobedience, some of them far from Boston, that year.

In one speech to the Boston Rotary Club, I said, "All of us must shoulder some responsibility for the city's difficult times. . . . Serious social and economic problems that beset our city are not being adequately solved. Busing is perceived as only one more in a long series of blows to neighborhoods that already suffer from sub-standard housing and unemployment. In South Boston and Charlestown, over 16 percent of the work force is idle. Among white youth, the figure jumps to over 25 percent, while black youth face a staggering 37 percent unemployment. In all likelihood, Boston's present situation, which appears on the surface to be solely a racial crisis, will not be calmed until these deeper problems are addressed. . . . we must all acknowledge that there is a middle ground in this city. Unfortunately, we have been quiet, too meek to speak out, the victims of the polarization brought about by the politically ambitious, the ideological purists, those who seek to profit from the divisions among us. Those of us who are moderates question why our schools are not producing better students while we are spending over $2,000 per pupil. We acknowledge the necessity of justice being done, but question the extent to which the judge has overtaken the prerequisites of our elected officials. We will not take to the streets to overturn the Constitution, yet we are not about to pat the judge on the back. We are worried; we are concerned: we are scared for our city. We love Boston. We stay here voluntarily. We aim to save it and that is our greatest challenge."

Anyone who invited me to speak and sent a plane ticket could get me. It was a great way to stay out of the line of fire in Boston. I signed on as a state co-chairman for Sargent Shriver's brief Presidential campaign in 1975 and 1976 and spent some time traveling the state with him. He was a delightful traveling companion and I was happy to be in places like Fitchburg rather than South Boston. So, in general, I kept my head down. I admit I was not a profile in courage. But I did refuse to endorse or contribute to ROAR or any other antibusing organization and I never attended any of their rallies in Boston or elsewhere. My absence was noted. I never did have the instincts of a martyr. Giving up my political career seemed unnecessary and extreme. Of course, I knew I might not survive the 1975 election regardless of what I did or did not do.

It was simply the worst year in politics in city history in my lifetime. The sense of betrayal and impotence churned in a cauldron that poured a poisonous potion into the very atmosphere. The evidence of political problems for me was everywhere. My mother could not shop at the local grocery store without some neighbor or friend accosting her with questions about why I was not supporting the cause. Many who had always pitched a DiCara sign on their front lawn refused to take my sign for this campaign. Others, including longtime friends and neighbors, just flatly told me to my face that they could no longer vote for me. Dick Kropas had always displayed a sign for me on Gallivan Boulevard. Not this time. He stopped speaking to me and never spoke to me again. They felt betrayed by one of their own. It was painful. Politicians not only love to be loved, they need to be loved. It is part of the DNA of a politician. I was not feeling the love that year.

For all my efforts to be relatively low key, I felt that I was sticking out. My colleagues on the City Council fell in line behind the antibusing activists. ROAR put enormous letters spelling out the acronym ROAR in the windows of the City Councilors whose offices faced the plaza, so the building itself acted as an advertisement and bastion for the antibusing movement. ROAR had so much clout at that time that it could count on the votes of 8 of the 9 city councilors and most of the state legislators from Boston. The organization even held its meetings in the Council Chamber. I would see them there when I stopped by my office after my last night school law class. In those days, the City Council was viewed as master of its own space. Allowing a public group that was engaged in public resistance against a court order to meet in the City Council chamber might not happen today. The antibusing forces went to Washington to hold a major demonstration just blocks away from a civil rights demonstration. Eight of the nine City Councilors went with them. I was the lone holdout. I sometimes felt as though I was walking around town with purple hair.

It was impossible to steer a moderate course on an issue that was increasingly dominated by the extremes. This often happens in grassroots movements. As time goes on, the loudest voices, the most passionate and certain, and those least likely to compromise, take over the movement. This happened with the antibusing movement. Louise Day Hicks created ROAR, but she soon found herself displaced by less politic and more uncompromising leaders, like Jim Kelly and Pixie Palladino. It is hard to believe, but some of the rank and file actually felt Louise sold them out.

Even the antibusing leaders sensed things were spinning out of control. Louise had attempted to calm an angry mob that nearly tore Ted Kennedy apart in September of 1974. Kennedy had to gallop beneath a hail of tomatoes and eggs and seek refuge at the federal building which is right next to City

Hall. The mob cracked the glass door in pursuit of him. It was an ugly, ugly scene. The mob ignored Louise's entreaties to go home and cease and desist. She was badly shaken when she returned to City Hall. From my seat next to her on the council floor, I noticed she was physically trembling for some time after that incident. "Larry," she said, "I created this and now I've lost control of it." She knew she could not undo what she had done. More zealous people were rising to dominate ROAR. As the frustration of the voters grew, so did their impatience with anyone who was not 150 percent with them.

In terms of my own political fate, I knew the numbers too well. I realized that any hope of holding onto gains in Charlestown had disappeared with the busing order. The high Irish in West Roxbury were just as angry as the working class Irish in South Boston. Not every voter was opposed to busing. There were many, like me, who found the remedy insane, but appreciated that the black kids of Boston deserved the same quality education as the white kids. Of course, plenty of white kids were not getting a very good education either.

I had received an excellent education in the Boston public schools but I learned that my experience was far from typical. The public schools in South Boston, Hyde Park and Dorchester were just as bad as the public schools in Roxbury. From my perspective, the system was letting down the average public school student in Boston—even before busing.

It has to be said that institutional leadership failed the people of Boston in those years. Judge Garrity was pigheaded in refusing to consult with people who knew Boston and its neighborhoods in devising a remedy to segregation. Most of the members of the Boston School Committee and City Council competed to be the most enthusiastic booster of ROAR, egging them on to greater flights of fury.

No institution covered itself with glory in those years and that included the Catholic Church. Boston was heavily Roman Catholic then and some parents found refuge in Catholic Schools. The Archdiocese had a policy to block its schools from becoming a haven from busing, but some schools ignored it and schools just outside of Boston could accept children using the suburban addresses of relatives or family friends without question. The Archdiocese was going through its own wrenching changes in those years so the mixed messages were understandable. Enrollment in Catholic schools in the Boston Archdiocese dropped by almost half in ten years from the all-time post-war high in 1964. In 1972, Catholic schools were closing at a rate of one a day across the nation. Nuns were leaving religious life in droves. The two orders that staffed Catholic schools effectively for free in those years, the Sisters of St. Joseph and the Sisters of Notre Dame de Namur, pulled out of dozens of schools in the area in 1975 because they did not have enough nuns to staff them. The parochial school system was heavily in debt and the new Archbishop of Boston, Humberto Sousa Medeiros, proved to be somewhat ineffective as a leader. Of course Cardinal Medeiros had a tough act to follow. His predecessor, Richard Cushing, was as charismatic and wily an Irish pol as any elected public official. Cushing knew how to lead and was a beloved figure in Boston. He presided over the marriage of John Kennedy and Jacqueline Bouvier in Newport, prayed at Jack Kennedy's Inaugural and said the funeral Mass when he was killed. Anyone would have had a tough time taking his place, but Cardinal Medeiros, a native of the Azores who grew up in Fall River, was culturally and stylistically out of sync with his flock.

And me? I put my head down, and kept up the grind of law school classes, went to every chicken dinner, every "time," every coffee klatch in places where I thought I might pick up a vote or two. After analyzing my vote in 1971, I realized that there were many wards in the city where I had an opportunity to pick up more votes: not necessarily the most votes, but enough to make an investment worthwhile. The beauty of running city wide is you can finish in the top 9 just by doing well enough in a lot of places, not all places, but enough places. I zeroed in on black wards, as among those where I might make some friends, and I did.

Mayor White was trying to do the exact same thing. In 1975 he faced the handsome State Senator and former Marine, Joe Timilty. White had won twice by assembling a progressive coalition that included the growing numbers of young professionals from Beacon Hill, the Back Bay, the Fenway and the South End; racial minorities from the South End, Roxbury, Dorchester and Mattapan; along with the Italians and few remaining WASPS and Jews left in the city. With some slight variations, this is the coalition I assembled to win election citywide.

While neither of us changed anyone's mind about busing, we survived the election that year. We both faced tough races. Timilty was within striking distance in what still is remembered as one of the nastiest, most bitter Boston mayoral races. Joe, to his everlasting credit, refused to play the race card and some say he probably lost because he did not stoop to that level. It will never be known.

White had opened up government to many who had long been shut out. He appointed women, Jews, and black men and women to senior positions in his administration. Deputy Mayors included a black man and an Hispanic woman. Of course, Kevin White was quietly undermining the opposition by tossing jobs and other favors to key people. Jim Kelly, a fierce ROAR leader from South Boston, got on the payroll of the Marine Industrial Park. Louise always played politics with Kevin. After she lost her council seat, the Mayor named her to the Boston Retirement Board, a no heavy lifting sinecure. Over the years, I have often been bemused by how tough talking people can be bought with a patronage job or a contract or another favor. Dapper O'Neil, the foul mouthed City Councilor, was a notorious cheap date in those years. Kevin could and did buy his vote repeatedly with a couple of meter maid jobs.

The Mayor and his people appreciated the need to pull votes out of Wards 16 and 17, so they were generous with summer jobs and other patronage positions during that campaign. There could not have been a single kid in Dorchester without a summer job during the summer of 1975. Bobby White, one of Kevin White's campaign coordinators in Dorchester, would call and ask if there was anyone who needed a summer job and, at one point, I told him I had run out of kids to employ. All those summer jobs helped me hang onto my vote in St. Gregory's Parish.

I had great confidence in the basic strength of my citywide organization. Since the first election, I had carefully built up my base of votes in the two big Dorchester Wards, 16 and 17; the liberal votes from Beacon Hill and the Back Bay and growing pockets of newcomers in the center city; the Italian voters of the North End and East Boston; and a growing percentage of minority votes from Roxbury and North Dorchester. I knew my vote in Dorchester would not hold completely after the desegregation order was issued. I could kiss goodbye to many votes in Ward 16 Dorchester and even many in my home Ward 17. I never did well in South Boston and never would. Some of my friends in Charlestown abandoned me because the busing order was of a moral order that outweighed any work I did on blocking an unpopular car wash from their neighborhood.

Voters in Boston had a lot to be unhappy about. The economy was still bad. Gasoline prices were sky high and gasoline was often in short supply. I remember hearing then about heroin overdoses in South Boston. For years there was a mythology that James "Whitey" Bulger, the head of the Irish mob in Boston and a South Boston native, had kept drugs out of Southie. It was never true. It was an urban myth. But Jim Bulger did have a reputation as a legendary defender of Southie Pride. One of Kevin White's top aides, who later became a prominent business leader in Boston, told me almost 40 years later that Whitey Bulger and his henchmen had threatened to shoot any black children who were bused into South Boston. According to the former aide, the Mayor was enraged. The two of them drove alone to South Boston in the Mayor's personal car and went straight to Senator Bill Bulger's house. Bill is nothing like his big brother. He is an erudite man, a lawyer, and later served as President of the Massachusetts State Senate and President of the University of Massachusetts. He was strongly opposed to busing, but Bill is not a thug. In the days before Whitey took off and became one of the FBI's Most Wanted Men, the best way to get a message to him was through his brother. The Mayor went into the house alone and afterwards told the aide that he told Bill that he and the FBI were aware of the threat. If one child was shot, there would be an all out war on organized crime in South Boston. The Mayor assumed Bill would make certain his brother got the message and evidently he did. There were serious violent incidents throughout the city that were unquestionably racial in nature, particularly in places like South Boston and Roxbury, but no black kids on school buses ever got shot in Southie.

In the end, I skinnied through in the middle of the pack in fifth place. I finished seventh in the September preliminary, but the higher turnout in November helped me. A higher general election turnout invariably includes more casual voters, younger voters and more minority group members. It is a rule of thumb in races from Mayor to President. The Mayor's vote was unquestionably helpful to me. While some Timilty people are convinced Kevin White stole that election, the numbers do not support it. Quite simply, black people saved us. The turnout in the black wards went up and we did well in those wards. I visited most every black church in the city more than once and Jerry Dunfey, then manager of the Parker House and a liberal Democrat with a strong interest in Civil Rights, hosted a cocktail party for me and invited every black person he knew. The demographic pattern established after World War II of white people moving from the city to the suburbs had continued and black people were making up a larger piece of the shrunken pie.

There was something of a diaspora from Boston. For example, my friend Bugs Connolly who grew up near me in Dorchester got married in 1969. The newlyweds moved to Plymouth and then to Braintree. John Hogan moved to Walpole. Tommy Serino moved to Peabody. Mary Currie moved from Dorchester to Randolph. Peggy Connolly moved to Canton. Frankie Pendergast moved to Sandwich at the top of Cape Cod. John O'Brien moved to Natick. Even before busing, the city was changing. In 1960, according to the U.S. Census, Boston had a population of 697,197 and 90 percent of the residents were white. By 1970, years before Garrity's order, the population was down to 641,071 and was 82 percent white.

Kirk O'Donnell was Kevin White's campaign manager and an adept get-out-the-vote (GOTV) guy. The campaign workers who get the vote out rank among the most important people in a campaign organization on Election Day. Before his death, he told me that he called one of Joe Timilty's senior campaign officials, who was a friend, on the afternoon of the election. He told him that White campaign workers were telling him that a lot of folks were showing up at the polls to vote who did not appear on any of their lists. In advance of the election, each campaign had dutifully identified their 1's and 2's, those most likely to vote for them, and the GOTV effort hauled those people to the polling spots. The Timilty aide told him that he was hearing the same thing. That told me that the population was changing. New people were showing up to vote.

Busing just slammed down the accelerator on the trend of white people leaving the city. Big families with lots of kids were heading down the Southeast Expressway in U-Hauls. After the court order, busing opponents were emptying out of the city. By 1980, the Census reported the population was down to 562,994, a precipitous drop of more than 12 percentage points in ten years, with 70 percent of the residents white and 22.4 percent black. It is safe to say that by 1980, those who could not tolerate busing and had the means to move out of the city had done so.

While the hint of change was contained in those results, the 1975 results were also the high point of the antibusing vote. Louise topped the council ticket with an astonishing 82,030 votes, a good 11,000 votes ahead of anyone else. She left us in the dust. She peaked politically that night in November. None of us knew it then but Louise would never win another election. While Gerry O'Leary, an incumbent, lost because he tried to straddle the busing issue and appeal to both sides, John J. Kerrigan, the former School Committeeman, who was the male equivalent of Pixie Palladino and an outspoken and crass defender of ROAR, won.

I felt relieved, but hardly satisfied. At the time, it felt as though I was running in place and I could see no way out. The city was still polarized and everyone felt on edge. But the year ended and while 1976 began just as badly as 1975, a change was underway that became more apparent literally by the month. With the benefit of hindsight, it is clear that 1975-76 was a tipping point for the city. Those who could not tolerate busing left almost immediately. No one expected things to improve when school classes resumed in September of 1976. However, the antibusing forces began to realize that the court order would stand. Their political leaders could not fix it, change it, or abolish it.

The ugliness did not go away completely of course. On April 5, 1976, Ted Landsmark, then a 29-year-old Yale educated lawyer, cut across City Hall Plaza. He was running late for a meeting on affirmative action in city construction projects. Ted is an African American. He rounded a corner and headed straight towards a group of South Boston High School students who were part of an antibusing demonstration. The kids spotted Ted and became inflamed. Joe Rakes, then 17, swung an American flag and struck Ted. The impact of the flag pole broke his nose and knocked off his eye glasses. The assault was captured on film by Stan Forman, the Pulitzer Prize winning photographer for the Boston Herald American. The dramatic image was searing. The photograph showed a furiously angry white man, his face contorted with rage, about to spear a black man with Old Glory, the symbol of America and freedom throughout the world. Stan won a well-deserved second Pulitzer Prize for the photograph. Decent people, and there were many decent people, were simply ashamed. Even Louise, ever the lady, was horrified. This was unacceptable. This was not Boston. The photo became a metaphor and triggered a subtle shift.

Several things happened that in my view helped the city turn a psychic corner. A month after Landmark's assault, a March against Violence and for Racial Reconciliation took place in downtown Boston. Mayor White and Senator Edward W. Brooke and Cardinal Medeiros were in the front row. I was in the second row right behind them. It still amazes me that not a single other member of the Boston City Council showed up that day. How could anyone be FOR violence and AGAINST racial reconciliation? It was an important moment, a public stand that said Boston is not only the home of racists.

The 200th anniversary of the United States of America took place in 1976 and the Commonwealth of Massachusetts and City of Boston, as the cradle of liberty and birthplace of the American Revolution, were front and center. It was a big deal with multiple celebrations. The Tall Ships cruised into the Harbor. Queen Elizabeth II came to Boston as part of the bicentennial celebration in July. The royal party crossed the Atlantic Ocean and pulled into Boston Harbor on the Brittania, the Royal Yacht. She visited all the usual places, including the USS Constitution in Charlestown, the fabled Old Ironsides', the Old State House, and City Hall. The Mayor hosted a lunch for her in the Gallery which now holds City Council offices. Every significant elected and civic leader from the city was there. She spoke very briefly, but I remember she repaired her lipstick in full view of everyone while seated at the head table. I was taken aback by that but I suppose if you are the Queen, you do whatever you want. My other recollection is Prince Phillip asked for a beer. It was a hot day and the planners assumed he would want a more genteel gin and tonic. He got his beer after a mayoral aide raced to the closest package store and bought a six-pack to fulfill the request. The Queen sat with Kevin White on a reviewing stand to watch a special parade. Despite the history of hostility between the Irish and the English throne, heavily Irish Boston was in a festive mood and greeted her warmly.

The very next month, the main building of the renovated Quincy Market opened with a flourish, three years after I led the floor fight on the appropriation needed to get the project underway. There was a huge party on August 25, 1976, the night before the ribbon cutting. I remember being struck by how young and relatively affluent the crowd was and by how many people I knew. There were not a lot of overweight ladies in flower print dresses chain smoking Lucky Strike cigarettes, which was what one encountered at most political events. The Mayor was being greeted like a conquering hero. It felt as though the sun had broken through after a particularly prolonged stretch of morning fog.

The pressure let up on me personally as well. I finally finished law school. I will never regret studying law and becoming a lawyer, but I still view those years of never quite catching up with my legal reading with real horror. I took the bar exam in February and learned that I had passed in May. I called home from western Massachusetts, where I was giving a speech, and my mother told me the envelope had arrived. I would not let her open the envelope. I waited until I arrived home to open it myself. My relief at passing the bar held no bounds. I suppose the prospect of failure terrified me. I never really had failed and flunking the bar exam would have been humiliating for me. More important, getting my ticket to practice law represented independence. I never ever wanted to be like those hat in hand supplicants begging for a job or other favor.

My proud parents hosted a sit down lunch for me at the Harvard Club to mark my entry to the Massachusetts Bar. The 60 or so guests were mostly old and Italian. I have vivid memories of those proud older people sitting at round tables chattering away in Italian. They all gave me money as gifts and that $2,500 became the down payment for a little house in Mattapoisett, a small bucolic seaside town on the south coast of Massachusetts. I did not want to go all the way to the Cape, for fear I would get stuck in those notorious bridge traffic jams. Mattapoisett was an hour away regardless of time or traffic. It was a place to recharge my batteries, take a swim and get away from the hothouse in Boston, where it seemed I would never be anonymous. I kept that house until I built a bigger summer house , after our three daughters were born, in the next door town of Marion.

In the fall of 1976, I went back to school. One would think I had enough of higher education by that point and it is not like I had a lot of free time. I enrolled in the Masters of Public Administration program at the John F. Kennedy School of Government at Harvard. The Kennedy School was still very small in those years and I had many friends there. The administrators wanted people like me, elected public officials with hands-on practical experience in government, to enroll at the school. We brought a fresh blast of cold reality to the idealistic college graduates who made up the bulk of the student body. My advisor at the Kennedy School was one Ira Jackson, the same Ira Jackson who had worked for Kevin White and counseled me on taking better care of myself. Ira was an associate dean at the Kennedy School.

I enrolled as a full time student. It was a wonderful experience. My experience at the Kennedy School was the exact opposite of law school: I loved everything about it. I loved the discussions, the reading, the lectures, everything. The campus is just a few subway stops away from downtown on the

Red Line. I had more control over my City Council schedule and could easily hold a hearing in the morning when I did not have class and then attend class in the afternoons if I did not need to attend a hearing. I never fell behind in my work. In fact, it stimulated my intellect in a positive way and raised my spirits. The juices were flowing again and I slowly emerged from the funk of the previous few years and actually started having a good time.

The Kennedy School, like Harvard's Business School, uses a case study model. My classmates were incredibly bright recent college graduates. Although I was only a few years older than most of them, I brought a very different perspective to class discussions. In Public Policy 240, one case study concerned the location of the University of Massachusetts Medical School in Worcester towards the end of the Sargent Administration. Many people thought it should be located in Boston, where most of the state's preeminent private hospitals are located. Others thought it should be located in Amherst, the location of the University of Massachusetts' main campus. But it ended up in Worcester, the heart of the Commonwealth, smack dab in the middle of the state. It was not merely a matter of geography.

I offered a theory that my more idealistic classmates found implausible, though all these years later I suspect I still was onto something. This is the DiCara theory of the location of UMass Medical School. After World War II, Republican Governors won election in Massachusetts with the help of a coalition of Italian-Americans and White Anglo Saxon Protestants or WASPS. The Democrats who broke that mold were Foster Furcolo, who was able to pull away the Italian votes, and Endicott "Chub" Peabody, who did the same with his fellow WASPS. Christian Herter, John Volpe and Frank Sargent, Republican Governors, each owed his election to this combination.

Sargent was governor when the decision was made. A top fundraiser to both Volpe and Sargent was Albert P. "Toots" Manzi, a politically active businessman who lived in Worcester. As an Italian, Manzi naturally went to his fellow Italian-Americans, many of them local contractors, when he raised money for his favored candidates. Sargent named Manzi to the Massachusetts Turnpike Authority. Toots later became a footnote in state political corruption history for his involvement in the shakedown of a New York consulting firm in return for help in landing state contracts.

So my theory was that the new medical school was put in Worcester as a thank you to Toots and his contractor pals. My classmates were askance. I still think I had it right.

The Kennedy School students are able to take classes throughout Harvard, so I took a graduate seminar on the New Deal taught by Frank Freidel, the esteemed historian and biographer of Franklin D. Roosevelt. I remember how much I enjoyed thinking, reading and writing about those programs and appreciating how FDR's vision changed and saved the country. It was real to me.

In the spring of 1977, I taught a course at Curry College that I later repeated as a seminar for Harvard undergraduates on American Urban Politics. I always enjoyed teaching and sharing my experiences with young people. My mind was simply in overdrive. It was an enormously rewarding and intellectually stimulating time. And it came at a good time in my life. The first terms on the City Council and my law school experience had left me depleted. Now I began to renew myself mentally.

As the months passed, I had a palpable sense that the city was changing in ways that were not necessarily yet visible, but the air felt different. The fever that had kept the city burning and almost delirious for years finally broke. Busing became a fact of city life. Busing effectively became the new normal. Those who felt strongest about busing had moved on. The economy began to improve. Congressman Thomas P. O'Neill, Jr., ("Tip"), the longtime Democratic powerhouse from Cambridge, just across the river from downtown Boston, became Speaker of the United States House of Representatives in 1977. Tip believed in taking care of his district and state. One of his closest friends was Congressman Joe Moakley, my former colleague from South Boston. Joe once told me years later that he had taken care of so many people, that he did favors for people he did not even like. Joe believed in taking care of Boston and did. Those two members of Congress probably had more to do with landing the federal funds that changed the physical face of Boston than any other public figures in the modern history of Boston.

Jimmy Carter, a Democrat, won the Presidential election of 1976. While the former Georgia Governor was not known as a king of patronage, he was still a Democrat and the wily Massachusetts Democrats made sure the state benefited from his administration. A friend told me that there were more Massachusetts people than Georgians holding key positions in Washington in the first year of Carter's single term in office. It may have had something to do with the fact that Carter named Jim King, the former advance man and district director for Ted Kennedy, to head up the White House patronage shop, in 1977. By all accounts, Jim King did a great job.

Louise topped the ticket by such a wide margin in 1975 that she was heavily favored to become President of the City Council in 1976. Three other successful council candidates pledged their votes to her before she even arrived at work the day after the election. She did not need my vote, but we did have a discussion about it. We agreed that a fifth vote from me would not be politically advantageous for either one of us. She made me chairman of the Committee on Planning and Development. I was thrilled. Although I did not know it at the time, that committee assignment set me up for my working career as a lawyer after I left elective office. The committee has oversight over the physical and economic development of the city. It includes everything related to economic development including financing, planning, zoning, land use policy, and the impact of development on the city and its neighborhoods. That position gave me an education about the infrastructure of Boston and how deals were done and the role economic development plays in a community.

To this day, I am bemused by politicians who question the value of public investment in infrastructure and development. The evidence is overwhelming that public investment, even a small investment, can make or break a development project that changes the economic course of a community. A hotel may get built because the city makes the right investment in road improvements or sewer hookups or gives the developer a tax break in return for locating the hotel in a key block. The government can seed development from the private sector by building a public facility or by promising to rent space in a new office building. Gov. Michael Dukakis systematically used the financial power of the state of Massachusetts to rescue aging urban downtowns throughout the Commonwealth during his time as governor. In Lowell, the worn out mill city on the Merrimack River, state investment, coupled with national legislation that turned the birthplace of the Industrial Revolution of America into a national park, literally transformed the city.

This was certainly true in Boston. I had an acute first hand appreciation of the value of public investment. Many friends and neighbors survived and thrived because of the helping hand of the city, either directly or indirectly. To have influence over the growth of the city was exciting to me. Not only was commercial development important, but I understood that construction projects generated jobs. The ripple effect from construction is considerable. Then, when a new building opens, the city gets property tax revenue and many people get permanent jobs.

I also understood that public projects can wreak havoc with urban neighborhoods. In my first campaign, I heard first hand from people living in the pathway of the proposed Southwest Expressway in Roxbury and Jamaica Plain. People in East Boston were in a frenzy over airport expansion at Logan International Airport. I had heard all the stories about the devastation of an old Italian and Jewish neighborhood in the West End, ostensibly done in the name of "progress." Construction of the Southeast Expressway chopped off a section of Chinatown and a corner of the North End, and put an ugly elevated highway right through downtown Boston that effectively divided the waterfront from the rest of the city.

The redevelopment and slum clearance efforts that took place in the 1950s were well intentioned, but by the 1960s, community activism was on the rise. Indeed, activism of all types was on the rise in that decade. There were demonstrations for or against almost everything: Civil Rights, the war in Vietnam, women's rights, environmental protection, and, in Boston, busing. So it was no surprise that community opposition to certain types of construction projects became organized and effective. That opposition ended up changing public policies and those changes affected the face and skyline of Boston.

This is the first formal photo ever taken of me. I look very much like my mother and our daughter Catherine in this picture.

My brother Vinny and I with our grandfather Lorenzo in front of our house in Dorchester in 1954.

First Communion was always held on a Saturday in May. Here I pose on the steps of St. Gregory's Church. Up until this time, no one had ever cut my hair other than my grandfather who was known as "Lawrence the Barber".

Despite my love of baseball, I was never very good at it. I could not hit a curveball or a fastball. This should not have been too surprising given I did not wear my glasses.

The Explorer Scouts on our way to Germany in June of 1965. At the age of 16, I spent my first night away from Dorchester and my parents.

Part of the Sunday ritual in the 1950s and 1960s was attending Mass and buying the newspaper. I often sold newspapers in front of St. Gregory's on Sunday.

I still have a picture of Robert Kennedy on my wall. I had a rare disagreement with my father when I suggested I drop out of Harvard to go to Indiana to campaign for RFK in 1968.

I had my first hard lesson about race and politics in high school when I was beat up after deciding that white and nonwhite children should play baseball and go on field trips together.

My grandmother accompanied me to the airport for my trip to Washington, D.C. to attend Boys Nation in 1966. It was the first time any member of our family had been on an airplane.

Mum and Dad posed with me at Quincy House on the day I received my Harvard diploma, June 17, 1971.

Bill Guenther, a Harvard student who was a year behind me, served as my campaign manager for my first campaign for public office. I campaigned against construction of a new highway—I 95—through the Boston neighborhoods of Hyde Park, Jamaica Plain and Roxbury. Little did I know that someday I would live in Jamaica Plain.

Mum and Dad and I stand atop three chairs as I declare victory just before midnight on November 2, 1971 and become the youngest person ever elected to the Boston City Council.

When the press visited the day after the election, on November 3, 1971, only my grandmother was home. She was very proud.

My first day as a Boston City Councilor.

I deliver a speech in front of a poster of Martin Luther King Jr. My generation was greatly influenced by MLK and John and Robert Kennedy.

Not unlike my mother, a lifelong music teacher, I was frequently in the classroom. Here I teach a class at Boston Latin School, my alma mater.

Mike Dukakis, the former governor and Democratic Presidential nominee, has been my friend and political ally for more than 40 years.

"The Soiling of Old Glory" © *Stanley J. Forman www.stanleyformanphotos.com. Stan Forman's incredible photo won the Pulitzer Prize in 1977. He took it on April 5, 1976 during an antibusing demonstration on City Hall Plaza. The photograph hurt the city's reputation. I contend the city bottomed out shortly afterwards.*

I actually enjoyed campaigning in parades, especially in warm weather.

Melnea Cass was known as The First Lady of Roxbury. She supported me in 1975 as I sought the support of Black Bostonians.

I accompanied Sargent and Eunice Shriver and the legendary farmworker leader Cesar Chavez down Hanover Street in the North End after Mass at St. Stephen's Church on February 29, 1976.

In January of 1978, some people were surprised when I won election as President of the Boston City Council.

I served on the Board of ABCD, the local anti-poverty agency, for many years. Here I am with Doris Graham of the Dorchester Area Planning Action Council, Bob Coard, the ABCD executive director, and a budding artist.

The statewide office holders for Boys State surround me in 1978. I stay in touch with many of these students. Years later, one became a legal client and another was a guest at our wedding.

Kevin White returns to Boston and takes command with the military on one side and Fire Commissioner George Paul on the other in February 1978 after I was Acting Mayor of Boston during the great blizzard in his absence.

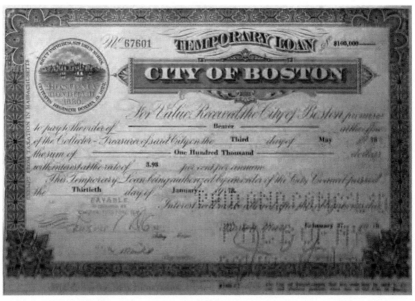

This is an authorization of a 1978 temporary $100,000 loan to the city of Boston which I signed in my capacity as acting Mayor.

I have been an active alumnus of Harvard University for many years. In 1996, I served as Marshall for my 25th reunion. In this photo I am standing with my wife Teresa in Harvard Yard.

This is one of the last photographs of me with my brother and sister and our remarkable mother shortly before she passed away.

And then there were five. August 28, 1982.

An Elsa Dorman photograph of the five of us, a year
or so after the girls were born. Teresa and I had our
hands full.

Sophie, Catherine and Flora (left to right) photographed in their graduation dresses as they completed Belmont Day School in 2012.

Building a New Boston

The modern era in Boston effectively began in 1949, when City Clerk John Hynes defeated James Michael Curley to become Mayor of Boston and with the passage of the American Housing Act of 1949. Those two events set the stage for the next decades.

John B. Hynes, the city's low key and hard working City Clerk, was acting Mayor in 1947, while Mayor James Michael Curley served a five-month sentence at the federal prison in Danbury on a conviction of mail fraud for war profiteering. Instead of thanking Hynes for his loyal service, Mayor Curley insulted Hynes on the very day he returned triumphant to Boston. The mild mannered clerk became so angry that he challenged Curley and beat the 74-year-old political legend in the election of 1949. Even then, Curley was an icon, but by the late 1940s he was becoming a caricature of himself and increasingly seen by Bostonians as a political dinosaur. His defeat signaled that Bostonians were looking for a bit of competence and a mayor with some administrative ability after the war. During his campaign, Hynes promised new housing to replace the ragged tenements and a new parking garage to be located underneath Boston Common. That election launched the modern era in Boston politics.

The city was in terrible fiscal and physical shape after the War. To be honest, it had been in terrible shape since the Great Depression of the 1930s. The old industries were long gone. The seaport was a shadow of its former self. The traditional immigrant ghettoes with substandard housing were collapsing from exhaustion and neglect and crowding the downtown commercial core. The tempo of Navy Yard work in Charlestown slowed as demand ebbed with the end of World War II. There had been no major commercial development in decades. The city's tallest building was the Custom House Tower. Its lower floors were authorized during the administration of President Andrew

Jackson in 1837. Before the waterfront was filled in, ships would pull up at the end of the city docks, almost touching the Custom House. In 1947 the old John Hancock Tower, a foot shorter than the Custom House Tower, was built. Those two towers were literally the only discernible landmarks on the city skyline. Downtown Boston, with its narrow curving streets that traced the long ago trail of cow paths, was also being overwhelmed by the automobiles of the commuters coming into the city each day to work. America's love affair with the automobile surged in the 1950s and there was simply no place to park all those cars.

Another major event occurred in 1949 that had lasting impact on the physical face of Boston. That was passage of the American Housing Act of 1949, a sweeping landmark bill that was part of Harry Truman's Fair Deal. The legislation expanded construction of public housing as well as the federal role in mortgage insurance. It provided for billions of dollars in federal funds for slum clearance, the construction of 800,000 public housing units and authorized FHA mortgage insurance. The housing crisis was severe, particularly with veterans returning home after the War. Millions were living in sub-standard housing. The cold water flats where my father grew up were still there and still completely inadequate. Public housing was considered a big step up from buildings that lacked central heat or hot water. The Congressman from South Boston, John W. McCormack was already U.S. House Majority Leader by 1949. He made sure that new federal housing projects were located in his neighborhood of South Boston, where they provided safe, clean and affordable housing for returning veterans and their growing families. Those projects remain in operation in Southie to this day.

Knocking down dilapidated slum tenements was universally cheered. No one wanted to keep those old firetraps so entire blocks and streets were eradicated to make way for new housing. The prevailing philosophy of urban renewal was knock down and build up; get rid of the old to make way for the new. It is a pattern seen in nature, where forest fires obliterate acres of old trees only to make way for new growth. It is also part of what Teddy White, a Dorchester native, called the ballet of urban life. Change is constant in urban America, although there are times when it is barely discernible.

This potent combination of slum clearance money and highway construction money after World War II transformed Boston. The Central Artery, named after Mayor John "Honey Fitz" Fitzgerald, the grandfather of President Kennedy, divided city neighborhoods and separated the waterfront from the rest of the city. It was an elevated highway that the passage of time only made more ominous, dangerous and ugly. Homeless people, drunks and criminals haunted its shadow. No law abiding person would venture underneath the elevated at night for fear of becoming a victim of crime.

In 1948, Department of Public Works Commissioner William F. Callahan, later head of the Massachusetts Turnpike Authority whose son's name is on one of the two old airport tunnels that link downtown Boston to Logan International Airport in East Boston, proposed a 25-year Master Plan for highway construction for the Boston area. The proposal called for a Southwest Corridor Expressway to run along the old railroad right of way from Rte 128 and the Dedham line straight through Roxbury and Jamaica Plain, ending in the South End. The goal was laudatory. Commuters could zip without pause from Dedham and Norwood and other points south right into town for work every day. The six lane expressway would run for 10.3 miles. Of course, the new highway would slice neighborhoods in two and displace thousands of residents. Hyde Park residents were so upset there was talk of seceding from Boston. To make way for the highway, blocks of factories and old residential housing in Roxbury and Jamaica Plain were knocked down.

But this time, the town rebelled. Bostonians had been informed by the experience with the Southeast Expressway and other controversial urban renewal projects and the opponents found allies in high ranking state officials. The times had also changed and ordinary people were becoming empowered. In the 1960s, massive public demonstration became a state of art that defined the decade with enormous marches opposing the war in Vietnam and in favor of Civil Rights. This filtered down to the local level of residents opposed to highway construction and airport expansion in Boston.

The very good thing about a democracy is that those in charge need to listen to their constituents—or else lose power. Governor Frank Sargent, an affable Yankee Republican at a time when Republicans championed the environment, listened. In February of 1970, Governor Sargent ordered a moratorium on the Southwest Expressway. He insisted the project be rethought and redesigned and include mass transit. By 1973, Interstate 95 had been rerouted along Rte. 128, the highway built in a loop around Boston. The city had to trade in some federal highway grant money for transit money. That switch was authorized by the Federal Highway Act of 1973. The Massachusetts Congressional delegation arranged for that little detail to make certain the state would not lose federal money because of the change of plans. The new transit money was used to build tunnels in place of the existing Elevated Subway line that created an eyesore down Washington Street. The subway tracks, commuter rail lines and the new Amtrak rail line went either underground or were designed at grade to become a seamless part of the neighborhood, rather than walls breaking up communities. Nine new Orange Line stations eventually opened, including several in Jamaica Plain, sparking a resurgence of that neighborhood, and a 52-acre linear park topped the whole thing with a ribbon of green through the neighborhoods. Governor Sargent's successor,

Mike Dukakis, was even more passionate about mass transit. During his time in office, Dukakis rode the Green Line subway to the State House nearly each day from his home in Brookline. Years later after leaving public office, he served on the Amtrak Board of Directors. None of this would have happened had it not been for the united front presented by Sargent, Dukakis and Mayor White. Leadership in this instance was crucial.

The Southwest Corridor experience is vital to understanding what came later, because nothing takes place in a vacuum. In government and politics, as in life, one event or incident triggers another and that triggers another. The chain reaction from either overt action, or sometimes from stubborn inaction, plays out for decades. In this case, the defeat of the Southwest Expressway led the way to the revitalization of entire neighborhoods and the creation of the Boston, celebrated and admired today.

Major construction projects take years to complete, because the prep work involved in taking property, clearing away old buildings and repairing the infrastructure can be as time-consuming as the actual new road construction. By the late 1960s, the negative fallout from four major projects had transformed the politics of development. Those projects were: the Southeast Expressway; the elimination of the old West End to make way for Charles River Park; destruction of seedy Scollay Square to make way for the new Government Center which included state, federal and city public buildings including the new City Hall, a still controversial structure in the brutalist style; and construction of the Prudential Tower, after years of battles over the size of the tax break the Prudential Insurance Company would get in return for constructing its new building.

In the context of the times, city leaders understood the need for economic development and growth and for new housing, and made decisions that made sense at the time. The city did what was necessary to get those projects built—but paid a price. I remember seeing a congratulatory photograph of Mayor John Collins and Cardinal Cushing at the groundbreaking of Regina Cleri, a residence for retired priests, right smack in the middle of the wildly controversial West End development site. The Archdiocese clearly had its price. The retirement community for priests is still operational after more than 50 years. Monsignor Francis J. Lally, the editor of The Pilot, the oldest Catholic diocesan newspaper in the country, served as chairman of the Boston Redevelopment Authority for years and shared the prevailing vision of urban renewal.

The passage of time changed the perspective. Neighborhood opposition grew too strong to ignore. Mayor Collins recruited Edward J. Logue, the New Haven City Planner, to head up the relatively new Boston Redevelopment Authority in 1960. He handed Logue a mandate and Logue ran with it. He created one of the most powerful urban development agencies in the country. He consolidated in the BRA the power to seize property through eminent domain, the responsibility for planning, and the authority to build. He was such a powerhouse that he ran for Mayor of Boston in 1967 in the election that White won. The churning of the 1960s on so many fronts included vigorous opposition to Logue's top down style of redevelopment and finally, Logue experienced more failures than successes in neighborhood redevelopment. To me, the Charlestown Redevelopment project, originally viewed as a massive slum clearing project, was the last gasp of that time. Opposition to the Charlestown redevelopment project was strong enough to cut that project to a fraction of its original vision, even with the support of Monsignor Lally and the local parish priests. Eventually, it just made more sense for the Mayor and the BRA to focus on downtown Boston, where there were fewer residents and where the commercial development represented a far bigger financial payoff for the city.

I developed an early interest in development projects. When I was a 14-year-old student at Boston Latin School, I wrote an essay about how Mayor Collins should be reelected because his urban renewal policies were carrying Boston to a bright future. Not long afterwards, I wrote another essay proposing that a facility be built on the Charles River Esplanade, so that Boston Latin School crew members could change their clothes indoors, rather than in the bushes. I did not succeed in getting a facility for the crew at the time, but I did identify the need. Louise Day Hicks did not know it at the time but when she made me chairman of the Planning and Development Committee, she gave me the opportunity to be involved in some of the projects that remade the city.

As the decade of the 1970s progressed, the city of Boston's financial problems grew worse. Residential real estate was wildly undervalued and the city tried to make up the difference by levying huge tax bills on commercial property owners. Norman Tregor put a stop to that. Norman Tregor owned a building in Boston that the city assessed at $320,000 and levied a property tax bill in 1977 of $80,928. The city assessed different classes of property at different percentages of fair market value. Mr. Tregor showed that his building was worth at most $87,904 and it generated an annual net income before taxes of $55,000. The Court agreed with his argument and ruled in his favor forcing a fairer, and less lucrative, system of taxation on Boston. It also cut revenues from property taxes, and forced the city to borrow money to pay back those who had been unfairly taxed.

Boston was not the only city to rely heavily upon the property tax. Virtually every town and city in the Commonwealth was in a similar position and in communities with large numbers of growing families with children who needed to be educated in public schools; the financial demands on the local government were enormous. All those people who moved to the suburbs—in search of that split level with a lawn—after the War created demand for more of everything: more roads, more sewage plants, more public schools, and more police and fire protection. That costs money. The property tax has no relationship to ability to pay. It is pegged on the value of the real estate. So inflation boosted the values of houses and the seniors on fixed incomes who had paid off their mortgages now were threatened with losing their houses because of escalating tax bills. Many younger families could not afford huge property tax bills on top of the other costs of raising a family. This made the state ripe for Proposition 2½.

Taxpayer rebellions began popping up all over the country and the Proposition 2 ½ campaign was orchestrated by a libertarian group called Citizens for Limited Taxation, headed by a North Shore housewife named Barbara Anderson, a dynamo who became a statewide celebrity. The initiative petition was approved by voters in 1980. It limited property tax revenues to 2.5 percent of the assessed value of property in a community and limited any annual increase to 2.5 percent. It also lowered the much hated excise tax on automobiles.

The Tregor Decision and Proposition 2 ½ had the force of law. Mayor White had few options left, so he started to sell city assets. All those public parking garages, low tech concrete structures tossed up in the 1950s to deal with the automobiles of suburban commuters, were in prime downtown spots. When the lots were sold, the garages were knocked down and new high rise buildings took their places. The St. James Avenue garage became 500 Boylston Street; the Fort Hill Garage became International Place; the Kilby Street Garage became 75 State Street;and the Lincoln Garage became One Lincoln Street. He sold the Prince School on Newbury Street and the shabby old school built in 1875 became an upscale condominium building with a concierge in the heart of the Back Bay shopping district. The old public grade school that I had attended in Dorchester was also turned into housing.

Kevin White reinvented city government in large part because of necessity. He simply did not have the money to run the city in the old way. He jettisoned water and sewer service, for example, and created the Water and Sewer Commission, putting that function on a pay-as-you-go basis under a separate administrative structure for the first time in history. As a result of the financial crises brought about by the Tregor decision and Proposition 2 ½, he closed police and fire stations in the early 1980s. In Charlestown, he closed two of the three fire stations and the police station. He was excoriated by Townies at the time, but property values in Charlestown have soared, probably 30 times, in 30 years.

From my perch as chairman of the City Council's Committee on Planning and Development, I had a bird's eye view of the transformation of the city. I scheduled committee meetings for 9 a.m. on Tuesday morning. I reasoned that anyone who cared would show up at that time, and it suited me. I am an early riser. Moreover, my colleague Dapper O'Neil could be counted upon to go to the Board of Appeal hearing on Tuesday where zoning issues were resolved. Dapper never really saw the big picture. Small bore deals involving a meter maid job or a liquor license were the coin of the realm for him and his primary interests, not high rise downtown towers.

Public money and public decisions were crucial to the transformation of the city. My committee had to sign off on all federal grants and city loan orders. A Democratic President, Jimmy Carter, and Democratic Congress kept public money flowing to the cities. An Economic Development Administration (EDA) grant paid for the improvements to the infrastructure needed to transform the Charlestown Navy Yard into the highly desirable residential area it is today. An $18.7 million Urban Development Action Grant (UDAG) helped build the platform over the rail lines at Copley Place. The platform, put in place with taxpayer money, cleared the way for construction of an office building, two hotels and a high end shopping area by a private developer. While I have always opposed sweetheart deals that give favors to preferred contractors who might happen to be great pals or great contributors to politicians in power, I do believe in using government money to leverage private sector investment. The dirty little secret of capitalism is that few wealthy investors are willing to take great risks with their money. They want a sure deal. It is inappropriate for government to eliminate all risk, but it can certainly minimize the risk. I believe that is a reasonable use of public money, so long as the payoff for the public is substantial. The projects the city sponsored in those years definitely paid off. They created new buildings in place of shabby underutilized or inefficient parking garages. They created private sector jobs, generated property and sales tax revenues, and injected old Boston with a jaunty new spirit. My friend Joe Moakley told me more than once that the "crane," the construction crane that is, was his favorite bird. Those construction cranes represented jobs and growth.

Boston has always boasted many universities and colleges and is a preeminent center of higher education in the United States. Thousands of college students bring energy to Boston that keeps the city ever young. The revitalization of Boston created restaurants, clubs, shops and other commercial establishments for the students to patronize. The young came out at night and kept the city alive after dark. It created a self-fulfilling circle that kept the young in Boston after graduation. The graduates worked in the new high rise towers, lived in the renovated apartments in the Back Bay and South End, and reclaimed old Victorian houses in Dorchester and Jamaica Plain, refurbishing them for their own families. When I was contemplating my future in the late 1970s, I remember speaking with a wise veteran political hand who lived at an apartment at the Prudential Center on Boylston Street. He told me he could look out his apartment window and see a gay bar just across the street from his apartment building which showed him that the city was changing a lot faster than anyone realized. That bar had long lines of gay men outside every night he said. The gay population of Boston proved to be explorers slightly ahead of other young professionals in reclaiming certain neighborhoods of Boston, such as the South End and Jamaica Plain.

The Bicentennial in 1975-1976 set a deadline for completion of the Quincy Market redevelopment, but it was only one of the elements putting pressure on the city to transform the waterfront area. My friend Bill McCue considered renting a one bedroom apartment at the then brand new Harbor Towers, high rise apartments on the waterfront, for what I recall was $135 a month in 1971. He invited me to take a look at it with him. Harbor Towers, two 40-foot residential towers, built in the same unforgiving brutalist style as the New City Hall, were intended to be affordable housing by the BRA and bring some nightlife to the waterfront area. At the time, the project seemed foolhardy. Crossing under the Expressway to get there from City Hall was a dicey trip and the high rise towers seemed completely out of place for Boston. Today the address is highly desirable because of the remarkable water views.

The change in the value of Harbor Towers came about because of the depression of the Central Artery, which gave energy to tremendous renewal of the old waterfront area which now features expensive lofts, condominiums, hotels, a convention center and other amenities that make it a vital part of the city. Once Quincy Market opened to great praise and popularity in 1976, the city became aware that tourists never ventured further because the forbidding overhead highway effectively acted as a barrier to the waterfront.

During Dukakis' administration, the brilliant Transportation Secretary Fred Salvucci, a Brighton native who had earlier worked for Kevin White as manager of the East Boston City Hall, aggressively championed the Central Artery project. Eventually, Speaker Tip O'Neill managed to get the massive federal funds needed to take down that ugly elevated highway and put it underground. When it was first proposed, Barney Frank, ever the quipster, joked that it would be cheaper to raise the city than depress the artery. He was not wrong, but the project has completely transformed the waterfront area. Tourists now can walk easily from downtown to the waterfront and development on the waterfront has made Boston a highly attractive location for national conventions. Motorists can now zip through Boston from points South to points North without any trouble. It is yet another example of a public project that changed the city in a profound way.

I enjoyed the economic development work immensely. The committee work gave me an outlet for the creative juices revived by my year at the Kennedy School. I felt I was making a real contribution to my city. It also made me think again of running for statewide office. The 1977 campaign for reelection was not particularly remarkable for me. I earned my masters degree in public policy from the Kennedy School at Harvard in the spring. My grandmother got all dressed up and even put on high heels to attend my graduation, despite her advanced age. I felt I had looked into the abyss and somehow survived in 1975. By the 1977 election, I was not feeling as much pressure, but I was still in something of a survival mode.

In 1977, I survived again but not everyone else did. Voter turnout spiked because of a ballot question on the structure of city government. I had been pushing it for years and it would not succeed that year, but it did have an impact on the turnout. John D. O'Bryant, an African American with an Irish surname, won a seat on the Boston School Committee. Even more surprising were the defeats of some of the pivotal leaders of the antibusing movement. Two years after topping the council ticket, Louise Day Hicks lost. She was stunned. John J. Kerrigan also lost his council seat and Pixie Palladino lost her spot on the Boston School Committee. The new councilors were Rosemarie Sansone, who had conducted a statewide referendum campaign on behalf of the Equal Rights Amendment and represented a young fresh face, and Raymond Flynn, a state representative from South Boston. Ray now would sit next to me at council meetings. The results were surprising at the time. The results hinted to me of bigger demographic changes taking place in Boston.

However, I was still finishing in the middle of the pack, the same place where I had finished in the past. I felt I was stuck on a treadmill on the Boston City Council and it was time to try again to move up. First, I really wanted to be President of the Boston City Council. There were some benefits to the job: a bigger office, more staff, and my own shower. The chaos of Council hearings frustrated me and I knew as President I could institute some changes in practices and rules. One of the changes I advocated was the "Freddy Rule," a firm limit of 10 minutes on any pronouncement by a Boston City Councilor during a meeting. It was necessary to curb the relentless rants of Fred Langone. I also abolished evening meetings. I had watched some of my colleagues return to work from the dinner break intoxicated. But I mostly wanted the bully pulpit and thought being President of the Council would be helpful in a statewide race. I had four votes: my own and those of Chris Iannella, Pat McDonough and Jim Connolly, who was a few years older than me but the closest I had to a contemporary on the Council. Joe Tierney wanted to remain as Council President and it was believed he had the support of Dapper O'Neil and Fred Langone. The three often voted together. That left the two newcomers: Sansone and Flynn. Sansone ended up voting present. Her father worked for the state Treasury and she could not risk a vote for me if I intended to run against Bob Crane. Flynn made himself scarce. I got to know his sainted wife Cathy very well in those days. He was never home and she was always very nice to me on the phone.

On New Year's Day, I ran into Fred Langone in the elevator. I often went to City Hall at night or on weekends and holidays to deal with paperwork. Fred invited me into his office. He kept his office dark. It was furnished with leather furniture, a brandy snifter and pungent with cigar smoke. Any conversation with Fred Langone was an adventure. Freddy could only speak with both hands in constant motion. As he frantically gesticulated, his tone of voice escalated. By the end of a paragraph, he would be at full shout. He explained that he would vote for me on the first ballot but only if I kept it a secret. He said he had been told that Kevin White and Bob Crane had lined up five votes for Chris Iannella on the second ballot to keep me from getting the presidency. He intended to frustrate his longtime rival. He said he wanted to see the look on Iannella's face when I won a first ballot victory. They had been feuding for years.

When I arrived at City Hall on the day of the vote, Ray Flynn was waiting in my office. He said, "I'm with you." I'm not quite sure why he was willing to vote for me after evading my strenuous courtship. I suspect he figured I was going to win anyway and wanted to be on the winning side. So I was elected on a 6-3 first ballot vote.

I knew when I was elected Council President that I would be acting mayor each time Kevin White left town. What I did not know was how often he went out of town. The Mayor had wearied of the day-to-day responsibilities of his job and was happy to delegate the tedious routine tasks to others. He no longer had a chance of winning national office since the busing debacle and his only attempt to run for governor had long ago ended in defeat.

Little did I know that within weeks I would be acting mayor during one of the most memorable natural catastrophes in city history. In New England there are snow storms and there are snow storms. New Englanders can deal with snow. Just after I became Council President, there was a snow storm on Friday, January 27. Kevin White was out of town and I was acting Mayor. Friday night is not a bad time for a snow storm. There is less traffic on a weekend and it is easier for the snow plows to move around the city. People are off work and in a more festive and relaxed mood. David Brudnoy, then hosting a radio show on WHDH, invited me on air. I spent four hours fielding phone calls, assuring Bostonians the plows were on the way, urging people to shovel around hydrants and check on their elderly neighbors. By Monday, the city was back to some normalcy. Two feet of snow is a lot of snow, but still manageable.

I flew to New York on the first weekend in February for a fundraiser; I was running for statewide office again, this time for Treasurer. I returned Saturday night and remembered as the plane touched down that I was acting Mayor again. Kevin had left town again and the City Clerk had notified me of his absence in keeping with the law. I went home to Dorchester that night but returned to downtown Monday, knowing another storm was on the way. And what a storm. The weather forecast became more ominous as the day progressed. I had slept on a pullout couch at the apartment at 52A Temple Street of two campaign workers, Wiley Bell and Kevin Connor, during the previous storm. The apartment was literally steps from City Hall, the State House and Suffolk Law School. I decided to bunk with them again because if the storm was as bad as predictions indicated, I could walk to City Hall.

The Great Blizzard of 1978, between February 5 and 8, was historic. An extra-tropical cyclone developed off the coast of South Carolina on February 5. It collided with an Arctic cold front which created an enormous and intense low pressure system. The result was a nor'easter with sustained hurricane force winds and 33 straight hours of snow. There was snow everywhere, an all time high in Boston, falling on top of the two feet from the earlier storm. The storm came at a time of a new moon, so the tides were unusually high and destructive. More than 100 people in the Northeast died. One little boy in western Massachusetts got lost in a snow drift steps from his front door and was not found until weeks later. Many lived without heat, water, food and electricity for more than a week. Nothing was working. Automobiles could not move. Public transit stopped. The U.S. government used military flights to get emergency supplies into the region.

And, I was in charge of Boston! Kevin White could not get back to town from sunny Florida despite valiant efforts. There are few things worse for a politician than being out of town during a crisis. He got as far as Washington, D.C. on an Amtrak train, but it was impossible to get into New England for days. He cooled his heels in Washington, ostensibly lobbying Tip O'Neill for federal disaster funds.

On the first night of the storm, Kevin Connor woke me just before dawn to tell me there was no electricity in the building. I called the 24-hour city service number. Joe Langille of Hyde Park was on duty. I told him there was no electricity on Beacon Hill. He told me there was no power anywhere in Boston.

"Is Kevin back in town?" I asked.

"No, he is not," he replied.

"Then I am in charge?"

"Yes, you are."

I headed for the bunker on the ground level of City Hall where the 24 hour service operated. I put on the warmest clothes I could find and headed out without benefit of a shave or shower. The winds were whipping at hurricane force and snow was drifting taller than I was. I avoided City Hall Plaza, where a good blast would have knocked me over. I weighed about 135 pounds at the time. Instead, I walked up to the State House and then down Bowdoin Street because I could not get over the snow drift at the intersection of Temple and Cambridge Streets, clinging to parking meters to keep on my feet. About 20 minutes later, 15 minutes longer than usual, I reached the bunker.

I did not do an Al Haig and laud my authority over anyone. It was a scary day. I offered my help. City work crews were completely overwhelmed. No one could have kept up with the storm. It just kept snowing on top of the two feet already on the ground. I told Joe Casazza, the legendary Department of Public Works Commissioner, to spend whatever he needed to clear the streets. It was an emergency. I authorized Joe Jordan, the police commissioner, to arrest people on sight to stop looting in Codman Square. The emergency trumped the Miranda Warning that day. The 82nd airborne was the first flight to land at Logan.

Before the Mayor finally managed to get back into Boston on Thursday, I had issued a proclamation turning Valentine's Day into Valentine's Month. The greeting card industry was apoplectic that sales would be lost. When I was challenged on that act, I noted that Cardinal Medeiros had declared that Ash Wednesday was the following Sunday. If he could change Ash Wednesday to a Sunday, why couldn't the acting Mayor turn Valentine's Day into a Month?

Years later, some have suggested the Blizzard of 1978 was like Woodstock with icicles. It was a full blown crisis but it was also a festive time that rolled back the clock by a century. People could not work or do anything routine or use any modern devices. Families cooked breakfast on outdoor grills and walked to Church. Neighbors reached out to one another. People used cross country skis to get around town. Neighbors built snow houses in the middle of the street, which was likely not going to be passable for weeks. Everyone was simply stunned by this display of natural power. With no electricity and in an era before ATM machines, people ran out of cash and resorted to bartering. It was an emergency and emergency conditions prevailed. We even pushed snow into the ocean; an environmental no no, but there was simply no other place to put it.

City Hall had emergency generators so the building had electricity and I could function efficiently from there and even take a shower in that private bathroom attached to the Council President's office. I am struck by how much simpler things were then. In those days, before beepers/ pagers, Blackberries, email and cell phones, I left on Tuesday night to have dinner with Jim and Janet Dolan in their North End apartment. The folks in the bunker could not have reached me easily. But I checked in with them often. The Dolans' had a gas stove and whipped up an elegant meal.

I still believed that the best way to be elected Mayor was from a position outside the Boston City Council. And I still wanted to be Mayor. This time I set my goal on ousting Robert Q. Crane, the state Treasurer and Receiver General, the man credited with bringing the lottery to Massachusetts. While the lottery was popular, Crane had nearly lost in a primary challenge in 1974 to Mark Furcolo, a lawyer and first time candidate, who was the son of former Governor Foster Furcolo. Crane skinnied to victory by a bare two points in the September primary in 1974. Crane was old enough to be my father, a World War II generation politician who grew up in Brighton, and, like Jack Davoren, the Secretary of State who lost his primary in 1974, did not spend much time at his government office. Crane had an outside job with a major food brokerage company which was controversial at the time. His style of politics had been vulnerable to challenge in 1974, when Mike Dukakis beat Bob Quinn for the Democratic gubernatorial nomination and Paul Guzzi beat Jack Davoren in his primary.

Our small family suffered a grievous blow that winter. My grandmother Josephine Alibrandi died at the age of 88. The Saturday night of the first blizzard in late January, my parents rushed her to the Carney Hospital. She had a massive heart attack. She was on her hands and knees scrubbing her hardwood floors up until then. She had never spent a single night in the hospital. It was terrifying for her. The sight of my much loved grandmother in the hospital bed with tubes and wires nearly broke my heart. But Grandma was still in charge. She gave me three orders: Lorenzo, she instructed, take care of your mother; you settle down; and when you get back to the house, turn down the thermostat. Why waste oil if no one is there?

She came home, but five weeks later suffered another massive coronary that killed her. She had a great run and a wonderful long life. We held a wake at Molloy's Funeral Home in Lower Mills. The first people to arrive were her niece Clara and her husband Louis who lived north of Boston. The snow was still making it difficult to travel, so they left their home in Malden and made their way on the old Rte 28, winding through every community in between Malden and Dorchester. The trip took them three hours. The second person to arrive was my colleague, Dapper O'Neil. Dapper had no love for me, but he went to every wake. He arrived and went into his routine of how my grandmother reminded him of his dear departed mother. We were cordial, but Clara and Louis who were a bit deaf at that point had a loud conversation.

"Louie," yelled Clara, "Can you believe Dapper O'Neil has the nerve to show his face here after not supporting Larry for Council President!" My mother and I kept our faces sober with great difficulty.

The extraordinary amount of snow prompted me to delay my formal announcement for Treasurer by three weeks. Then, in late March, I criss-crossed the state in a six city announcement tour. My campaign manager Mark Roosevelt and I drove from Boston to Pittsfield, where I announced on a Tuesday night. We went to Springfield to announce there on Wednesday morning. We flew from Barnes Airport outside Springfield in a tiny airplane to New Bedford. We hit massive snow squalls over Rhode Island on the way. I pulled out the Italian prayers my grandmother had given me from my wallet during that turbulent white knuckle flight. After announcing in New Bedford, Mark arranged for a better airplane and we flew to Boston then drove up to Lowell and then Worcester. It was frenzied and crazy and exhilarating. I literally never stopped moving for the next six months. I barely slept and every waking moment was overflowing with campaign events, council meetings and fundraisers. I was having the time of my life.

Crane had felt his vulnerability acutely in 1974 and saw the same signs I did. So he tried to convince me to run for another office. Bo Holland, a Boston political operative who was close to Kevin White and Crane and something of a legend in Boston political circles, acted as the go-between. He proposed a face to face meeting with Crane on a Sunday in June. Crane invited me to follow him in my car from the Marriott Hotel in Newton to his house in Wellesley. His lovely wife Mary offered me a ham sandwich. We talked. Crane offered help if I would run for Secretary of State. His people would raise money for me and his friends at The Boston Globe would not take issue with my switching races. Although Paul Guzzi had been elected Secretary of State just four years earlier, he had decided, after considerable internal debate and public procrastination—which badly hurt him—to run for the U.S. Senate. Senator Ed Brooke was clearly in political trouble and there was blood in the water. The Democratic primary for the Senate seat became crowded.

Crane is an extremely likeable and affable guy, but what he was asking made no sense to me. I felt it was too late to switch races. I had already raised money and put myself out as an advocate for certain fiscal issues specific to the Treasurer's office. So I respectfully declined to get out of the race. We parted amicably.

I only told one person, my campaign manager Mark Roosevelt, who is now the President of Antioch College, about my secret meeting with Crane. Mark, on his own, leaked the story to the Boston Phoenix, the alternative weekly newspaper. The part about Crane's columnist friends, David Farrell, Mike

Barnicle and Robert Healy, being willing to do his bidding at The Boston Globe caused quite a ruckus at the newspaper. Years later, the Pulitzer Prize winning cartoonist Paul Szep told me that he had been instructed to draw a negative cartoon about me showing me as the David to Crane's Goliath flinging mud. Tom Winship, the Globe editor, later told me that "you have your friends and Crane has his friends; three of his friends happen to work for the Globe."

To say I really had no idea what I was getting into is to understate my naiveté. Dorothy Curran, a sweet woman who had worked at the city Department of Parks and Recreation since James Michael Curley got her the job after she was widowed young, warned me. "They will hurt you," she cautioned. "They will not let you win." Dorothy had a way of knowing things she was not supposed to know. She had it exactly right.

The year 1978 proved to be a very strange and turbulent year in Massachusetts. Edward J. King, the former director of the Massport Authority, beat Governor Michael Dukakis in the September primary for the Democratic nomination. One of King's political operatives, Angelo Berlandi, famously said that "we put all the hate groups in a pot and stirred." In November, Senator Edward W. Brooke lost the Senate seat to Congressman Paul E. Tsongas, who had beaten Guzzi and several others to win the Democratic Senate nomination. Brooke had not lived in the state full time for years and had marital problems. All this personal difficulty cost him in a year when voters were upset about inflation and the soft economy. These titanic struggles dominated the news coverage. My earnest efforts to highlight better ways of investing state funds barely rated a mention in news coverage.

When Crane could not get me out of the race, he stacked the ballot with names intended to confuse the electorate and reduce my vote. It is an age old practice that has never fallen out of fashion because it invariably is effective in spoiling challenges for low ballot positions. John F. Kennedy did it in his first 1946 congressional race; James Craven, a longtime state rep from Boston, did it repeatedly in Jamaica Plain. When I helped our neighbor, William F. Keenan, in his state legislative race in Dorchester in the first campaign I worked on as a boy, a candidate named Edward Keenan appeared on the ballot. Even though Edward Keenan never once appeared in the neighborhood or actively campaigned, he pulled more than 1,000 votes on Election Day.

The 1978 primary ballot listed the incumbent first with the challengers listed alphabetically. This is how it read:

Robert Q. Crane, Treasurer
Lawrence E. Blacke, Boston
Paul Cacchiotti, City Councilor
Lawrence S. DiCara, Boston City Councilor

Thomas Lopes, New Bedford
Dayce Moore, Braintree

The biggest threat to a vulnerable incumbent is a one on one challenge. It crystallizes the fight. Voters can only vote for one person if they have some grievance with the incumbent or are just feeling grumpy and want to take it out on someone. Lawrence E. Blacke was a classmate from Boston Latin School and a lawyer. He had run for the City Council the year before, for the first and only time, and would never run for public office again. His first name and Boston address were intended to confuse. Paul Cacchiotti was from Everett. He was a city councilor who never before displayed any interest in running for statewide office and never would again in the future. He had an Italian surname, just like me. I never did figure out where Lopes and Moore came from, but their names came after mine in the alphabet so I was sandwiched. Lopes had an address less than 8 miles from my summer house in Mattapoisett and many of my Dorchester neighbors had moved to Braintree. Bob Crane was kept under 50 percent of the vote, but he did get more votes than anyone else including me. The old sandwich trick worked.

Throughout the mid-1970s, I was befuddled each time I was confused with the then state Senator from Revere, Joseph J.C. DiCarlo, who was the Senate Majority Leader. Although the confusion likely helped me carry Revere in 1978, it did not help me anywhere else, given that Joe was convicted and imprisoned on federal extortion charges. When asked if I had ever held public office in Revere, I would attempt to clarify the difference by replying: "I went to Harvard, he went to Jail." Believe it or not, even today, I sometimes get asked whether I am a former elected official from Revere.

The Treasurer's race was the first nasty campaign of my career and I did not enjoy it. There were a few mysterious events that with the benefit of hindsight still leave me wondering what was really going on. I received a letter one day from the allegedly estranged wife of a local school committee member in the southeastern part of the state. She complained about her husband and said she was looking for a man like me. I never responded. I barely knew her. She and her husband had attended a barbeque at my house in Mattapoisett. The letter just seemed odd to me. Later I learned her husband got a part time job with the state lottery. Of course, I have other friends who got those jobs, too, but I still do wonder about that peculiar letter.

There were some comic moments. I nearly always had a driver and these young men had varying abilities. One time, Patrick Burke of South Boston was driving me to Sheffield to deliver a commencement address. We were stopped for speeding on the Massachusetts Turnpike by a State Police Trooper. He let us go after noting that he had spent some time at South Boston High School and understood people from South Boston had a lot on their minds. That night we stayed at a friend's large house in Longmeadow. The friends were away but told us where to find the key. We had to hunt for some time to locate it and all the while joked that the Longmeadow Police might be suspicious of two Boston kids prowling around this mansion in the dead of night. Another time Christopher Burke, the youngest of six sons of the Burke family of Canton, was pressed into service as my driver after I broke a collar bone in a softball game. Chris was a really terrible driver and I finally asked him how long he had been driving. It turned out he had just secured a learner's permit one week prior.

On the 15th of August, I wandered through the campaign headquarters and spotted some campaign volunteers just hanging around. Since time immemorial, people have been hanging around campaign headquarters for no good reason. I suggested everyone should go out and distribute campaign leaflets. One of the volunteers was Michael Teplow, a teenager who had been an intern in my council office. Michael was a quiet Jewish boy who wore a yarmulke. When he grew up, he became a lawyer, immigrated to Israel, where he still lives and serves as a councilor on the local Karnei Shamron Town Council. August 15 is the Feast of the Assumption, a holy day of obligation in the Catholic Church which meant every practicing Catholic should attend Mass. I suggested Michael go to the corner of Franklin Street and Arch Street, because hundreds of people would be there at noon. Michael got lost and asked a number of people where "Arch Street" was. He eventually found the big building with the big cross on the wall and stood out front of St. Anthony's Shrine in his yarmulke distributing leaflets for my campaign on the Feast of the Assumption.

The only thing that softened my own blow at losing was watching Mike Dukakis concede that September night. He was shellshocked and still had money in his campaign account which he had held off spending because he did not realize he was in trouble. I was denied the chance to win another office, but Mike lost his job. It was far worse for him.

The Treasurer's race in 1978 was the last time I ever tried to run for statewide office. Although my two efforts to run for state office did not succeed, I still remember with great gratitude and fondness, the wonderful people I met. I have a theory that has never been disproved, that the greater the distance from Boston, the friendlier the people. In the days before cell phones, I would stop at pay telephones to call into the office and headquarters. The press paid little attention so there was time on those long drives between events to think or nap. I kept a list in the car glove compartment of all the radio stations that carried Red Sox games live so I could listen to the Sox wherever I might be. Emily Sullivan, now departed, was a kind and generous woman in Holyoke who always made me a meal and offered me a free place to sleep. One day, my driver got us lost on the way from Adams to Holyoke. When we arrived, Mrs. Sullivan was still waiting up for us. Jim Rowley in Adams and Remo DelGallo in Pittsfield, who still runs a restaurant there, always welcomed me with a meal and smile. Friends I made on those campaign swings remain friends to this day. They bring their sons and daughters to Boys State and Girls State; greet me warmly at state Democratic conventions; and provide useful information when I have an out of town real estate deal.

So there I was after the election of 1978, still on the Boston City Council. My tenure as President of the City Council was ending and I had no success convincing my colleagues to vote for me as Council President again. I sunk into a blue funk.

Riding the Roller Coaster

A political campaign is a relentless race to beat the clock and make a compelling case to the electorate before it is too late. Election Day is the absolute final deadline. Every potential voter needs to be contacted and persuaded before that deadline. No opportunity is wasted. There are drive-time radio interviews at dawn, breakfast meetings, press conferences, repeated visits to senior citizen Bingo games, door to door pleas, speeches, television tapings, cocktail party fundraisers, and late night strategy sessions. Then the clock stops and the polls close at 8 p.m. and the voters' verdict rolls in.

There is an inevitable let down when any campaign ends, but a losing campaign is particularly devastating. The aftermath can be crushing. Even campaign reporters talk about "post-election depression." For a candidate it is far worse. Putting yourself out for judgment by the public is a tricky exercise. If voters reject you, it is tough not to take it personally and allow the defeat to become an assessment of your sense of self worth. In the crowded multi-candidate City Council races, I had never personally experienced the type of tactics directed at me by the Crane campaign in 1978. No one had ever targeted me so specifically, even during the difficult 1975 busing year election. I took everything personally.

The let down was profound because it was not just the end of a losing campaign for state Treasurer. I was also losing the Presidency of the City Council with the bigger office, larger staff, prestige and clout that went along with it, and going back to being a back bencher on a body I increasingly saw as a dead end.

I was completely broke. I mean really broke. Old friends had loaned money to my campaign and I had to figure out how to pay them back. Debt in the DiCara family was not something taken lightly. The campaign debt weighed me down like a boat anchor. I could almost hear the jangle of the anchor chain as I dragged myself through the days as autumn faded into winter in 1978.

My campaign schedule and my own inclination and style to be busy had kept me moving from dawn until long after dark, day after day. A friend once said that I had two speeds: fast and holy shit. I had been moving at holy shit warp speed for months. The sudden stop was almost disorienting.

I felt profoundly alienated. I was so lonely. I tried to keep busy going to three, four or five parties and events in a single day; making brief stops, like a candidate would on a campaign schedule. Looking back, I see it as a bit pathetic, a desperate attempt to avoid being alone and to feel among friends. In contrast to the frenetic pace of the campaign, I had little to do. The phone quite literally stopped ringing. I was literally uncomfortable in my own skin. I suffered from a skin problem, hives or psoriasis. I never knew which one, but it is worth noting that both conditions are closely related to stress. My own body was screaming at me.

My social life was hardly typical for a guy in his twenties. I looked a good ten years older than my years and behaved older as well. I always had the courtly demeanor of a man from a different generation, a combination of my proper upbringing and my own sense of how a public official ought to behave. This did not make me date bait for the bright young women I met in the late 1970s who were members of a far more casual generation of women who were breaking into and progressing in professions that had been reserved for men in the past. That December, I invited five different dates to accompany me to the Harvard Coop annual dinner. Each declined. I went alone and sat next to an 81 year old woman. Alice Knox was lovely; a longtime employee of the Coop, but it just seemed par for the course that I would be seated with someone's grandmother. I had friends whose marriages were beginning to become undone and it struck me that they were getting divorced and I hadn't yet even gotten close to getting married a first time.

My dear grandmother, Josephine Alibrandi, who played such a crucial role in my life, had died the previous winter, just short of her 89th birthday. I went through the motions of the rituals of death with my parents: the wake, the funeral and the burial; but I never took the time to truly grieve because I did not have time in an election year. The delayed trauma of that loss hit me after the primary election. My grandmother was the rock in our family, one of the pillars upon which our family rested. This diminutive strong willed lady had an inner strength that inspires me to this day. She baked macaroni from scratch, every ingredient infused with care and love. I have never, in all the years of dining in expensive Italian restaurants, ever tasted any baked macaroni more delicious than hers. Each Monday, she boiled her white cotton sheets on the kitchen stove in an enormous pot, stirred them with a long stick, and then hung them out to air dry. Later in the day, she ironed each sheet with a big, black flat iron that she heated on the stove. The iron made a very satisfying thump each time she put it down on the ironing board to press each cotton sheet crisp and wrinkle free. She was the personification of common sense, duty, constancy and great love.

Every Election Day, I drove her to the polls to cast her vote. As a naturalized American citizen, my grandmother took this civic duty particularly seriously. She felt honored to vote, particularly with her grandson on the ballot. That September 1978 primary was the first in which I voted without her at the "Woody"—the Woodrow Wilson School in Dorchester. I felt her absence acutely. I felt very alone.

Ken Hartnett, a Boston Globe columnist with a tart pen, had described me as a modern day Calvinist during the campaign, a young guy who behaved like an old prig and took himself just a bit too seriously. His assessment was harsh but not completely wrong. I didn't watch television. I railed against the way the state lottery fostered a get rich quick mentality on the poor who could ill afford to spend food and rent money on lottery tickets. I recoiled at the sight of elderly women clutching $20 bills in their gnarled arthritic hands at church-sponsored bingo games. Gambling of any sort just struck me as a risky activity for those with little income. Countless studies have subsequently shown that government sponsored lottery programs exploit the poor, who have no realistic chance of achieving great wealth in any other way.

At the age of 29, I felt positively ancient. When I spoke to the young boy selling the Boston Sunday Globe at St. Gregory's after Mass, I sounded like a grandfather talking about the good old days when I sold newspapers there. In seven years on the City Council, I had grown old in some ways. I had made a conscious choice to pursue public office and I did it with a focus that meant I did not have a lot of fun in my twenties. Now that I am more than twice that age, I see I was still impossibly young at age 29, still idealistic, still easily bruised.

There were a few bright moments as 1978 counted down. One came when my mother brought her students to City Hall for their annual Christmas concert. By 1978, mother was teaching at the Richard J. Murphy School, an elementary school in the Popes Hill section of Dorchester. She had previously taught junior high school students at the Russell School in Dorchester. Each year groups were invited to sing in the cold cavernous lobby of the new City Hall at Christmas time as the season was called back then in those politically incorrect times. The rosy faced students and their sweet voices warmed up that cold space considerably. I always hosted her students in the Curley Room for donuts and hot chocolate. The kids loved it and my mother would beam with pride at her son, the City Councilor.

Many of her students, particularly the children she taught for many years at the Russell, which served the Columbia Point Housing Project, were so poor they did not own a dress white shirt or blouse. She liked her students to dress in white shirts and red ties for the Christmas concerts. When my brother Vinny and I outgrew our white shirts and my sister Ginny outgrew her white blouses, she would save them in a box. Every December, she took them out, carefully washed and pressed each one and lent them to her students along with the red ties. Mother did this on her own for no extra compensation or even for thanks. She believed the children learned something useful from being dressed up in public that would serve them well in life. There was not a lot of talk about self-esteem in those days, but that is what she consciously built in her students. I have spent much of my own life mentoring and helping young people and find it deeply satisfying; and each time I do so I think of mother and her glowing example.

I belonged to many, many civic and charitable boards at that time. It was part of a conscious networking strategy but also a way to keep myself busy. This is a theme in my life, keeping busy. I served on the Boy Scout Board, the Kennedy Action Corps Board, the Harvard Coop Board, the Harvard Club Board, Action for Boston Community Development (ABCD), and probably a few others. It was a bit over the top but reflects my sense of myself as a young guy in a big, big hurry. I felt I was rushing but making no progress, running in place on a treadmill to nowhere.

I felt my political career had ground to a screeching stop. My campaign manager, Mark Roosevelt, had not helped matters by endorsing the Republican candidate for Treasurer, Lew Crampton, on his own. My colleagues on the Democratic State Committee were peeved at this violation of party loyalty and demanded an explanation. Mark's mailing to my political list without my permission, was the sort of thing that happened that fall. Nothing seemed to be under my control. Every slight felt like a blow. Despite my best efforts, I was unable to secure a job for Pat Landers, one of my administrative assistants. Pat was a native of Dorchester and a Williams College graduate and had served me well. Not being able to help him land a good position made me feel powerless. Pat ended up working at the State House and later attended the Yale School of Organization and Management and Yale Divinity School. He did well.

When Melnea Cass, the First Lady of Roxbury, died on December 16, I did not rate a seat in the church to attend her funeral, despite our long and warm friendship. I went to the Community Awards Dinner for ABCD, the city's leading anti-poverty agency, and David Finnegan, the School Committee member, sat at the head table. I was not invited to sit there even though I had been a member of the board and the City Council President. Those with political DNA require constant reassurance. I was no exception to that general rule. I was not feeling the love. It was quite a comedown.

My natural optimism eluded me. During that bleak December, I had a seasonal lunch at the historic Union Oyster House across the street from City Hall with two old friends: Kirk O'Donnell, the political operative who was working for Tip O'Neill in Washington by then, and Bobby Hanson, another skilled operative who was living in Dorchester and a friend from City Hall. I believe Kirk was home for the holidays. I could be honest with these old friends and told them I was seriously thinking this term might be my last on the Boston City Council. They argued fiercely but kindly with me. You can't go out a loser, Larry, they said. You need to go out a winner, even if you never seek political office ever again in life. Do yourself a favor and run one more time so you go out on top with a victory and the "W" for winner next to your name. I agreed to follow their advice, even though I did not have the heart for another campaign at that point.

I had made a practice of staying at my office late on the eve of holidays. As a single guy, it was no great sacrifice for me and invariably someone needed help. One memorable Christmas Eve, I got a phone call from Kenny O'Donnell, the legendary political organizer from Worcester. Kenny was a special assistant to President John F. Kennedy and one of his closest aides in the tight knit Irish Mafia of the Kennedy White House. He had been Robert F. Kennedy's roommate and football teammate at Harvard. He was campaign manager for Robert F. Kennedy when he ran for President in 1968. Kenny came home and ran for governor of Massachusetts twice, in 1966 and again in 1970. The last time he finished last with about 9 percent of the vote. He developed a serious drinking problem after JFK died. I remember having lunch with him and Phil Johnston and the District Attorney from Hampden County, Matty Ryan, in 1970. Kenny had two double martinis and a beer and almost no food. I was amazed. I had never before seen anyone literally drink his lunch. I saw him around town and got to know him pretty well.

So he called me on Christmas Eve, a Thursday night, and begged for a favor. "Larry," he pleaded, "if you can help me, you are my friend for life." He said he had a "friend" living in the Back Bay who had lost her heat. If she did not get the heat restored right away, she would have to wait until Monday because Christmas fell on a Friday and no one worked on the weekend. It was a long time and a bad time to be cold in Boston. I called the city Housing Inspection Commissioner at home, who tracked down the inspector for the Back Bay. At five minutes before 5 p.m., Kenny called back. The heat was on. He was thrilled and grateful.

In January of 1977, Kenny's wife Helen, the mother of his five children, died. According to a memoir written by their daughter Helen, both parents suffered from alcoholism. Three months later, I was invited to a bachelor party for Kenny at the Sheraton Boston Hotel. Among those in attendance was Judge W. Arthur Garrity, a friend of the O'Donnells' from boyhood in Worcester. Kenny was marrying the lady who had lost her heat, his exercise therapist, Asta Steinfatt, a native of Germany. The wedding was held at Memorial Church at Harvard. Kenny did not live for long after his wedding. He died much too young in September of 1977 at the age of 53.

The timing of Kenny's remarriage so soon after his first wife's death was remarked upon at the time. His second marriage took place on the same day as a celebratory anniversary event at the Institute of Politics at Harvard. I remember hearing Dave Powers, another longtime JFK aide, say that Ella Grasso, who then served as Governor of Connecticut, was asking whether the flowers from Helen's funeral were recycled for the wedding. It was a tough crowd. In Kenny's defense, his heart broke and life collapsed after the assassinations of John and Bobby Kennedy. Bobby was his best friend. Like so many, he sought in drink the solace which can never be found.

After the holiday lunch with Kirk and Bobby, I felt committed to one more term and resolved to make the best of it. I had one intriguing opportunity to go another way. I received a call from Amos Hostetter, a Harvard Business School graduate who had founded Continental Cablevision Inc. He wanted to talk so I met him for lunch at the Harvard Club in downtown Boston, very early in 1979. At the time, the cable television business was still in its infancy. The notion of people actually paying to watch television—when anyone could get the big three broadcast stations and public television for free—seemed almost foolhardy. But visionaries like Hostetter saw the potential in specialized channels on sports, news, cooking, interior design, movies and all the other options viewers enjoy today. Back then, he was primarily concerned with securing licenses from towns and cities in Massachusetts. Each municipality negotiated a separate deal with one cable television provider. The value of those leases was obvious. He felt my political skills, energy and statewide campaigning experience would be helpful to his company. He offered me a job. I turned him down. Had I accepted, I might have been on the ground floor of a billion dollar plus cable television industry. But at the time, I still burned to be mayor someday and still believed it feasible.

Although I viewed myself as "old" months before my 30th birthday in April, my mood brightened as the year drew to a close. The Kennedy School of Government had moved into a spanking new building next to the Charles River in Cambridge. The school had been housed for years in a rabbit warren of offices and classrooms at the Lucius C. Littauer Building, just north of Harvard Square. Lucius Littauer, Harvard class of 1878, served in the U.S. House of Representatives, and left a philanthropic legacy that benefits the university to this day. Harvard President Derek Bok decided the Kennedy school warranted its own space as a living memorial to the late President and as a way to bring professionalism to those who pursued a career in government. The John F. Kennedy Library on Columbia Point in Dorchester would not open for another year. The new school seemed enormous at the time. In those early days, I was invited to help fill it with students.

The dean of the Kennedy School, Graham Allison, offered me a job. The job entailed me acting as a consultant to him for 50 days in the first six months of the new year, 1979, for $100 a day plus expenses, which were to be charged to my own American Express credit card. My job was to recruit new students for the public policy program, work with the alumni, raise money and build up the programs. During his long tenure at the school, Dean Allison built the school into a major professional school for public policy and government and served in senior positions at the Pentagon as an expert in nuclear strategy and national security. I was so excited. I needed a diversion and really needed more income. This job called upon my inherent strengths: talking to people, persuading people, making a sales pitch for an academic program I loved. The part time job revved me up again.

I had a great time. I rode the Amtrak train down to Newark, New Jersey and recruited two new students. I flew to Cleveland three times. I traveled to Flint, Michigan and Columbus, Ohio and made frequent trips to Washington, D.C. It was fun to reconnect with old friends and acquaintances, make new friends and acquaintances, link up the disparate elements of my life and talk about something that mattered to me. In a democracy, anyone can run for office and win, but government and politics benefit from the experience of thoughtful, informed people with real practical know-how. Knowledge and expertise matter. As our country has become larger, more diverse and more complex, there is an even greater need for public employees and public officials to be smart and informed about everything from the intricacies of Wall Street bonds to the causes of poverty. The Kennedy School experience gives its students that knowledge. I felt good about my role in building the institution.

Michael Dukakis had joined the Kennedy School faculty after leaving office in January, after his defeat by Ed King. Eddie King was always something of an aberration in state politics. He was a genial man but stuck in another generation. He often seemed out of sync with modern times. His Secretary of Human Services, Charles "Chic" Mahoney, had been a whiz kid in the administration of former Governor Foster Furcolo and was considered a bit "affected." In other words, he was gay before people acknowledged it. Someone once told King that Chic followed a "gay lifestyle." King reportedly replied that he had no problem with the guy having a good time. He apparently did not understand that gay meant homosexual. Mike Dukakis set up a government in exile while at Harvard and began to plot the rematch campaign of 1982, when he would snatch back the corner office at the State House to serve two more full terms and run for President as the Democratic nominee in 1988.

Meanwhile, I had requested and been granted the chairmanship of the City Council Planning and Urban Development Committee, so once again I was presiding over Tuesday morning sessions that nurtured a new era for economic development in the city of Boston. One of the tools we used repeatedly in those waning days of the Carter Administration, when interest rates went sky high, was Industrial Revenue Bonds.

Borrowing money was extremely expensive during the Carter years. I had opened a fledgling law practice and did a lot of house closings and knew many individuals who got first mortgages for their first homes and had to pay 16.5 percent interest, which is almost inconceivable at a time the rates can be as low as 3 percent. These were people with excellent credit histories. Commercial borrowers did not fare much better. An Industrial Revenue Bond reduced the cost to commercial developers by a significant margin in certain Commercial Area Revitalization Districts. The city created those districts in downtrodden sections of the city, particularly ringing the downtown commercial zone, in an effort to create more economic opportunities and generate more tax revenue for the city. The bonds, combined with federal tax credits awarded for saving historic structures, helped to revitalize the Russia Wharf Buildings and parts of the waterfront; the North Station area, which had fallen on hard times; and transformed the Financial District, including Liberty Square. These tools effectively turned the urban renewal strategy from tear down to rehabilitation and dozens of historic buildings, with their unique features and quirks, were saved and reused. The pace of using these tools to spur economic development in Boston accelerated in 1979.

My colleagues did not always see economic development as I did. I remember that I was coming up short on approval of the UDAG grant that would lead to development of Lafayette Place in Downtown Crossing. Ray Flynn kept proposing crippling amendments to mandate construction of affordable housing in Chinatown, which would have killed the deal. I kept losing 4-5.

I told Eddie McCormack, the former Attorney General who was representing the developers, a Canadian group, that I had doubts we would get the grant application approved. The Council took a dinner break. After dinner, Dapper O'Neil said he decided this project was good for the city and he would make sure it happened. He asked me how he would know the right way to vote. I told him that when I nodded my head up and down, it meant vote yes. When I nodded my head left and right, it meant vote no. For the rest of the evening, he followed the instructions and did as he was told. That is how the UDAG grant won approval and why we have Lafayette Place today. I have no idea what happened at dinner.

I was usually in sync with the Boston Redevelopment Authority and the White Administration, but not always. The committee sometimes handled requests that struck me as odd. One day a request came for a federal UDAG grant for John A. O'Connell, the owner of O'Connell Seafood Co., to build and expand a dry dock on the waterfront which would allow him to grow his fishing business. As chairman, I always got to ask the first question, so I asked Mr. O'Connell about his background and experience. He said he had worked in the fish department at a local supermarket. This struck me as inadequate credentials for a large public grant.

The request, however, held the highest priority in the White Administration. Ed Sullivan, the Vice-Mayor and a truly decent man and a gentleman, pulled me aside to personally advise me that this was a critically important request. Something just seemed off to me and I reported it out of committee with an unfavorable report. However, it passed the full City Council easily. The late Dave Farrell, then a Boston Globe columnist and confidante of the Mayor and Bob Crane's, attacked me for shilling for my Harvard classmate John Fulham, whose family owned an existing ice business, serving the fishing fleet. I knew John, but we were hardly close and his family business had nothing to do with my reservations about the grant request. I never did learn the source of Mr. O'Connell's clout but my instincts were confirmed a few years later when O'Connell was convicted of defrauding the federal government in connection with the very same UDAG grant.

Along with all my other woes, I was also really tired of being broke. Because I was turning 30, I felt it was past time that I got my financial act together. I began to focus more energy on my fledgling law practice and slowly but surely took on real estate closings and other mundane bread and butter legal tasks to build up a clientele, hone some expertise, and make a little money. Charging people for my services was initially a struggle because as a politician, it felt natural to just do favors for people for free. But I learned.

At the same time, I provided plenty of free legal advice. Throughout the 1970s, I was intimately involved in the creation of three health centers in Dorchester: Uphams Corner, Codman Square, and Bowdoin Street. They have become important community institutions in the subsequent decades.

To say I was less than enthusiastic about running again is to understate it, but I had taken to heart the advice Kirk and Bobby had given me the previous winter and hired a campaign manager, Fred Geyer. Because I was having a lot more fun working for the Kennedy School, chairing the Committee on Planning and Development, the reelection campaign did not draw my full attention. I went through the motions: senior citizen picnics and bingo games, the church and veterans dinners, and the subway stop "meet and greets." But the campaigning had a desultory air to it.

I turned 30 in April and my reelection committee threw a huge birthday party on the top floor of the Harvard Club. It was fabulous. A slogan of many in my generation had been "don't trust anyone over 30," but that was long before we all turned 30. The attitude changed substantially as we each reached that milestone birthday. Being 30 felt momentous to me and I wanted to mark it properly. I also wanted to thank those who had helped me in the past. I had been running nonstop for public office for eight years and had asked much of my friends and supporters. There was always another DiCara campaign. The party drew a huge crowd and I drew great consolation in seeing so many people. It made me feel that I still had friends.

There were a few warning signs that spring. When I called the first organizational meeting for my council reelection campaign at the Knights of Columbus Hall in Lower Mills, only 19 people showed up and the group included my parents, my godfather and his family, and people who were paid to work for me. It was not a good indication of my electoral prospects. I had been fortunate over the years in recruiting friends and supporters to my campaigns, but it is possible to ask too much. Campaign workers, virtually all volunteers who take on the humble tasks of a campaign, do get tired. They have their own responsibilities and lives. They move on. My political career was not the center of their universe.

The year 1979 represented something of a lull before the storm in politics. Joe Timilty was challenging Kevin White for Mayor for the third time. This time they both looked as though they were going through a kabuki dance. There was no heat. Dukakis was in exile at Harvard. While Ed King got off to a rocky start as governor, he had a four-year term and wasn't going anywhere anytime soon. Jimmy Carter was struggling in the White House and our own Ted Kennedy was sending off unmistakable signals of his intent to challenge the sitting President of his own party in the 1980 Democratic primaries.

It ought to be noted that Massachusetts politicians have their own unique view of the world. Having produced so many House Speakers and Presidential candidates, it just seems normal to see national politics as a natural extension of state politics. In my own life time, I have seen three House Speakers from Massachusetts: Joseph D. Martin (a Republican), John W. McCormack and Thomas P. O'Neill, Jr.; and six Presidential candidates: John F. Kennedy, Edward M. Kennedy, Michael S. Dukakis, Paul E. Tsongas, John F. Kerry and Mitt Romney, the lone Republican. Massachusetts political operatives become as familiar with the precincts of Des Moines and Manchester as they are with those of Boston and Worcester. The national exposure gives Massachusetts political operatives a leg up over those from other states. They learn about the complexities of national politics first hand. The late Mary McGrory, herself a native Bostonian and graduate of Girl's Latin School, who worked at the Herald with my Dad, once wrote that everyone in Massachusetts considered himself a political pundit. No one who has ever lingered at a neighborhood tavern would disagree.

The 1979 September preliminary campaign results shocked me out of my complacency. I came in eighth, almost out of the running and a worse finish than my first run for public office eight years before, when I finished seventh. I was flabbergasted. It was a sucker punch that caught me totally by surprise. The eighth place finish meant I could easily fall below the critical line and be out of a job. I had seen others drift down and out of the money between September and November. On the other hand, Tom Atkins, in 1969, and Jimmy Connolly, in 1975, had bounced back. It was way too close for comfort. I was not always thrilled with my job, but I felt strongly about my career in public service and the prospect of losing ginned up my competitive instincts. I shifted the campaign into high gear.

What sometimes happens when an incumbent official is in obvious peril is that friends and supporters spontaneously rally. When public opinion polls showed Mitt Romney running essentially even with Ted Kennedy in the 1994 U.S. Senate race, people from Kennedy's past, including staffers dating back 30 years, left jobs, homes and families to come to Massachusetts to help him. He won reelection by 17 points that November, his closest reelection margin, but a landslide by any measure. A similar thing happened to me. My friends showed up to hold signs, make phone calls, address envelopes and donate money. The rallying cry was "Let's not lose Larry." I was grateful and I also worked like a demon. As Kirk and Bobby had advised, I did not want to go out a loser. I did not stop moving for six weeks. Impending defeat does concentrate the mind and focus energy.

On election night that November, the hard work paid off. I not only won reelection easily for the fifth consecutive city election, but I topped the ticket. I came in first with 69,102 votes, something I never anticipated in my wildest most optimistic dreams. Six weeks earlier I had feared defeat. We partied hardy at the Hampshire House on Beacon Street that night and on this joyous night no one was inclined to head home early.

So what happened?

Kevin White easily won a fourth term, beating Joe Timilty in their third face off by 10 percentage points. Joe only won 3 of the 22 wards: Hyde Park and parts of Jamaica Plain, Roslindale and Dorchester. By then, Kevin had mastered the use of his Little City Halls to provide jobs and services to people in every neighborhood. Even the hard line "antis" in Southie backed him. Summer jobs and other favors trumped antipathy over busing by then.

A comparison of my votes between 1971 and 1979 tells part of the tale. I received almost 8,000 more votes in 1979 than 1971, despite a precipitous decline in both population and registered voters during the 1970s and a smaller voter turnout. The city had 52,031 fewer registered voters in 1979 than in 1971. By the 1979 campaign, the families most concerned about busing to integrate the public schools had long moved out of the city. The population of Boston had been dropping steadily for 30 years, since it reached an all time high of 801,444 in the 1950 federal Census. In 1950, the city was full of veterans returning home from the war, attending school and beginning careers that launched the extraordinary postwar economic boom.

In 1950, the city was 95 percent white and 5 percent black. There were not enough Asians or Hispanics to register in the government head count. The population dropped steadily each decade according to the decennial Census figures as the trek to the suburbs began. Between 1950 and 1960, the city lost more than 100,000 people. The population was 697,197 in 1960, the year John Kennedy won the Presidency, and the number of white residents was 90 percent, with 9 percent black. By 1970, before busing, the population had dropped another 50,000 to 641,071. By 1970, the city was still overwhelmingly white at 82 percent with 16 percent black. As an aside, I ought to point out here that the small black population of Boston in 1970 suggests it would have been possible to integrate the public schools if the Boston School Committee had chosen to do so without undue turmoil or pain. And while some new black people were moving into Boston, the real change in proportion came because more white people were leaving the city. So any sense that minorities were flooding Boston reflected fear more than reality.

By 1980, the population dropped again to 562,994 and the white population was 70 percent with 22.5 percent black, 2.7 percent Asian, 4.7 percent "other" and 6.4 percent Hispanic. The 1980 census figures represent the bottoming out of the population loss in modern times. Subsequent census counts show a steady increase in city population each decade to the present.

Although the population was going down, the city did not remain static. Theodore White writes of the urban ballet of constant motion and change in American cities. It was so in Boston. Nature does abhor a vacuum. While families moving out of the city tended to be white people of European ancestry, probably barely a generation or two removed from the immigrant experience, those who took their place were far more diverse. The demographic mix of the city was undergoing a subtle change. As the white population dropped, the minority population expanded, becoming a larger slice of the smaller pie. But there was something else different about many of the newcomers, they tended to be single, more affluent and better educated than the people they replaced.

In some neighborhoods, including the South End and Jamaica Plain, gay and lesbian couples were on the cutting edge of a wave of urban pioneers who recognized the beauty and potential in the worn out Victorian town homes. In others, including my own neighborhood of Dorchester, young professionals, both black and white, spotted the real estate bargains in mixed race neighborhoods and bought and renovated houses. These young urban professionals, the famous Yuppies, were eager to embrace the city experience, take on the challenge of rehabilitating a beat up Victorian era house, and ride the subway to work, or better yet, walk to the office. The lifestyle suited them. They stayed downtown after work, meeting friends for a drink or dinner. They were moving into new apartments and condominiums refurbished from the small colleges being closed in the Back Bay. For example, Garland Junior College in the Back Bay and Grahm Junior College in Kenmore Square shut down, opening up blocks of real estate for other uses. They transformed warehouse space into homes with sweat equity and imagination. The Waterfront Urban Renewal Plan and a federal Economic Development Administration (EDA) grant were slowly changing the battered industrial waterfront area of Boston, particularly in Charlestown and the North End. Eventually, the downtown section and South Boston parts of the waterfront caught up and became redeveloped as well—in one of the more stunning reversals of Boston real estate fortunes in my lifetime. Back in the 1970s, old timers were beginning to bemoan the loss of the "old" ethnic neighborhoods as young professionals paid astronomic rents to live in the quaint little apartments of the Italian North End. The increase in rent, often to Italian landlords, encouraged many of my countrymen to move north to Malden, Medford, Woburn and Swampscott. Just as the high tide swings back every 12 hours to cover up the beach laid bare during low tide, the empty buildings of Boston were once again filled with new Bostonians. Depopulation was followed by repopulation.

Demographics is destiny in politics. However, it is worth noting here that the newcomers did not all vote in municipal elections. In fact, many of them never voted in a city election. They did not feel connected to Boston City Hall. Most did not have children, or if they did, they sent their kids to private schools. They did not need summer jobs or government jobs of any sort. They were relatively well educated, relatively affluent and decidedly independent. Many of the newcomers voted in Presidential elections and often voted in statewide Senate and Gubernatorial elections, particularly if there was a contest. But municipal elections did not concern many of them. For many, the only connection to city government came in the form of parking tickets, trash pick-up and perhaps the odd burglary or street mugging. This has proven true to the present day. Although the population of Boston was 617,594 in 2010, only 111,000 people voted in the 2009 city election.

Not all the newcomers were affluent. There was also an uptick in immigrants. Boston has been a destination for immigrants seeking freedom and opportunity for centuries. When I was still in office, there was a huge wave of Irish immigration. Unlike the desperately poor farmers who fled poverty in the 19th century, these Irish immigrants were often well-educated. The Irish economy at the time was so bad that the young high school and college graduates came to Boston and worked as waitresses and house painters. Much later, the famed Celtic Tiger economic resurgence, between 1995 and 2007, which transformed Ireland from one of the poorest to one of the wealthiest countries in Europe, drew them all back home again.

After I left public office, the immigration wave surged again—with so many Vietnamese that Dorchester Avenue looked like one long "pho" or soup shop. Another wave of immigration from South and Central America and the Caribbean islands followed. There is a substantial lag, however, between the arrival of immigrants and their impact on an election. It takes years to become a U.S. citizen and for those who arrive without the ability to speak English, it can take even longer. One of the reasons the Irish seized control of Boston as quickly as they did more than 100 years ago, is that they spoke English when they arrived.

In any case, I was watching the urban ballet dancing through the streets, abandoned by the Irish and Italians fleeing the busing order, as well as the new sections reclaimed from the transit improvements in Jamaica Plain, and the "urban renewal" projects of the South End, the West End and the Waterfront.

My election results showed the unmistakable trends underway in the demographics of Boston. I always relied upon a coalition built upon my sturdy Dorchester base. I lost 1720 votes in my home Ward 17 between 1971 and 1979, a whopping 35 percent decline, but I came in first in the ward and those votes still represented a good solid base. I would have been in trouble if I had to rely upon traditional Dorchester votes, given the decline in population. I finished first or second in Allston-Brighton, Jamaica Plain and the Back Bay/ Beacon Hill wards, all neighborhoods growing with newcomers. I also picked up a lot of new black votes. My vote total in Ward 14, for example, in Dorchester and Mattapan, doubled between 1971 and 1979. Ward 20 (West Roxbury) was a socially conservative ward of mostly white middle-class Catholic voters who strongly opposed abortion, an issue that was becoming heated at that point. It was not a favorable environment for a pro-choice candidate. The first of what became a sizeable community of lesbians had moved into parts of that ward close to Jamaica Plain. I finished third in Ward 20, and picked up 1,778 votes over my 1971 showing. Jamaica Plain is a case study in how a neighborhood can be transformed from a down at the heels community into a vibrant and upscale one because of the proximity of new subway stops.

Nearly every resident of JP today can walk to a subway or bus stop and ride to downtown Boston within minutes. It shows how careful government investment and spending can generate enormous private sector profit, and lead to greater affluence and tax revenues.

In the euphoria of coming in first, I was convinced that I could be elected Mayor. After all, I came in first! That must mean people like me! The new Bostonians tended to be more liberal and more like me. I knew this from my own campaigning throughout the city and the election results confirmed the demographic trends underway. The results created a sense of invincibility that others had experienced before me. Although Kevin White had just been elected Mayor for the fourth time, most thought this would likely be his last term. The Mayor had lost interest in his job and from my perspective as a 30-year-old, he was getting old. The supreme irony, as I look back, is that Kevin celebrated his 50th birthday that fall. He left office at the age of 54. When John Collins left office in 1968, he was only 48. It says something about how the personal perception of age changes in the course of a lifetime, as well as how aging has radically changed in the course of my own lifetime with the extension of the average life expectancy. My parents seemed quite old when they reached their 60s, the decade I am in now. But I still play squash, swim in the ocean, and work long hours. I am "younger" in outlook and activity level and health than my parents' and grandparents' generation, just as many of my peers are.

A first place finish in a Boston City Council or Boston School Committee contest does not directly translate into votes for Mayor. I should have known better as a student of city politics. I could have asked "Mayor" Peter Francis Hines, "Mayor" Chris Iannella, "Mayor" Louise Day Hicks and "Mayor" John L. Saltonstall. In each instance, they topped the ticket in a previous City Council or School Committee race and ran for mayor in the next election. Each one came up short. Mike Flaherty topped the ticket in his city council races in 2003, 2005 and 2007. When he challenged Mayor Tom Menino, who was running for an unprecedented fifth term in 2009, he lost 57 to 42 percent.

There are many reasons for the discrepancy. I suspect one of the biggest is that the vote for City Council is a far more casual vote than the vote for Mayor. In choosing a Mayor, people consider a number of factors, among them the candidate's suitability for the job. The City Council vote is almost a throwaway, a vote for a familiar name, a name with a certain ethnicity or a name of someone who lives in your neighborhood. But I was floating after that election. As 1979 drew to a close, the telephone was ringing off the hook again! I was energized and focused and set my sights on the 1983 mayoral contest when I hoped to realize my longtime dream.

Reaching for the Dream

The 1979 first place city council finish injected renewed optimism into my life. I felt energized and alive again. My focus returned and narrowed on one goal: the 1983 mayoral election. Of course, there was no guarantee Kevin White would step aside and not run for reelection, but it seemed very clear to me that he had lost interest and was ready to move on. His departure promised a huge field. When one incumbent holds a high level position for a long time, there is tremendous pent up demand when a vacancy finally occurs. After 16 years of one mayor, a new generation of ambitious politicians was literally chomping at the bit, like a pack of restive race horses. I knew the election would be competitive but after my first place council showing, I felt I was in as good a position as any other candidate, perhaps better than many. After all, Boston voters had become accustomed to voting for me; they knew me and now I had evidence they liked me! I had worked hard, foregone vacations, stayed late in the office, attended every health center opening, bingo game and Knights of Columbus breakfast, and arranged for countless summer jobs and other favors. I felt just as smart as anyone else—smarter if I was going to be totally honest. I had experience. I had a vision for Boston. I felt unstoppable.

The plotting began right away in my own mind as to how to best position myself for 1983. I decided I would be a stronger candidate if I were an outsider and not an incumbent city councilor. The modern history of Boston campaigns suggested strongly that voters liked the idea of someone riding in to rescue the city from outside. I reminded myself often that it had been many decades since an incumbent City Councilor had been elected mayor. The high jinks of the Council did not comport with the public image of a mayor as all powerful and above the fray. So I decided not to run for re-election to the Council in 1981. Walking away from a paying job was not something I did easily. I let each of my colleagues know personally of my intent. My colleague Chris Iannella, who so often acted as a kindly uncle to me, was concerned and pulled me aside to urge me to reconsider. "Do you know what you are giving up?" he demanded. I knew I was giving up a job that paid $32,500 (after a recent pay raise), an office and staff, and proximity to phones and a Xerox machine. In the early 1980s, access to telephone lines and a Xerox machine was a bigger deal than it is today. He replied with genuine feeling: "You're giving up a free parking space in downtown Boston!" As a longtime subway user, I was probably less worried about that parking space than others might have been, but even in 1981 free parking downtown was a big deal. Many times over the next few years, as I became completely lost in the Congress Street garage or waited impatiently for a Red Line car, I remembered Chris' words.

But I was ready to roll the dice. I did not want to be a lifer on the Boston City Council. By the end of the decade, I was building a decent law practice. I was not pulling down huge fees but was doing well enough that I felt confident I had the chops to make it as a lawyer if my career as a politician were to end. Through the years, I developed a specialty in real estate and development law and found my experience on the council allowed me to help developers and businesses build, buy and renovate throughout the city. I derived great satisfaction from helping clients build a new Boston and still do. It is difficult to develop property in any well established city. The zoning laws and inspection and permitting processes, so critical to order and safety, can be daunting. I began to develop expertise in guiding clients through the labyrinth of regulation and bureaucracy of city, state and federal government to achieve their goals. At the same time, I could help clients understand the needs of the city and its residents and the benefit of making their specific projects fit neatly into a bigger, more dynamic urban whole. Smart development is a win-win for everyone. The city and its residents benefit from the jobs, shops, housing and tax revenues from new development.

My world view was also expanding from the narrow focus of the boy who grew up in Ward 17. I was beginning to appreciate that there was a broader world beyond the 47 square miles (that includes the islands) of Boston. Bostonians are just as notorious for parochialism as denizens of Manhattan, whose world view begins and ends with that tiny congested island of land in New York City as demonstrated by that famous New Yorker cover. My out of state trips for the Kennedy School stretched my consciousness and awareness. I was increasingly seeing my life in a bigger and broader context.

Boston celebrated its 350th Jubilee anniversary in 1980 and the Mayor, as usual, put on a grand show. The festivities ran from May through the end of September, when he hosted the Great Cities of the World Conference in

Boston. Given the economic problems, turmoil and population loss of the previous decade, it may have seemed a bit pretentious to some for Boston to put itself in league with cities like Rome and London. But Kevin White always thought big, and to be honest, hindsight shows the city had bottomed out a bit before 1980 and was beginning to show signs of a steady come back. The high class Jubilee festivities celebrated Boston's long and rich history with parades, receptions, a balloon race, a special Jubilee concert at Symphony Hall and even a visit from Canadian Prime Minister Pierre Trudeau on the fourth of July.

The Jubilee celebration culminated with the Great Cities of the World Conference, which featured representatives from 36 cities on four continents. The intent of the conference was to help the developing world learn from the experience of the past and to share information that would help all cities plan for the 21st century. It says something about Bostonians and the fierce pride and love we have for our home town that none of us thought it odd that Boston still regarded itself as the hub of the universe.

Kevin White always enjoyed the trappings of office. He increasingly spent most of his time at the elegant Parkman House mansion on the top of Beacon Hill. The house had been left to the city and the Mayor essentially used it as an alternative home as well as an official meeting spot for dignitaries. He particularly enjoyed hosting this international gathering, and especially a dinner for the mayors represented by the Great Cities at the Museum of Fine Arts.

The jockeying for position for the next campaign began almost immediately after Kevin White won election to his fourth term the previous year. David Finnegan had served on the Boston School Committee for two terms, the second as President of the Committee. He ran for mayor in 1979 and finished fourth, but it was widely viewed as a warm up to establish himself as a strong candidate for the office in the future. He was seen as an up and comer. Ken Hartnett, the Globe columnist, lavished praise on the defeated candidate after the 1979 race as a contender for the future. Finnegan prudently hosted a radio show in Boston after he left public office. Talk radio was extremely popular in Boston back then. There were a number of all news radio stations and radio was an effective way to communicate with voters.

David was the second highest vote getter on the School Committee in 1977 and I suspect he interpreted those results much as I had viewed my own vote as a sign of political popularity. However, there is a big difference between being the single choice of a voter and being one of multiple choices as each of us eventually learned. But those few years were a bit heady. I felt that I was in a select group of potential mayors. The Italian Vaticanologists coined an expression, *papabile*, a reference to a Cardinal who is a potential candidate for Pope. It literally translates as "one who might become Pope." The list of *papabili* is made up of insiders who mention this or that Cardinal as a possible successor to the chair of Peter. In political chattering classes, I was among the *papabili* in Boston in the mayoral competition.

I could see and feel the difference in how people viewed me. My credentials looked strong: I was young, just 30 years old; I now had ample practical experience in government and politics for someone my age; I was clean as a whistle, without a hint of scandal or corruption; I had consistently won election with the same coalition that elected Kevin H. White and other successful modern day mayors; I retained strong roots in Dorchester and was showing strength among the high growth areas in the city and among minority group voters. As a potential mayor, I was invited to many functions and accorded a deference that was decidedly different from being just one of nine City Councilors.

Of course, being among the mayoral *papabili*, also made me a bigger target. I was acutely sensitive to the vulnerability of serving on the Boston City Council with colleagues who would routinely bring to a vote extremely controversial issues. Ray Flynn, for example, was a leader of the anti-abortion movement and would introduce meaningless resolutions on behalf of the Right to Life forces to cement his ties to conservative Catholic voters. Even Louise Day Hicks, a devout Catholic, once told me she thought abortion should be available "if God forbid, something bad happens to one of my granddaughters." Louise was as conflicted about the abortion issue as most everyone else!

When Ray Flynn served in the state Legislature, he co-sponsored legislation with Rep. Charlie Doyle of West Roxbury to prohibit the use of state funds in paying for the abortions of poor women. Charlie used to perform these incredible rants on the floor of the Massachusetts House bellowing about "Sayyyyleeeeen abortions!" at the top of his lungs. The saline abortion was a procedure used to induce an abortion after the first trimester. The Hyde amendment, sponsored by Rep. Henry Hyde, an Illinois Republican, prohibited the use of federal funds for Medicaid abortions. Hyde announced his intent to file that amendment at the National Right to Life Convention in Boston during the summer of 1976. Gov. Mike Dukakis vetoed the Doyle-Flynn bill when he was in office. But Ed King was a pro-life governor and he signed Doyle-Flynn into law after he took office in 1979. Eventually, the state's highest court ruled it unconstitutional, deeming it illegal to deny a legal medical service to women simply on the basis of income. This was one of many decisions, the most recent being gay marriage, that shows how the Massachusetts Constitution, which is older than the federal Constitution, is actually stronger on civil liberties and personal freedom than the U. S. Constitution.

The abortion issue was a hot one in Catholic Boston and Catholic Massachusetts. Even though national surveys show that Catholic women undergo more abortions than Protestant women, the Roman Catholic Church in Boston had considerable clout and the Church, then and now, vehemently opposes abortion.

Just nine months after the Supreme Court made most abortions legal with the Roe v Wade decision in 1973, Kenneth C. Edelin, an esteemed African-American medical doctor and then the chief resident in obstetrics and gynecology at Boston City Hospital, aborted a fetus by hysterectomy of a 17-year-old unmarried girl. The teenager and her mother wanted the procedure and wanted to terminate the pregnancy. Not long afterward, the assistant District Attorney in Suffolk County, Newman A. Flanagan, indicted Dr. Edelin for manslaughter, arguing the one pound fetus was old enough to survive outside of the womb.

After a highly publicized trial, Dr. Edelin was found guilty of manslaughter in February of 1975. He was on probation for a year, a sentence that suggested the trial was more about making a political point than punishing a true criminal. Nearly two years passed before the Supreme Judicial Court tossed out the conviction and cleared him of all charges. The case attracted intense media coverage and kept the abortion issue in the news. Newman Flanagan, a classic Boston Irish Catholic politician, double Eagle graduate of Boston College High and Boston College, longtime Knight of Columbus and father of seven, rode the fame to election as District Attorney in 1978 and served until his retirement in 1992.

By not running again, I could spare myself the fallout from votes on hot button issues and remove myself from the day to day distractions of the Council. I took other steps to prepare for a mayoral campaign. I kept my campaign office operating in an efficiency apartment I rented at 21 Beacon Street, the Bellevue Hotel, then an old shabby rooming house where John Kennedy had maintained a voting address back in the 1950s. The room cost me about $135 a month and I set it up with a pull-out couch and odds and ends of furniture. It was unusual then to pay rent for a campaign office in an off year. Some of my colleagues ran their campaigns from their City Council offices, a violation of law, but one frequently overlooked in those days. I used the room as a crash pad at times when I needed to attend an early morning event downtown after a late night. More important, I kept a campaign staffer working there full time on my mailing list. I had been building a list of supporters and contributors for years. It began with friends, neighbors and Boston Latin School classmates and their families. By the end of 1981, that list was transferred from thousands of cards into my first electronic list of 5, 500 names. "The Larry List," as my colleagues call it, has been maintained and culled and expanded over time so I now have 10,000 telephone numbers on my Blackberry. I sometimes wonder what life would have been like if such technological advancements had coincided with my political career.

It was also past time that I moved out of my parents' house. I had always enjoyed living with my extended family but it is hard to be taken seriously as a mayor if you are living in your parents' attic. I was 32. It was time I got my own place. I looked for the proper house for a long time because I wanted a house that looked like a mayor lived in it. I finally found a handsome brick house at 311 Ashmont Street in Ward 16, about a mile from my parent's house and near the border of St. Gregory's parish. The house was suitable for entertaining, an essential for an upwardly mobile politician. The four bedroom house, custom built in the 1920s for a Miss Whelan, had cedar closets and a huge living room. My mother remembered that I knew the former mayor of Gardner from Boys' State and she suggested I give him a call to find out where I could get some deals on furniture. Gardner was known as the Chair City and the Furniture Capital of New England because of the large number of furniture manufacturers based there in the early part of the 20th century. It was still the place to go for a great deal. As always, Mother gave me great advice. I furnished the house with purchases from Gardner. I still own one of the couches.

The house was too big for a single person, but it conveyed the gravitas and seriousness of purpose of a Mayor. Honey Fitz Fitzgerald, the former Mayor and father of Rose Fitzgerald Kennedy, the mother of John F. Kennedy, had owned a big house at the corner of Welles and Harley Streets in the same neighborhood. Rose Fitzgerald married Joseph P. Kennedy in that house in 1914. That house burned down in 1938. The neighborhood was filled with houses built in the late 19th and early 20th century that were being snapped up by younger people as families moved to the suburbs. The Ashmont Street house was also a short walk to the Ashmont subway stop. I moved in on Columbus Day in 1981. It was just perfect.

I enjoyed hosting gatherings at my house. I always invited the new fellows from the Institute of Politics at the Kennedy School over for a cocktail party. The term cocktail party is a bit of a grand description for the gatherings which featured beer and wine with potato chips and pretzels that I served. But the events were always a great success. The politicians from other parts of the country welcomed the invitation from an elected official and liked getting out of the Harvard bubble to learn about Dorchester and Boston. I remember Rep. Geraldine Ferraro, the Democrat from Queens who ran as the first female vice presidential candidate on a major ticket with Walter Mondale in 1984, came to one of my parties and was delighted to be back in a neighborhood that reminded her of her own District in New York. Ed Fouhy, a longtime television network producer who later oversaw the presidential debates, also attended.

The 1981 election was a bit strange for me because I was not on the ballot for the first time in ten years. National politics was undergoing a sea change. Ronald Reagan had won the Presidency in 1980, signaling a turn to the right—not only for his Republican Party but also for the country. Ted Kennedy had failed in his attempt to take the Democratic nomination away from President Jimmy Carter. Many progressives felt disillusioned. There is no question that a more conservative political philosophy was on the ascendency by 1980.

I was not the only incumbent to walk away that year. Two of my colleagues, Rosemarie Sansone and John Winthrop Sears, also decided not to seek reelection. The three of us were the three most progressive members of the City Council. Our decisions to leave the Council were all different and all personal. Nevertheless, three vacancies at the same time were unusual and triggered a lot of interest on the part of potential candidates. It is much harder to knock out an incumbent than to win an open seat. For an off year election, a total of 40 candidates decided to run. For comparison purposes, it is worth noting that there were 41 names on the ballot when I first ran in 1971, when there were also three vacancies.

The business community in Boston backed "Four Fresh Faces." They were Terry McDermott, Mike McCormack, Bruce Bolling and Maura Hennigan. Terry, Mike and Maura were Irish and decidedly younger than the mean on the City Council at that point; Bruce was African American. Maura was the daughter of James W. Hennigan, Jr., a longtime fixture in Boston politics who served as state representative, state senator, and register of probate and on the School Committee. Her grandfather was a state senator and a great uncle served on the Boston Common Council in 1900. Maura carried on a family tradition and reflected the style and approach of her father. This is all by way of suggesting that youth did not necessarily equate with change.

Mayor White saw an opportunity to strengthen his hand on the City Council with the three vacancies that year as well, and he threw his political muscle behind a slate that became known as the "Kevin Seven": Bruce Bolling, Pamela Gillman, Steve Michaels, Fred Scopa, Dick Hogan, Gerry McHale and Brian Hickey. Only three, Gillman, McHale and Bolling, progressed from the preliminary to the November ballot, and only Bolling won a seat on the City Council. Bruce was the son of a longtime state Senator, Royal Bolling, Sr., a popular figure in the black community. The failure of the Mayor's political machine to come through for his slate was revealing. It showed he could not transfer his power and influence to others and contributed to the overall sense that it was time for him to hang up his gloves. Bruce went on to have a long distinguished career and became the first African-American President of the City Council. His election in 1981 was also another indication of the

changing demographics of the city and the growing size of the minority community. Terry McDermott, one of the fresh faces, and Pamela Gillman, one
of the Kevin Seven, met on the campaign trail, fell in love and married, had
two daughters, and eventually moved to the suburbs.

Although I was not a candidate, I was heavily involved in the election as
co-chair of the committee pushing for a ballot question to restructure the
Boston City Council. Massachusetts is one of the few states that allow citizens to pass a law through petition under certain circumstances. In this case,
a special act of the Legislature permitted a vote concerning the structure of
city government, provided enough valid signatures were filed on a timely
basis. This procedure is a leftover from the progressive era of the early 20th
century and is a way to bypass a recalcitrant legislature. If proponents of a
new law can gather enough signatures of registered voters, the question goes
to the electorate for an up or down vote. If people vote for it, the measure
becomes law with the same force of law as one written and passed by the
state Legislature and signed by the Governor. Lawmaking by referendum is
not always good for a city or state because a popular position is not always
the correct position. California, for example, has gone through all sorts of
contortions because of various tax referenda. Obviously, no one likes taxes
but taxes are necessary to pay for public services, such as California's once
vaunted university system that was free to those who qualified. Lack of tax
dollars has sadly changed that. Massachusetts also approved tax limitation
referenda that starved local government and created turmoil at the local and
state level for years.

District representation was a direct challenge to the status quo and the only
way to change the status quo in Boston would be through some sort of outside force, such as a court order or a ballot question. District representation
was a cause I had championed since my days as a Harvard undergraduate.
Boston is widely considered an Irish city because of its most famous politicians: Fitzgerald, Kennedy, Tobin, Hynes, Curley, Collins, White and Flynn.
Indeed, city government was still overwhelmingly Irish in the 1970s but the
city itself had been less Irish than the outside world realized for decades and
was becoming more diverse with each decade. For example, Boston boasted
a vibrant black community of people who arrived before the Irish. After
World War II, they were joined by blacks making the Great Migration from
the South and Jim Crow, black people from the Caribbean, and then Haitians
and Africans, creating a diverse black community that has never been as
monolithic as the data would suggest. The Hispanic community is equally diverse with Dominicans, South Americans, Puerto Ricans and Cubans. Some
remnants of the old White Anglo Saxon Protestant population remained as
did some Jews, though neither group can muster the numbers needed to win

election. But even those groups with large numbers of residents, particularly minority groups, could not win a citywide race.

Even when I was running for public office, those of Irish and Italian backgrounds made up at least 50 percent of the vote in a city election, although they made up a smaller proportion of the total city population. They were the most faithful and reliable voters in the city and, as a result, had more political clout. It was always a case that there were wards that voted as regularly and systematically and routinely as going to Mass on Sunday. The system was self-perpetuating. People from South Boston, for example, an Irish neighborhood, voted in high numbers for Irish candidates who won. In turn, those candidates lavished attention and favors on South Boston and neglected wards where they did not get many votes. Allston and Brighton, for example, neighborhoods loaded with students, were low voting wards in a city election. I suspect some of my council colleagues thought visiting those wards was as useful as paying a call in Somerville or Cambridge. Transient younger voters, such as college students in Allston or young professionals living in the Fenway, were not likely to vote in a municipal election. I was always struck by how many more requests for city jobs and contracts came from neighborhoods like my own in Dorchester or West Roxbury and South Boston. It was clear that the residents of those neighborhoods understood how the system worked. They benefited from the status quo in a very concrete way.

But there was something fundamentally wrong about a system that kept neighborhoods from getting a fair shot at having a representative on the governing body of the city. No one had been elected from East Boston for 25 years, for example, where 40,000 people lived. Allston /Brighton represented 10 percent of the city population, yet there hadn't been a councilor from those communities since the late 1950s. Nearly all the city council members from the 1960s and 1970s came from a handful of neighborhoods: South Boston, Dorchester, Jamaica Plain, Roslindale and West Roxbury. That was great for those neighborhoods, but not good in the long run for an increasingly diverse city or for neighborhoods with different needs and priorities.

Now, I did not want to take anything away from Dorchester but it just struck me as unfair that residents of Allston, Roxbury, Mission Hill and East Boston did not enjoy the same benefits as people in South Boston, Dorchester and West Roxbury. They all were citizens. They all paid taxes. They were all Bostonians. My colleagues on the Boston City Council thought I was out of my mind because they understood better than anyone else the intrinsic advantage each enjoyed from keeping things just as they had been since 1951, when the current system for electing the City Council was put in effect.

Before 1909, Boston's legislative structure was more like the state and federal systems of a large House of Representatives and smaller Senate. There was an 8 member board of Alderman and a 75 member Common Council, which included three members from each of the then 25 wards. The city charter was rewritten in 1909 to replace that system with a 9 member City Council. The Mayor also got veto power in that charter change which enhanced the power of that office. The Republican-controlled state Legislature imposed charter changes upon Boston over the years, at one point returning to the ward system in the 1920s. But, in 1951, the nine member at-large City Council returned.

The ballot question in 1981 expanded the nine seat council to 13 seats with four at large positions and nine elected from districts. This reform guaranteed representation for every section of the city and gave black, Asian, Hispanic, and gay candidates a better shot because they only needed to persuade their friends and neighbors in their district, not the entire city. An attempt had been made in 1977, with a similar ballot question which I also supported, but it fell short in part because there was no money behind it. This time would prove different.

I was approached by a small group of business leaders which included Robert Beal, who had been president of the Greater Boston Real Estate Board in the late 1970s, and the late Jack Delaney, who was then executive secretary of the Coordinating Committee, a group of preeminent Boston business leaders. The Coordinating Committee was nicknamed The Vault because its meetings originally took place at the Boston Safe Deposit and Trust Co. The Vault was created in 1959 to help Mayor John Collins with redevelopment in Boston. Boston has had an elite group of influential business leaders and bankers since the Puritans. The Vault was a behind the scenes quiet force in the 1960s, 1970s and 1980s. These business leaders acted out of self interest. A bankrupt Boston, the existence of ghettoes, the possibility of rioting, or a high crime rate were bad for business. They also realized the city was changing and felt it would be better for Boston if the City Council was more representative of the diversity of its residents. Beal and Delaney asked me to get out front on this effort because of my longtime commitment to district representation and because I was stepping aside so I had no vested interest in the outcome. I agreed. I have never had a problem with enlightened self interest.

This stealth group raised money to pay for public opinion polls and advertising. The polls conducted by the pollster Tom Kiley, a onetime seminarian who became a nationally regarded master of urban polling, showed us early on that the voter turnout that year in the minority community was likely to be exceptionally low without a concerted effort to get voters to the polls. Identifying the problem early meant we had time to develop an aggressive get out the vote campaign in the black community. We also targeted younger, better educated newcomers, who were traditionally less likely to vote in an off year municipal election. The involvement of the business community was kept very quiet. It would not serve our purposes to give opponents the chance to say the business community was trying to influence the election which, of course, was exactly what was happening.

We faced an entrenched attitude and a way of doing business politically that was so "normal" few questioned it. That attitude was hard to change. It was also tough to convince people who lived in neighborhoods where a city councilor had always lived on the same street or on the next block that a change would be good for the city. They certainly did not see any change as good for them. A lifetime of being able to buttonhole the councilor at Sunday Mass or at the neighborhood coffee shop or dry cleaner was taken as an entitlement. That kind of easy access translated into results and clout. No one likes to give up even an ounce of power.

The campaign focused on the future and the fact that a more representative legislative body would move the city forward. Little did we know that the new district system would launch a number of political careers, including those of Bob Travaglini, who later became state Senate President; Dan Conley, who later became District Attorney; and Tom Menino, who would serve an historic tenure as Mayor of Boston. The forward focused message resonated with the newer younger voters. The black community got a clear message, too. Change meant they could elect one of their own from their own neighborhood. Except for Tom Atkins, an African-American Councilor who won in 1967 and 1969, every other member of the city council had been white since the council went back to the at large system in 1951. That all-white streak ended with the election of Bruce Bolling in 1981.

The black community had become more consolidated in Mattapan, Roxbury and Dorchester because of a well intended, but misguided, effort by bankers to increase home ownership, by giving no money down mortgages to black people. As hard as it is to believe, a federal agency, the Federal Housing Administration, created in 1934, fostered policies that made it almost impossible for certain categories of people, including people of color, to obtain mortgages. Federal law did not rectify that discriminatory policy until the mid-1960s with the Civil Rights legislation pushed into law by President Lyndon B. Johnson. By the time of the urban race riots in 1967 and 1968 many bankers were openly worried about the fate of cities, where a majority of residents, minority group members, did not hold a stake through home ownership. Although well intended, the Boston Banks Urban Renewal Group proved to be an early and telling demonstration of the folly of giving mortgages to people who cannot afford to own homes, a practice that led to a housing bubble 40 years later, which burst with devastating consequences for families and the economy. This story is told with compelling detail by Hillel Levine and my old school mate, Larry Harmon, in *The Death of a Jewish Community: a Tragedy of Good Intentions.*

They describe how the bankers in a contorted version of redlining literally drew a line on a map around a specific section of city where they would approve these loans which were guaranteed by the federal government for low income residents. The area happened to coincide with the largest Jewish community in the city, a robust and thriving community straddling Blue Hill Avenue not far from my grandfather's barber shop. For bankers, the Jewish community with its many small business owners was unprofitable because so many residents had paid off their mortgages. As hard as it is to believe, the bankers would only approve loans to black people who were buying in that section of the city. Unscrupulous blockbusters and mortgage and real estate agents took full advantage by terrorizing the Jewish homeowners and convincing them to sell and move. These unscrupulous blockbusters would take a random street crime and use it to convince longtime Jewish residents that they or their wives or daughters would be next. Within a few years, a robust Jewish community of 90,000 had been decimated. In its place were poor black people who defaulted in record numbers on those loans they could ill afford. Studies show that the default rate had little to do with race. The middle class black homeowners in the more stable sections of Dorchester and Roxbury did not default on their mortgages. They had sufficient income to afford the payments, unlike many of those who were enticed into home ownership they could ill afford between 1968 and 1970. I remember the lightning speed of the turnover and the empty store fronts and temples. For years, the city campaigns ended with an election eve rally at the G & G deli on Blue Hill Avenue. By the time I ran in 1971, there was no longer a rally. The G & G, a neighborhood gathering spot for decades, had shut down in 1968. Moreover, Chief Levine, the proprietor of a funeral parlor in the Jewish Community and a major player in the 1967 mayoral campaign as a Kevin White supporter in the Jewish community, was no longer a significant political player. In fact, by 1971 there was only one precinct in Ward 14, the one on Wellington Hill, where any Jewish voters remained. During the four years I attended Harvard, the families of nearly every Jewish friend from Boston Latin School had moved out of the city. The departure of the Jewish community from Dorchester and Mattapan was a big loss to Boston.

There was no nostalgia among the newcomers who were moving into Boston in those years. They were young and hopeful for the most part and the future-oriented message delivered during the campaign for the ballot question in 1981 resonated with them. Voter turnout was about 32 percent higher in 1981 than it had been in 1977, when the districting question had lost. Some

neighborhoods changed position in response to the better financed and targeted message. East Boston, for example, switched position and voted aye.
Subsequently, East Boston sent one of its own to the Boston City Council.
Dorchester Wards 13, 15 and 17, where racial change had been significant
and where young professionals were moving in, also flipped from four years
earlier. Turnout in the overwhelmingly black wards of 9 and 14 increased dramatically. Those voters got the message loud and clear and the margins were
revealingly lopsided. In Ward 9, a total 1,644 voters voted "yes" and only
86 voted "no." In Ward 14, a total 2,359 voted "yes" and 123 voted "no." In
Ward 21, the heavily liberal ward of Allston, turnout was appreciably higher
than it had been in 1977 and the supporters' side of the question benefited.
By contrast, turnout in Charlestown of "no" votes barely moved, going from
1,714 "no" votes in 1977 to 1,783 in 1981. The " yes" votes in Charlestown
almost doubled from 480 in 1977 to 811 in 1981. These "yes" votes were
obviously newcomers who had moved into the town at the beginning of the
gentrification that would eventually change the neighborhood almost beyond
recognition.

I was heartened by the results of the ballot question in 1981. It confirmed
my earlier analysis and my impressions. I moved around the city constantly
and I could see the changes underway. Indeed, I could see the change around
my own home on Ashmont Street. Young professional couples were slowly
but surely moving into many of the Victorian-era houses and using sweat
equity to recapture their old grandeur. Not all of them stayed. Many moved
to the suburbs when they had children. The Boston public schools sadly only
got worse in terms of general quality after busing. It took a dedicated and
adroit parent to get any child a proper education in the public schools and it
was easier for many to just move to Milton or Newton and send their kids
off to excellent public schools. Larger numbers of professionals, particularly
professional women, were staying single longer and that affected the composition of many neighborhoods.

Terry McDermott was given the task of drawing the districts. We sat at my
kitchen table at Ashmont Street and looked at a map of Boston. I argued that
if most of Roslindale were attached to West Roxbury, as nearly always happened in Ward 20, the West Roxbury candidate would win. But, if Roslindale
and Hyde Park were joined, then almost anyone, including an Italian candidate, had a shot at victory. The district emerged that way and Tom Menino,
an Italian from Hyde Park, ran and won a District seat. The rest, as they say,
is history.

Although the deep funk that persisted through my years in law school had
long since dissipated, I often felt that I was running out of friends when I
reached that big milestone birthday of 30. My long time friends remained

friends, but their circumstances had changed. As they married and had children, they simply did not have the flexibility and time to join me for a late night dinner or go to a movie or a Sox game. I began to use the little house in Mattapoisett more by myself. The south coast of Massachusetts, the area that rims Buzzards Bay between Fall River and the Bourne Bridge to Cape Cod is one of the great delights and secrets of the state. The little seacoast towns have stayed small and free of the crowds, overdevelopment, fast food joints and tourism that plague Cape Cod, but they enjoy the exact same weather, ambience and warm ocean water. Being in Mattapoisett for even a single night refreshed me. I always slept better there and for a few hours felt free of the responsibilities of office. I sometimes brought a campaign staffer with me and would have them read out a name from my vast collection of 3 X 5 cards and I would recite back the address, ward and precinct.

Being out of public office was a harsher experience than I expected. The invitations that were automatically extended to a member of the Boston City Council just stopped coming. I still received invitations but not the sort of select invites that go only to elected officials. For example, Frankie and Billy Chin, the longtime proprietors of China Pearl, a landmark restaurant in Chinatown, had always invited me to their remarkable Chinese New Year's dinner because they always invited the entire Boston City Council. I was no longer able to advocate for causes, such as community schools, which I had supported for a decade. I was no longer on TV, on radio, or as frequently quoted in the Boston papers. I had gambled in walking away from the City Council and giving up the perks of public office. But I was convinced that it would be tough enough as an Italian-American to be elected Mayor of Boston without also being an incumbent Boston City Councilor.

Many of Kevin White's top people were encouraging me to run. That told me as clearly as anything else that he was not going to run again. But the Mayor kept his own counsel. Then on Bastille Day on July 14, 1982, The Boston Globe lead editorial not so gently told Mayor White that it was time to retire to private life. I later learned the back story of the editorial. Martin F. Nolan had become editorial page editor of the Globe in 1981, after 20 years as a political reporter, columnist and Washington Bureau Chief. Marty was an Irish-Catholic native of Boston, graduate of Boston College and seasoned political observer who did not pull any punches. He brought a new muscularity to the editorial page of the Globe. He decided Mayor White had reached the end of his political career and wrote an editorial firmly telling White decided Mayor White had reached the end of his political career and wrote an editorial firmly telling White that it was time to go. He did not share it with anyone else at the paper except for the Boston Globe publisher, William O. Taylor. Over lunch at Maison Robert, a very good French restaurant located in the beautiful old City Hall, the Beaux arts building where Kevin's father Joe White had served, Marty showed Bill the editorial. Bill Taylor agreed with the sentiments. The irony of the publication date of the editorial, July 14, 1982, the anniversary of the day that celebrates the day the French mob stormed the Bastille prison in 1789, was not lost on me. Kevin Hagan White, the brooding loner in love with the city who preferred the comfort of Parkman House to the grittier precincts of his city had become our very own version of Louis XVI. The editorial said Mayor White had lost his credibility, that his administration had become corrupted by power and ended by advising Kevin that the city would treat him more fondly if he realized it was time to leave gracefully.

In the context of Boston politics, that editorial said it all for me. At that time, the Boston Globe exerted a tremendous influence in city and state politics. Everyone read the paper and paid attention to its editorials and columnists. It is hard for young people who surf the web on smart phones to appreciate the power that newspapers had in the days before widespread Internet use and cable television news. The Globe set the agenda and could make or break a candidacy with a single editorial. Back when Boston had 5 robust daily newspapers in the 1950's, the Globe was considered the Irish maids' newspaper with folksy front page editorials signed by ``Uncle Dudley''. As competitors fell by the wayside and closed, the Globe emerged as the loudest and clearest liberal media voice in New England. The editor, Tom Winship, was a Harvard educated Yankee with liberal politics and an activist bent. He hired young and smart reporters and gave them the freedom and resources to investigate and write in depth. The Globe was one of the first newspapers to call for withdrawal of the U.S. from Vietnam. It was the third major newspaper to publish the Pentagon Papers. It began racking up Pulitzer Prices.

Until the pivotal 1967 mayoral election, the Globe had refrained for endorsing in political races. That ended in 1967 because the publisher viewed the choice facing the city, Kevin or Louise Day Hicks, as too important to stay on the sidelines. The paper stuck with Kevin for four consecutive mayoral campaigns, Breaking with him before the fifth sent such a strong message that I could not believe even Kevin would ignore the instructions to hang it up. So moving towards 1983, I felt confident and optimistic about the future.

The Last Campaign

In those years, a mayoral election held momentous import in Boston. It was the equivalent of the Olympics, a quadrennial competition and clash of political superpowers. Those of us eager to run for Mayor kept one eye on Kevin Hagan White who went into a Hamlet act about his intent to seek reelection; teasing the public, delivering mixed messages to his closest aides, and playing out in public the excruciating process of letting go of the job. Most political observers felt that if he had survived the tough climate of 1975, when the busing order was handed down, he could survive anything. That is not to say he would win a mandate. The best and smartest politicians leave when the crowd is still cheering. Those who do not, or who cannot let go of power, often end up ignominiously tossed out of office and end their careers as losers, broken hearted by what feels like a personal rejection. It is extremely difficult to walk away and Kevin White loved being Mr. Mayor. Yet Kevin had gotten the message that it was time to go loud and clear from The Boston Globe editorial the previous summer, and public opinion polls were not any more reassuring. A poll conducted in January by WBZ-TV found that only 18 percent of Boston voters favored the reelection of White. Not helping his cause was an aggressive investigation into the alleged money laundering of his associates by the federal prosecutor, William Floyd Weld.

Weld, a brilliant summa cum laude graduate of Harvard, where several buildings carry the Weld family name, was the most exotic of political rarities these days, a liberal Republican. He eventually became a wildly popular two term governor of Massachusetts. He came to public notice as a crusading reformer as the U.S. Attorney for Massachusetts, and Kevin H. White fell squarely in his crosshairs after sufficient numbers of city employees complained about being shaken down to attend a "birthday party" for the Mayor's wife, Kathryn, in 1981. The party was called off, but the feds thought Kevin was trying to launder money for personal use. The Mayor was never indicted. It is worth pointing out that such "times" had been routine for generations in Boston. In the past, petty cash funds, financed by "times" and other questionable means, were not unknown, but another sign of a smart politician is to recognize when the rules change and adjust behavior.

I was convinced he would not run again and planned my campaign accordingly. Others were not so prescient. David Finnegan, for example, had a slogan that he put on everything: billboards, campaign leaflets, and house signs, that said "Finnegan or him again." It was a clever way to set up a two man race, a clear choice between the incumbent and Finnegan. It proved to be a fatal strategic error for Finnegan when Kevin did not run, but White's presence promised to loom over the race whether he was in or out. He defined what it meant to be mayor for a generation, for good and bad. His time in office set a certain standard and expectation. Every election is a reaction to the past. There were those who could not imagine anyone else being mayor and sought the candidate who most reminded them of White, while others reacted strongly against White and sought out the anti-White candidates. His vacillation also froze in place many big donors, members of the business community, and rank and file campaign workers who happened to be on the city payroll.

Mayor White was not beyond using this period of indecision to have some fun. Speculation about the mayor's intent became a parlor game. On March 20, the Mayor told Frank Avruch, a reporter for WCVB-TV, that he planned to run for a fifth term. Afterwards, his aides retracted the statement claiming he was joking.

He also wreaked revenge. Peter Lucas, a veteran political columnist for the Boston Herald and a savvy insider, had mocked Kevin in print many times for his aloof loner in love with the city persona. He labeled him "Kevin Deluxe" and "Mayor of America" and needled him mercilessly for his elitism and pretentious airs. However, the two men had known one another for years and the Mayor knew that Peter wanted the scoop when he made his decision. So the Mayor called Peter himself on the eve of his announcement, May 25, 1983, just before Memorial Day, and the traditional kick off for summer, and told him he intended to run for an unprecedented fifth term. The next morning, May 26, the feisty tabloid's headline blared "White Will Run" with a story under Peter's byline. That evening, Kevin announced he was sailing off into the sunset and not running for reelection. Peter was so humiliated that he tried to resign from the paper on the spot. I understand his editor dismissed the resignation out of hand because the embarrassment was great for circulation. Peter Lucas remains convinced to this day that the Mayor's deception was deliberate. George Regan, White's press secretary, claims he had two press releases in his pocket that day: one if he decided to run and another if he decided to retire. But Bob Crane, White's best friend, said he did not doubt he was retiring. I agree with Peter Lucas and Bob Crane.

Each of the nine candidates who would eventually be on the ballot in the preliminary mayoral election had announced his or her candidacy before Kevin's declaration of intent. I announced on Tuesday, May 3, at seventeen places throughout the city. My slogan was "Larry DiCara Everybody's Mayor" and by announcing in every neighborhood, I underscored my commitment to represent everyone in the city, not just a favored few. Kevin White had increasingly become seen as the Mayor of the downtown business community and there was a palpable yearning in the neighborhoods for a mayor who would pay attention to the decaying infrastructure and specific needs of each community. Kevin White had also become more autocratic over time and many city residents wanted to be heard and involved in city government.

When Kevin White first became mayor in 1968, he staffed city government with a diverse and talented group of people. A generation of political leaders had CVs that included a stint as an aide to White. He appointed the first black and the first woman and first Hispanic woman as a deputy mayor. He fielded a team of very smart, politically adroit men and women. But, over the course of his time in office, the A team moved on to other career opportunities and the Mayor used city jobs to buttress his political operation. The patronage army was driven by self-interest and greed and a few ended up in prison.

One of the great frustrations of 1983 for me was that the news media focused more on the horse race and peripheral matters than the substance of position papers and question of qualifications for office. For example, Wayne Woodlief, the Boston Herald columnist, led off his piece on my announcement day by focusing on the pivotal issue of whether I was too short to be mayor. I am 5 feet 4 1/4 inches tall, and I am aware that I am shorter than many other men. But I am taller than one of the greatest mayors to ever serve in the United States, Fiorello LaGuardia of New York City, the Little Flower (an English translation of his Italian first name) who was either 5 feet tall or 5 feet 2 inches tall, depending upon the source—and height has nothing to do with ability.

I was also very aware that I did not fit the public preconception of a typical Boston Mayor. My own baseline poll conducted in the early spring showed that only about nine percent of the voters thought I looked like a mayor. As long as anyone could remember in the city, Boston Mayors had been Irish Catholic married men with lots of kids. I was single and Italian, as well as short. Any politician whose image deviates sharply from the norm is going to face a challenge in surmounting the psychological bar of acceptability. Women, for example, who run for mayor, governor, or president, still face this barrier because some voters have a hard time seeing women in executive positions. Candidates who are members of minority groups also often face a subtle psychological barrier from voters who just cannot overcome a preconception that an elected public official looks a certain way. Progress and the passage of time fortunately have changed those preconceptions.

There were nine names on the ballot in the preliminary election for Mayor, including my own: state Rep. Melvin H. King, a towering bald African American legislator and former social worker with a bushy beard, who favored jump suits and dashikis; Ray Flynn, the City Councilor from South Boston, who had been a leader in the antibusing and anti-abortion movements; David Finnegan, the former School Committeeman, who grew up in Dorchester but lived in high voting West Roxbury; Dennis Kearney, the sheriff of Suffolk County, who was from East Boston; Fred Langone, the City Councilor from the North End; and Robert R. Kiley, the former deputy mayor and head of the MBTA and a brilliant turnabout management expert. Bob was from Minneapolis and had little chance of persuading Boston voters to make him Mayor despite his considerable talents and brains. There were also two fringe candidates: Michael Gelber, a follower of Lyndon LaRouche, and Eloise Linger, a member of a socialist workers party. I viewed David Finnegan and Ray Flynn as my biggest rivals, but eventually realized the greater problem was that I was everyone's second choice and I was competing with Dennis Kearney and Bob Kiley for the same progressive constituency. Dennis Kearney and I were too much alike. We were the same age; we graduated from Boston Latin School and Harvard and earned master's degrees at the Kennedy School and law degrees from Suffolk; we each won election to public office at an early age; he was an Irish kid from an Italian neighborhood—East Boston—and I was an Italian kid from an Irish neighborhood—Dorchester. We were on the progressive side of the political spectrum. Dennis is also short, though a couple of inches taller than me. Kiley had no real neighborhood base in the city, although he had amassed an impressive record of public service. He would later go on to revitalize the transit systems of New York City and London. Fred Langone was never really a serious contender but his presence on the ballot would pull away a couple of thousand votes that I may have gotten. I always suspected someone put him up to it, most likely someone in the Finnegan camp, but never learned who even after his death; I delivered the eulogy at Freddie's funeral.

I believed in process and transparency and citizen involvement and ran a campaign that reflected those beliefs. I assembled task forces of various experts, neighborhood activists and just plain people to give me input on more than a dozen position papers on the issues that affected Boston and its neighborhoods. The position papers ranged from Arts and Culture to Women's

Issues. I labored over those white papers because I wanted to be seen as the candidate of substance, yet I did not want to make promises I could not fulfill. I truly wanted my campaign to be a forerunner of a DiCara administration, so the position papers made proposals which were measured and achievable. My experience at the Kennedy School of Government and as a student of government made me a believer in devising systems and following processes to make government more effective and efficient. While I did not want to generate controversy with my position papers, I did make my philosophy clear and came out squarely in support of full rights for women, gay people and minority group members. I took positions on historic preservation, neighborhood services, and public safety, and called for a more lucrative linking between downtown and neighborhood development. I called for cooperation among the alphabet soup of agencies responsible for cleaning up Boston Harbor. The harbor was badly polluted from literally hundreds of years of neglect. The need for a massive new waste water treatment facility was clear. Eventually, the old House of Corrections was moved and a new Deer Island facility was built pretty much as I proposed, thanks to Governor Dukakis and a hefty infusion of federal money obtained by the able Massachusetts Congressional Delegation. I got a lot of compliments for the substance of those position papers . . . but compliments do not necessarily turn into votes.

The city was on the verge of a new day. Time Magazine had named "The Computer" the Man of the Year in its January issue of 1983. The personal computer was just then beginning its ascendency and the technological revolution that has transformed the way people communicate, do business and live was underway. The campaign did not reflect the fact that we were standing on the edge of a radical transformation in the national economy of the United States or that Boston would become the poster child, many years later, of the new prosperity. At the time, the public schools were in miserable shape with a high dropout rate and were fast becoming majority-minority with all the inherent problems an urban system loaded with poor children entails. The housing stock in certain neighborhoods was literally falling down. Working class people simply could not afford to make the expensive renovations to their own tired real estate and many landlords were not in any better position to invest in their property than their tenants. Crime was a growing issue. The racial turmoil of the 1970s, coupled with high unemployment among young white and black men, created a toxic mix.

The challenge any candidate faces in a multi-candidate field for mayor is to cobble together enough votes to get a plurality. For the preliminary campaign with a crowded field, no one needs to get 50 percent of the vote, just more than anyone else except for one candidate. Each candidate, except for the two fringe candidates who would never get more than a few hundred votes at most, could count upon a certain number of votes from family, friends and neighbors. I naively thought that my ten years of City Council votes, the countless appearances at dinners and events, the many summer jobs and other favors would translate into votes for mayor. I was wrong.

Charlie Spillane was then head of the Greater Boston Building Trades. He was a terrific guy, who began his work life as a member of the cement masons' union and moved up to become the top labor rep for the building trades. He was born in South Boston and lived in West Roxbury with his wife and 10 children. (My wife, Teresa Spillane, is not related to Charlie.) I knew him well because he also served as Secretary for the Board of Appeal which heard zoning cases in Boston. I had even socialized with him. I remember him dancing with his sister, a Catholic nun, at a Spillane family gathering. I had voted with the building trades on every major vote to come before the City Council for ten years. The vote was not always an easy one. For example, I voted against rescinding the bond the city issued for the controversial Park Plaza project in 1974, at the behest of the building trades, and took a lot of heat for that vote. When I began running for mayor, I went to see Charlie. Before I had a chance to ask for his support, he shot me down: "We're with Flynn." I was stunned and incredulous because Ray Flynn had voted against some of the projects that meant jobs for Charlie's members; projects I helped push through the Council. When I asked why, he replied: "He's from Southie; we're from Southie. Don't waste your time." There were many disappointments like that during that campaign.

When I moved to 311 Ashmont Street, I took along the phone number which I had had installed at 86 Codman Hill Avenue when I was elected in 1971. I also installed a second line. I only gave the number to my parents and, and sometimes, to whoever was working for me at City Hall or in a campaign. It rarely rang. Late on a hot summer night, it rang. It was Bob Page, the then publisher of the Herald (the Herald had had many changes in leadership since the Hearsts bought it in the summer of 1972), who was in a rage, perhaps influenced by a bit too much alcohol. He had learned that the next day my campaign, in one of many failed efforts to jump start our valiant effort, had purchased a full page ad in the Globe. He warned me, in terms that I considered a threat, that if I did not advertise equally in the Herald, I would pay for it.

This was not my dad's Herald. It was a very different newspaper, with very different standards and what appeared to be a revolving door of personnel at most all levels. Herald coverage of me was never good, but it became perceptively worse as they pushed David Finnegan throughout the end of the summer, and began ignoring me. The good news was that this was not a phone call telling me that a beloved relative had died, which are the types of phone calls I was accustomed to receiving late at night.

David Finnegan had lined up everyone who was against Kevin White and he was pulling down substantial contributions from the same people who had supported Louise Day Hicks and Joe Timilty. The rest of us could count on a core of supporters who could afford the $1,000 maximum contribution, but many of the big givers were on the sidelines until Kevin made his intentions clear.

An open race for mayor inspired every constituency group and organization in Boston to host a candidates' forum. I attended nearly every one. There were dozens and eventually I realized that most only attracted a handful of people who almost always were already committed to a candidate. I could have been the second coming of Demosthenes and my performance would not have persuaded a single one of them to support me.

There is a tendency in crowded candidate fields for the media to "tier" the contest, both consciously and subconsciously. Invariably, frontrunners or those deemed frontrunners get the most attention and more coverage results in more support. It is a self fulfilling mechanism. Similarly, those who do not get attention or who get relegated to a second or third tier are seen as unlikely to win. This makes potential supporters look elsewhere, because no one wants to vote for a loser. My campaign pollster, the very able Peter Hart, did a baseline survey that showed my approval ratings were as high in the black community as in the white. This is unusual in Boston, particularly after the racially fraught decade of the 1970s. So I felt I was well positioned to put together the same coalition that had elected Kevin White for four successful terms.

I was not the only person who thought that way. I was approached early on by Jerry Rappaport, the developer of the West End and the wunderkind from the administration of John B. Hynes. He allowed that I would make a terrific Boston Redevelopment Authority director in a Finnegan administration. He made it very clear that he was in a position to make that happen. Given Jerry did not have a crystal ball any better than mine, I declined, even though the BRA job is a great job in Boston. Perhaps it was a bit of hubris, but I had been pretty lucky in politics after winning my first public office at the age of 22. Although my efforts to run statewide had never been successful, I still felt confident that Boston, my home town, would come through for me, or at least I could cobble together enough people to get me into a final. I had great confidence in my ability to persuade, in my education, my experience, and my temperament. I just felt I was the best guy for the job.

I had another intriguing offer by WBZ Radio during the campaign. Chris Cross, the WBZ Radio program director, took me out to lunch towards the end of the campaign and asked me if I would be interested in the talk show host slot that had once been held by David Finnegan. Talking is something that comes naturally to me and the offer was interesting, but I declined. I wanted to see the campaign through to the end. It also occurred to me that this might be yet another Finnegan campaign ploy to clear the field of competition. But the station evidently was really interested because Chris Cross took me to lunch again after the preliminary election and asked me to sit in as host one Saturday night. The topic that evening was the U. S. military invasion of the little island of Grenada. WBZ General Manager Anthony William Hartman, who was known as Bill and had an Italian mother, and I had a pleasant conversation afterwards. He told me he thought I did well, but the station decided not to hire me because I was not Irish. They had studied the demographics of their listening audience and decided an Irish talk show host worked better. They subsequently hired Peter Meade, who held the job for years and did an excellent job.

I did attract some boosters during the campaign. I was endorsed by Jason H. Korell, the managing editor of the Parkway and West Roxbury Transcripts; WEEI Radio; my former colleague from the City Council, John W. Sears; The Boston Business Journal; and State Rep. Angelo Scaccia, a popular lawmaker from Hyde Park and Roslindale. And Bob Kiley withdrew from contention in September and endorsed me as "the class of the field." It was flattering and welcome, but Bob had not been able to gain any traction at all as a candidate for mayor, so he could not transfer many votes to me. I deeply appreciated then and now all the support I did get.

I invariably fell into the second tier. Thirty years later, I am still playing "coulda, shoulda, woulda." A number of factors could have been different that might have made a difference for me. The Globe could have endorsed a candidate but chose not to after having said any of the candidates would be better than Kevin White the previous year. The publisher decided to let the electoral process work on its own and I'm told that most of the top editors and columnists were not particularly invested in an election they viewed as a transition election. Kirk Sharfenberg, an editorial writer who befriended Ray Flynn, was the only advocate for Ray on the editorial board. He subsequently became editorial page editor of the Globe and tragically died young at the age of 48 of cancer in 1992. I am told that his influence in the 1983 choices was not as great as perceived by those of us on the outside looking in. Marty Nolan, the editor of the page who did have clout, was on my side but he deferred to publisher Bill Taylor's decision to stay out of the race.

I got excellent reviews from the first major televised candidate debate at Faneuil Hall in August, but the Herald poll that was conducted after that debate had me in fourth place. The Herald pollster only surveyed people who voted in the 1979 election as a way to identify those most likely to vote in a mayoral election. Past behavior is often an excellent barometer in public opinion sampling but the city population had changed a lot in those four years and the newer people were more likely to be my kind of voters. Had I been presented as a first tier candidate and had I secured the Globe's backing in August, it might have elevated me as the progressive choice and convinced those folks in the Back Bay and Beacon Hill who voted for Mel King to stick with me, and might have convinced Bob Kiley to withdraw sooner, and maybe even convinced my doppelganger, Dennis Kearney, to withdraw and wait for another time to run for mayor.

It is amazing that I got good reviews for my performance at the debate given how physically uncomfortable I was at the time. In the middle of the campaign, a woman who was then married to one of my supporters decided I needed to upgrade my wardrobe. So we went off to Newbury Street, and purchased two Italian-cut suits, one dark, one light; a shirt from Germany which had a very stiff collar; and a very fashionable tie. She was pleased.

It was decided I should wear the dark suit, an elegant wool blend suit which included mohair, for the first mayoral debate. The debate took place on August 17, the height of the summer, at a time Faneuil Hall had no air conditioning. The temperature in the hall had to be 100 degrees. Moreover, my campaign staff had arranged for a phone book or two to be placed under the cushion of the seat so I would not look shorter than the other candidates. The bright TV lights only made the oppressive summer heat worse and that stiff German collar felt like cardboard. It was one of those times when image trumped comfort.

There were some other memorable moments. The day before the preliminary election, I marched in the Columbus Day Parade that started at Dartmouth Street and Commonwealth Avenue in the Back Bay and ended up in the Italian North End. I felt like Lawrence of Arabia in a three piece gray suit, marching through the streets where I had some of my strongest supporters.

Ray Flynn once paid me an interesting compliment at a candidates' night. We participated in nearly every one and often sat next to each other. We sat next to one another at City Hall and I had grown to know some of his children and helped out one son on a few occasions. At a candidates' night focused on housing policy, Ray turned to me after I answered a question and said: "You know more about this stuff than anybody else. You would probably make a great Mayor, but I don't think anybody's going to vote for you." He was not making an endorsement.

On another occasion, a reporter for Bay Windows, the gay newspaper in Boston, asked me if I was gay. Any single man over the age of 25 was somewhat suspect in those days. Today many professionals delay marriage until much later. I was ahead of my time in that regard. In response I paraphrased Ed Koch, a lifelong bachelor, who was often asked the same question: "I am not gay, but if I were gay I would be very proud of it." I was one of the few Boston City Councilors to ever stand up for gay rights.

I remember when David Brill, a gay activist and investigative reporter for the Gay Community News, died tragically young at the age of 24 in 1979. He specialized in reporting on violence against gays, a critical issue in those years when many gay people were first coming out of the closet. Gay bashing was sadly condoned in some quarters even by police officers. The Stonewall riots, viewed as the pivotal moment in the gay rights movement, had taken place in Greenwich Village in June 1969 after the police raided a gay bar. I convinced Police Commissioner diGrazia to sit down with leaders of the gay community. That meeting led to a wholesale change in attitude at the police department and is something I remain proud of to this day. One of my Harvard classmates had sent me a note in 1975, commending me for insisting the police address gay bashing. "I know that defending the civil rights of homosexuals isn't necessarily the most popular action for a politician to take," he wrote, "and I admire your courage."

I knew I might take some heat from conservative voters if I attended David Brill's memorial service at the Arlington Street Church. I went to the service anyway. David Brill was a courageous young man and it was an honor to know him.

In 1983, supporting gay rights was hardly a majority position, even in Boston. To me, it was a no-brainer. I was the boy in kindergarten who was told to not speak Italian. I was the grade school student whose mother went back to work soon after my sister turned two, and later became the family's primary breadwinner. I was the earnest young Boston Latin School student who followed the civil rights battles of the 1960s by watching the evening news and devouring print media of most every variety. I was the college student whose honor thesis focused on the failure of the Boston public schools to educate Spanish-speaking students. I had always understood the importance of civil rights. To me, gay rights is a civil rights issue. How can anyone condone discrimination on the basis of sexual orientation any more than race, gender, or national origin?

Thankfully, after the passage of time, many other American people have seen the light. For younger people, my students at Boys State/Girls State, for my daughters and their friends, gay rights is yesterday's issue. It was not that way in 1983. Mum and Dad heard frequent unhappy comments at the Star Market in Dorchester Lower Mills after Mass, but I have no regrets.

Boston has never been a unified city in the European sense as much as it is a coalition of neighborhoods. Each neighborhood has its heroes and villains, its bosses and precinct workers, its own political history, and its own pattern of voting. I studied the election results for years and became adept at predicting behavior. I knew Boston was changing. The clues were visible if you were looking. When campaigning in more traditional middle class Irish and Italian neighborhoods, I frequently told voters that Boston was a very different city from the city of my childhood. When I was just learning to toddle in 1950, Boston was 95 percent white, with a black population of five percentage points and not enough other racial minorities to be measurable. By 1980, the city was 70 percent white with 22.5 percent black residents with other racial minorities, particularly Hispanics, beginning to grow. By 1983, no single ethnic group much exceeded 20 percent; the Irish population of the city was then about equal in size to the black population; the Asian and Spanish-speaking population was greater than the Italian population and the most significant emerging group was the non-ethnic young professionals. By 1983, one out of every three households was a person living alone; a great majority of those people were in their twenties and thirties and college educated, politically my likely voters.

The economy of the city was also changing, but the campaign rhetoric was relentlessly grim. Campaigns tend to replay the last song over and over again. We were all still predicting fiscal calamity and talking about jobs and lifestyles that were never coming back to Boston. In a weird way, we were all running against Kevin White, who was not even on the ballot. We were intently focused on talking about how terrible conditions were in Boston in order to convince voters each of us was the right candidate to lead the city in the future. Of course, the city had not completely turned the corner, though my sense now is that it had bottomed out long before 1983. But the city's books were still in tough shape.

The economy had sunk into a brief but deep recession in 1982 costing the Republicans more than two dozen seats in the U. S. House. Boston had still not figured out how to resolve the assessment problem created by the Tregor decision and the population was still in decline. Whoever won the election faced some difficult decisions. The union work rules governing the police and fire departments were long overdue for change. There were far too many people on the Boston city payroll. The school system was fast becoming dysfunctional. The atmosphere was not as pessimistic as it had been during the height of the busing troubles, but it was not exactly optimistic either.

Weeks before the preliminary election on October 11, I knew it was over. My campaign manager and good friend, Bobby Hanson, also recognized the reality and pulled me aside. He was only 35, just a year older than me. Bobby was a trained economist who studied at Yale and earned an MBA at Boston University's School of Management. He was extremely bright and a serial problem solver in every job he ever held. He had taken over my campaign that summer after running into me in Dorchester. Bob was raised in

Watertown but had recently moved to Dorchester. Campaigns are chaotic by definition and mine was particularly unfocused until Bob took over. In late September, he bluntly told me I was not going to win and he was going to stop spending money of any consequence because he did not want me to end with an overwhelming debt. I had loaned my campaign literally every penny I had and depleted my modest savings. Bobby was clear that he would not condone any debt that could not be wiped out with a single big fundraiser. He wanted me to remain positive and upbeat and go out with style and panache. I knew he was right and will never forget his candor and initiative. He was a true friend. We wiped out that debt, about $30,000, the following March 27 with one big event—just as he planned.

The preliminary election results were a surprise to almost everyone. The candidate with the deepest pockets who had been presumed the winner, David Finnegan, finished out of the money. Instead, the insurgent candidates, Flynn and King, topped the ticket; each pulled 28 percent of the vote. Ray got slightly more: 48,118 to King's 47,848, but they were essentially even. Neither had raised much money. In fact, they ran guerrilla campaigns, real grassroots ground wars to cobble together the plurality each needed to best the rest of the field. Finnegan ran third with 41,657 or 25 percent of the vote. I finished fourth with 15,148 or nine percent, the same nine percent I got in the first benchmark poll conducted by my campaign the previous spring; the same nine percent of people who thought I "looked like a mayor." Dennis Kearney did even worse, finishing fifth with 6.5 percent or 10,992 votes. Dennis at least carried his home ward of East Boston. As the sheriff of Suffolk County, Dennis controlled a lot of jobs. I am convinced there were very few families in East Boston that did not have a member working for the sheriff. I lost my old home ward, Ward 17. The overwhelming sense that I was not in contention led even my own neighbors to vote for someone who had a better shot at winning.

I found Mel King's vote fascinating because for the first time in Boston political history, the minority community truly rallied behind one of their own. He pulled an astonishing vote from the black wards, helped by an intense voter registration drive and several campaign appearances by nationally prominent black leaders including Harold Washington, the mayor of Chicago; Andrew Young, the mayor of Atlanta; and Jesse L. Jackson, the civil rights leader. In a speech I delivered at Boston University just days before the general election, I noted that he did exactly what Irish ward bosses did so well in the first years of the century; he pulled out black people, young people, feminists and others who had never participated in the process before.

He carried Wards 8, 9, 10, 11, 12 and 14—Roxbury, Mission Hill, Dorchester and Mattapan—by enormous margins. He even carried Ward 17, because the ward had a significant black population by 1983. From the standpoint of the city, this was a good thing. Black voters needed to realize they had clout. People died for the civil right to vote just 20 years earlier and from a strictly civic standpoint, I had to applaud this turnout by the black community. By not running for reelection, Kevin White liberated the black community to vote for King. White had done extremely well in the black wards in the past for several reasons: he appointed black people to senior leadership positions in his administration, but more important, he controlled jobs, housing, and grants that made a huge difference in the lives of low income people. Mel King also drew a significant feminist vote. The gender gap was impressive. Not too many liberated women were voting for anti-abortion leader Ray Flynn. It was enormously disappointing to me to see places where I knew I had good support go for other candidates. Ward 5 on Beacon Hill and the Back Bay, for example, went for Mel King, while I finished second.

Flynn cobbled together his vote by drawing on the anti-abortion voters in the high voting wards. He ran a decent second to Finnegan in West Roxbury. The Southie vote for Flynn in Wards 6 and 7 was almost as monolithic as the black vote was for Mel. My new home ward of 16 in Dorchester went to Finnegan with Flynn running second. Flynn managed to run second in high voting wards and carry his own constituency in Southie and Charlestown by a healthy margin. Ray Flynn managed to emerge as the choice of the blue collar conservatives still in the city, just as Mel King became a rallying point for the growing numbers of minority group members. It was enough.

In the years since that election, I have met far more than 15,148 people who swear they voted for me. It is like the large number of people who claim to have seen Ted Williams hit a home run in his last at bat at Fenway Park, a number that magically inflates with the passage of time. When one of my daughters went through a rough patch at school and was disappointed by a teacher's decision, I told her that I sometimes write down 15,148 even now to remind myself what a real disappointment is. I had drawn more than 69,000 votes when I topped the City Council ticket four years earlier.

Finnegan was disappointed as well. He raised more money than any of us and was viewed as the frontrunner by many. But he made a fatal error. Kevin White may have defined what it meant to be mayor for Bostonians, but a clear majority was sick and tired of his act. When asked to describe White in a single word, one third of the electorate said "arrogant" in a survey conducted for a Boston radio and television station. Finnegan was cocky and came across as a little too sure of himself. He did not campaign very hard and sidestepped attempts to nail down his positions on specific issues with a breezy joke or aside. In the end, I am convinced he came across as a little bit too much like the aloof incumbent mayor.

Being in the second tier meant I got fewer contributions and fewer resources to get my message out to voters. It was a self-fulfilling dynamic.
Less attention from the press means fewer contributions and less support.
Ironically, being in the first tier ended up hurting Finnegan because it attracted more scrutiny from the press and he did not hold up well under it.
Shortly before the election, Andy Hiller, a longtime Boston TV reporter,
convinced Flynn and Finnegan to appear with him for a live interview in front
of City Hall. Flynn was steaming about a Finnegan radio ad that called him
a political chameleon who shifted colors and positions with the audience he
was addressing. Flynn shouted, "You called me a racist! You called me a liz-
ard!" . . . two lines that were the only ones remembered from that encounter.
The chameleon incident helped Flynn because it showed many people that
Finnegan was Him Again, a replay of the arrogant Mayor who had overstayed
his welcome, and Flynn somehow came across as the common man.

There was one other factor, that could not be anticipated, which hurt me.
The election was postponed by a court order from late September to October
11 because of a lawsuit brought over a dispute over the new city council
district lines. The extra three weeks meant three more weeks of television
advertisements, telephone bills, rent, and other campaign expenses that I
could not afford.

On preliminary election night a few hundred of my strongest supporters
and best friends gathered at Chelsea's bar on State Street. The proprietor offered use of his club for free, reasoning correctly that he would do a healthy
business selling booze to the crowd. A longtime Boston television reporter
covering me that night, privately told me that, "Everybody realized you
would have been the best mayor," just before I went up to concede. I heard
that a lot. It was cold comfort. I wished she and others had said it on air. The
disappointment from that loss remains with me to this day. My slogan of
wanting to be "everybody's mayor" was not in sync with those residents who
wanted their own personal mayor who reflected their views, and my relentless
efforts to show voters I was the most qualified were not responsive to their
personal concerns.

I went to the temporary podium set up at Chelsea's and thought briefly
that there was something very familiar about that podium. As I delivered my
speech, the television stations pulled away because David Finnegan, the man
expected to be one of the victors, had begun to concede at his headquarters. It
was somehow fitting that I did not even get unbroken TV coverage at the moment of defeat. Weeks later, a priest at St. Gregory's called me and asked if I
would please return their lectern for midnight Mass. The campaign had borrowed it from the Church for my election night party. No wonder it seemed
familiar. I had read from that lectern at Mass every Sunday for many years.

The outcome of the general election was a foregone conclusion. There were not enough black votes or liberal votes in a two-person race to get Mel over 50 percent. On Election Day in November, Raymond Leo Flynn was elected Mayor with 128,578 votes or 65 percent of the vote. Flynn's victory turned upside down the path to electoral victory for successful mayors. For the first time since 1949, the best educated candidate and the most progressive candidate did not win. Flynn beat King because a black candidate simply could not win in Boston in 1983. He was literally the last white guy standing. After Flynn left office, the old electoral pattern reasserted itself and that familiar coalition of liberals, minorities with a strong neighborhood base, would prove to be the key to victory for Thomas Menino, who has served an unprecedented five terms.

When I look back at that election, it is very clear that I may have been ahead of my time. The demographic changes in Boston then underway had not reached the point where they are today. Today a conservative candidate would have a very difficult time winning election in the city. Timing is almost everything in politics. The right candidate at the wrong time will not win. I was convinced I was the right candidate, but it clearly was not my time.

Was my dream delayed or denied? Unlike past defeats, I did not allow myself to wallow in misery or fall apart. The candidate of 1983 had learned a great deal since the young idealistic 22-year-old who won his first campaign in 1971. I took better care of myself. I knew more about human nature and human frailties. I understood more about myself and appreciated acutely that hard work, brains and tenacity are not always enough. Life, as John Kennedy once famously said, was unfair. I was not cynical, however. I still believed strongly in government, the political system and the basic goodness of people. My friend Bobby Hanson had done me a huge favor in psychologically preparing me for election night. I knew it was coming and could handle the disappointment far better than I could have a few years earlier. Bobby Hanson and I had agreed to a timetable for shutting down the campaign. By the Friday after the Tuesday preliminary election, the phones were turned off and removed from the headquarters; the files packed in boxes and stored in my basement; the staff dispersed; the headquarters was broom clean.

I was 34 years old and it was time for me to get on with the rest of my life.

The Rest of the Story

That deep aversion to being in a position of need and groveling for favors helped me move on from the loss. When I left the City Council, I knew I could survive financially without that job. After the 1983 election I was in even better financial shape: I was a single guy with two modest mortgages, and I was earning enough money as a lawyer to pay my bills. On October 12, 1983, the day after the preliminary election, after about four or five hours of fitful sleep, I got up, showered and shaved, and rode the subway to my law office just like every other day. I needed to keep moving forward and it was a comfort to have some place to go.

One of the benefits of living near Ashmont Station was that everyone boarding there could get a seat because it was the first stop on the line. So I settled into my seat on the Red Line train with my copies of The Boston Globe and Boston Herald that morning, reading the stories about my own defeat. I know I attracted a few bemused looks from fellow commuters. It did not feel like the first day of the rest of my life. I was putting one foot in front of the other. After a hard fought campaign with such high personal stakes for me, I felt physically exhausted and emotionally drained. I cannot deny I felt deeply disappointed. But I am not someone who hides under the bed covers.

Although I would never hold public office ever again, my involvement in a lifelong love affair with Boston as a private citizen continued unabated. My relationship with Boston began when I was a child. I learned how to navigate the subway system as a boy and never hesitated to walk, sometimes for miles, to get to a destination. For example, I often walked from Charlestown to downtown Boston with my classmate Connie Doherty. The iconic stores and restaurants that represented Boston at that time remain with me: the original Filenes' Basement, where everyone's mother found remarkable bargains, Bailey's ice cream next to the Boston Common, the elegant hat and jewelry stores. I remembered the clatter of the old elevated train rumbling from North Station across the bridge to Main Street in Charlestown. I learned the streets of Jamaica Plain, Roslindale and West Roxbury by walking to the houses of Boston Latin School classmates. This was long before MapQuest and Google Maps and GPS devices. That knowledge came in handy later when I went door to door as a candidate. My services have frequently been auctioned off for charity as a tour guide because I can tell a story about why a neighborhood starts or stops in a particular spot, about the history of that corner, about the family that once lived in that house and about the long gone deli that served the best Reuben sandwich in the world.

The Boston of today is full of immigrants from places some of us cannot find on a map. Entire streets are full of Vietnamese and Dominicans. Entire buildings in Brighton and Mission Hill are full of Russians who tormented the Brookline Public School system administrators for years by sneaking their kids across the border into the excellent Brookline public schools. It is remarkable that these Russians, after years of life in a closed autocratic system, figured out immediately where their children could get the very best free education. In Roxbury, Nigerians and Somalis bring new vitality to a neighborhood that was once made up of first generation Irish-Americans. The gay community has filled in many of the missing pieces in the city by revitalizing down-at-the-heels neighborhoods and causing property values to skyrocket.

At the same time and somewhat inexplicably, the Boston accent is fast disappearing. I'm not quite sure why; perhaps it is the proximity of neighbors from someplace else and the homogenization of culture from television. Fortunately some of us are far too old to ever learn how to pronounce the letter "r" and we will always "pahk our cahrs near the fi-ah depahtment."

It has been obvious for some time that I like to keep busy and there has been no lack of opportunity of worthwhile projects to keep my non-work hours full. Since boyhood, I have always loved to teach and mentor young men and women. I suspect this is something I inherited from my mother, a lifelong public school teacher. My involvement in Boys State/Girls State, the American Legion programs that train young men and women in the democratic political process, has been constant since my own days as a student delegate in Massachusetts and Washington, D.C. Boys State has become my second family. For a week each June, I move onto a college campus to teach classes on government and the political process and each year never fail to be impressed by the energy, potential and idealism of the young. I have spent many hours debating the merits of this college or that university and finding ways for these talented and eager teenagers to pay a college tuition bill. They renew my faith in human nature and have made me very, very proud.

Many of my early Boys State students have been elected to public office, in Massachusetts and elsewhere. At one point, five of the forty members of the Massachusetts State Senate were graduates of Massachusetts Boys State. One Boys State veteran, Mark Gearan, served as director of the Peace Corps and is now president of Hobart and William Smith Colleges. I also take considerable pride in the accomplishments of the young people who worked on my political campaigns and on my city council staff. When I was City Council President, we designated an entire room "intern city." Those young people brought sunshine into the cloudiest day. They came from varied backgrounds, ranging from prestigious private schools to public universities. Each one was special. I like to think I have probably signed more letters of recommendation than anyone outside of the academy. Many of them went on to enjoy great success with families, jobs, community engagement and a few even distinguished themselves in politics and public service. Terry Miller served as Lieutenant Governor of Alaska; Marty Fridson became a well-known columnist on financial affairs; and Michael Brown co-founded City Year. One member of the New Hampshire Legislature recently told me that his interest in public service was piqued by an internship at my City Hall office forty years ago.

I have served on the Democratic State Committee for more than four decades. I keep in contact with friends across the state who once helped me on my own statewide campaigns and still thoroughly enjoy the state nominating and issues conventions. I was appointed to the Board of Trustees for the University of Massachusetts in 1987. The public community college and university system is critical in providing opportunity and an excellent education to Massachusetts kids who come from families that cannot afford a fancy private higher education. It was gratifying to be involved in the expansion of the university to five campuses and construction of the 10,500 seat Mullins Center at the Amherst campus during my seven years on the board. The center has become the premier venue for sports events and entertainment for western Massachusetts.

My friends in the real estate business community convinced me to co-chair the Commonwealth Housing Task Force which led to Chapter 40R, which provides incentives for construction of smart growth transit-oriented housing all across the state, and I worked hard to pass that legislation in Massachusetts. As a diehard city dweller, I have seen the value of public transit for individuals, families and businesses over and over again and frankly cannot understand those who question the public investment in it.

I was named a trustee of the Franklin Foundation and the Franklin Institute which were created by a trust left by the legendary Benjamin Franklin to the city of Boston. When Benjamin Franklin died in 1790, he left 1,000 pounds silver each to his two home towns, Boston and Philadelphia. The money was intended to provide loans at 5 percent interest to young married artisans under the age of 25 who were apprentices in trades in each city. Franklin was fascinated by the potential of compounded interest and it was his intent that the funds increase in size and be perpetually self-sustaining. Over the course of 200 years, the trustees let old Ben down. Had the trustees done what he instructed, the trusts would have had a combined value of $36 million after two centuries. Boston's share was only worth $4.4 million in 1991, the time when Franklin's will said that 75 percent of the money was to be spent on a public project decided by the citizens of each town. I helped steer a home rule petition through the Boston City Council to get the money to the Benjamin Franklin Institute of Technology, which was created with the trust money and which awards nine associates degrees in engineering and industrial technologies, keeping up a modern day version of Ben Franklin's old apprenticeship system. It was the right thing to do and Benjamin Franklin would take great pride in the expertise and work ethic of these modern day artisans.

The state Legislature has hired me several times to sort through the decennial federal census and provide counsel on the best and fairest way to draw congressional district lines. The complexity of the task, a mind boggling puzzle of demographic trends, political considerations, and legal challenges, is one I look forward to tackling every ten years. I have stayed on the board of the Harvard Cooperative Society for decades; served as a trustee and overseer of The Children's Museum; and as chairman of the Boston Municipal Research Bureau, which maintains a tradition of honest insightful analysis of city finances.

When the Big Dig project was about to begin, many business leaders worried about the impact of years of construction on the city. The construction project was massive and it promised to bring complete gridlock without adequate planning and a lot of mitigation measures. I was invited by Boston developer Norman Leventhal to help create the Artery Business Committee (ABC). The business leaders who worked downtown were particularly worried about the impact of construction on their businesses. The Artery Business Committee had three purposes: keep downtown Boston accessible during Big Dig construction; make sure the completed project adequately served downtown; and be certain that political and legal controversies did not derail the project. Norman was a genius at pulling together 150 of Boston's leading experts in construction, design, permitting, and public relations, and putting everyone in the same room. It made a huge difference. ABC helped keep Boston open for business throughout the lengthy construction project. Indeed, the city had the lowest vacancy rate and the lowest unemployment rate in history during construction. This was not totally a result of the committee, but I have to believe the organized leadership and coordination of ABC helped a lot. I would point out to my then very young daughters the beautiful bridge being built as a northern gateway to Boston. They called it "Daddy's bridge."

The Artery Business Committee transformed into A Better City after the Big Dig was finished. I was honored to become chairman. The nonprofit organization continues to bring together private, public and community partners for work on new challenges facing the city.

And it took me awhile, but I finally found love. I was serving as President of the Boston Latin School Association in 1988 and helping to develop a capital campaign to raise money for the school. The association hired a young recent Williams College graduate to edit the Boston Latin School Bulletin. I noticed her right away; she was smart, cute and not too tall. Teresa Spillane grew up in West Roxbury and graduated from Boston Latin School many years after I did. Despite the immediate attraction, I hesitated. She was only 22 years old. I was 39 and I thought probably too old for her. I finally worked up my courage to ask her out the following spring. Well, it was clearly meant to be. I courted her. We fell in love and married on October 6, 1990. All of our guests wore blue and white political buttons printed up for the occasion that said, "Larry and Teresa: A Team for the Future." This was one campaign that would prove to be a huge success.

Soon after we married, we decided Teresa should pursue her doctorate. When she was admitted to the Massachusetts School of Professional Psychology, we celebrated with a wonderful dinner at the Ritz. For four years, we scrimped and borrowed and made the same kinds of sacrifices that our parents made for us. I was honored to be in cap and gown to present her with her degree in the spring of 1995. Teresa became a licensed psychologist with a specialty in the issues surrounding pregnancy and childbirth and helping mothers maintain and achieve emotional wellness at a challenging time. She has taught at Harvard Medical School and helped found Isis Parenting.

Two years later, on August 7, 1997, after much prayer and the help of modern medicine, we became the proud parents of triplets; three girls who are as different and unique as three children born of the same parents at the same time could ever be. Catherine, Sophie, and Flora changed my life and brought me great joy. They arrived early as multiple birth babies often do, but were healthy and quickly grew. I got up every night when they did when they were infants. A nanny handled Wednesdays so Teresa and I could sit in bed and read. Within minutes, both of us would be fast asleep. By the time the girls could sleep through the night, I could change and feed all three in 35 minutes flat. I chose to restrict my travel schedule because of my desire to be home with them. Teresa and I once took a rare trip to Bermuda to visit the U. S. Consul, the charming Bob Farmer. I came home a day early to find four of six ears were infected.

Soon after the girls were baptized by Teresa's Uncle Billy at Mission Church, my favorite Aunt, Auntie Jo, passed away. My dad followed, dying quite suddenly on Holy Thursday in 2001. Mum was with us until shortly after Thanksgiving five years later, spending time both at Standish Village in Dorchester Lower Mills and then at Eventide Home in Quincy. She never missed a beat mentally, but Parkinson's disease took a huge toll on her physical condition. Just as nature replenishes itself, so does the human race. Three adults who enjoyed life and one another's company were replaced by three young women, one more articulate and intelligent than the other.

Like any parent, I want the best for my children. I taught them how to ride the subway; how to toss a softball and swim in the ocean; how to root for the Red Sox; and even how to analyze election results. My daughters clearly know they can get anything out of Dad, so I am the favored designated shopping chauffeur. I hope that I have been a better father because of my relative maturity. By the time of their birth, I was 48 and wiser than the brash 22 year old who won his first election to the Boston City Council. I know I have done things for my daughters that I would never have done for myself. I learned from the example of others, both good and bad, and took copious mental notes. I am also acutely aware that I will only be their Dad once. I am grateful that I can pass on to them the values I learned from my grandparents and parents and provide them with opportunities to learn and flourish in this highly competitive world. I try to teach our children that each person has dignity and that dignity does not require wealth, fame, the ability to speak the King's English, or even a good education. From time to time, if we are exasperated by one of our daughters, one of them will suggest: "you're a lawyer, she's a shrink. What do you expect?"

After a few years in a small firm which carried my name, I joined Peabody Brown in 1990; the firm became Nixon Peabody in 1999. My partners understand that I have many interests beyond the practice of law. I have extraordinary flexibility and frequently take advantage of our office in Washington, D. C. It has been a good balance.

I have kept a hand in the extraordinary renaissance of Boston as a lawyer specializing in real estate. In the thirty years that have passed since my last run for public office, the trends that began to emerge in the 1970s continued and grew and became more pronounced. Today Boston is a very different city from the one in which I was born in 1949. The demographic diversity of its citizens from a racial, generational, income and ethnic standpoint could not have been imagined just after the Second World War. The economic development, growth of new business and industry, and sheer wealth now evidenced by elegant pricey restaurants with martini bars and million dollar condos would not have been guessed at by John B. Hynes when he ran against James Michael Curley in 1949 and began to bring the city into the modern era.

The word "organic," like the word "holistic," is frequently used, and often misused, these days. I especially object to any references to the changing demographics or economics of a city as being "organic." After more than forty years of being in the room, I am convinced that major changes in Boston, or in most any other city, result from the actions of elected officials and the government over which they preside. These changes are rarely the direct result of grass roots and well-meaning bottom up participatory efforts. Some of the major projects in Boston; Quincy Market, Copley Place, Charlestown Navy Yard, Central Artery/Tunnel, the Norman Leventhal Park at Post Office Square, the South West Corridor, the Silver Line, would not have taken place but for activist government and elected officials who acted with vision—and often not in agreement with the desires of the majority. Statues are not constructed to honor those who waited for the crowd to gather and then ran to the front of the parade.

Few things give me more pleasure than to walk through Norman Leventhal Park in Post Office Square. Norman's nephew, David, was my Harvard classmate, and I became friendly with Norman and his late brother Robert during my first campaign. We have been friends and allies ever since. Norman brought me in as a member of the legal team that helped to bring about the development of the park. It required enormous political courage by the Flynn Administration to break the lease with Frank Sawyer, who operated a very old and ugly parking garage on that site. The city is a far better place because of Norman's vision and the good work of John Connolly, Bart Mitchell, Steve Coyle and their colleagues in the Flynn Administration, who helped create this beautiful park. I am delighted when I spot Norman strolling through his park when he is in town.

Shakespeare wrote that past is prologue, and the knowledge I gained as a city councilor informed my legal career. I have had a seat at the negotiating table for a great many economic development projects in Boston. When I stroll through downtown with one of my daughters, I can point to nearly any building or complex and tell her a personal story of how the building came to be bought, sold, renovated, built or repurposed. It is a very good feeling . . . and not just because it makes the three DiCara girls proud of their Dad. Those deals created jobs and homes for all kinds of people, transformed decrepit shells into viable businesses, and generated millions of dollars in tax revenues. More important, those deals brought Boston back as one of the preeminent cities in the United States and one of a handful of truly international cities in this country. When fiscal conservatives rail against government spending, I point to these multiple examples of prudent government investment which have brought an incalculable improvement in the economy and quality of life of the city.

Alvaro Lima, the talented director of research for the Boston Redevelopment Authority, compiled some data for me at the request of my old friend Peter Meade, the BRA director, which explains Boston's economic development. In the 1980s, more than 13 million square feet of office space was added in Boston, along with more than 5,000 hotel rooms and 40,000 new jobs. The growth continued for the next 20 years. By 2010, Boston had almost doubled the office space available in 1960, added more than 62,000 housing units, and more than 100,000 jobs. Most extraordinary of all, Boston's population began to grow again. While there are fewer residents in 2010, a total 617,594 according to the federal census, than the 697,197 recorded in 1960, the sharp decline of the 1950s, 1960s and 1970s switched to growth in the 1980s. The city kept on growing even though Boston housing and the cost of living became far more expensive. Lifestyles changed radically as everyone who lived through those years knows well. The notion of someone like me, a lawyer who was gainfully employed, living in his parent's attic in the same house as his grandmother with three generations under one roof is no longer even close to the norm. More college educated people live alone than ever before. Couples have far fewer children. Indeed, there are one-third fewer school age children in Boston now than when busing began. I have friends who live alone in luxurious multi-million dollar homes in a neighborhood which was once a slum teeming with extended families of immigrants living in two room hovels and sharing a single bathroom with other families. It is truly remarkable that this sort of change could happen in one place in a matter of a century.

The changes within neighborhoods have been equally dramatic. While entirely new residential neighborhoods have been created on the Waterfront, at the site of the old Navy Yard in Charlestown, and in the Seaport section of South Boston, the old neighborhoods changed as well. The racial shift was seen most dramatically in Roxbury. Today most people think of Roxbury as a community of African-Americans. But in 1950, a year after my birth, Roxbury was 80 percent white. In 1980, it was only 10 percent white. South Dorchester was almost 90 percent white when I first ran for public office in 1971. By 1990, the neighborhood was barely 50 percent white. These patterns, however, are beginning to shift again. When I drive down Columbus Avenue in Roxbury today, for example, I see more white people going about their business as the gentrification that transformed the South End creeps over the neighborhood line towards the south. Theodore's White's urban ballet is often improvisational, with new and different groups moving to fill a vacuum, take advantage of a deal, or just seek an opportunity to claim a piece of Boston. Census data analyzed for Alexander Von Hoffman's book *House by House, Block by Block: The Rebirth of America's Urban Neighborhoods*, shows amazing demographic change in certain neighborhoods. One that leapt off the page at me is the number of college graduates in the South End. A college education is probably the most reliable barometer of economic prosperity there is. In 1970, fewer than 17 percent of the people in that neighborhood had attended or completed college. Thirty years later, the number was almost 62 percent. That single statistic speaks volumes about the change that took place in that community.

The large tenements in the downtown wards so common before and during World War II were replaced as a result of the urban renewal plan, which wiped out the West End, and by construction of the Central Artery, which chopped the North End and Chinatown into pieces. By 1960, the downtown population was far lower than it had been just decades earlier. In recent years, large residential buildings have been built downtown which house hundreds of condo owners and apartment dwellers under one roof. As a result, the biggest precinct in Boston, with more than 8,500 residents, is the downtown precinct which includes Chinatown. This has diminished political power in long powerful neighborhoods. South Boston, for example, has about a third as many people as it had a century ago. Even political powerhouse neighborhoods like West Roxbury have fewer residents than just 20 years ago.

We see similar shifts on a bigger scale in the entire country. The Northeast and Midwest lost population to the South and West after World War II. In 1960, when John Kennedy narrowly beat Richard Nixon for the presidency, Pennsylvania and California had the same number of Electoral College votes, 32. Today California has 55 votes to Pennsylvania's 20. In 1960, Massachusetts had more Electoral College votes than Florida, 16 to 10. Today Florida has 29 votes to Massachusetts' 11.

Real estate development is not the only thing that made Boston what it is today, but the development effectively acts as a visible metaphor for recovery. I have often cited a vote I made as a City Councilor in 1976 to borrow money for the city at 9.22 percent tax-free. At the time, the federal marginal tax rates were greater than 50 percent. A comparable private loan would have violated state usury laws. While New York defaulted, Boston teetered, as did Cleveland and Detroit. But Boston turned a corner and I will argue that it did so because of an alchemy of factors that came together at the right time.

One of Boston's greatest strengths is brain power. This has been true since the first Bostonians settled here. Generations of bright young people have come to Boston and Cambridge to earn a higher education at the region's superb colleges and universities. Many of them stay to work, create new businesses, and raise their own families. Harvard students come from all over but after graduating most invariably settle on either the west or east coast, though some do return to the South and Midwest. Boston attracts many because it became a center for high technology, cutting edge health care, financial services and education at the very time those industries became the new engines for prosperity and success in the 21st century. Boston was not the only place where those economic sectors thrived but it was a key locus. As the capital city of Massachusetts and the largest city in New England, with a seaport and international airport and some of the best hospitals and universities in the world, Boston was primed to roar back. Mike Dukakis won the Democratic nomination for President in 1988 in part because of the power and appeal of the "Massachusetts Miracle."

Political leadership in the 1970s and decisions to invest public money and clout behind certain economic development projects laid the foundation for today's prosperity. Had Kevin White not sold all those downtown parking garages and pushed for the revitalization of the Faneuil Hall Marketplace and the Charlestown Navy Yard and development of all the "Places" that dot downtown—Lafayette Place, Copley Place, International Place—Boston would not look or feel the way it does today.

Political leadership also made a difference in terms of the federal resources that came to Boston. The Big Dig that depressed the central artery and built the Ted Williams third harbor tunnel to the airport are the most vivid examples of the difference smart public investment can make in a city. The powerful and long serving Massachusetts Congressional Delegation always put the interests of Massachusetts and Boston first. Ted Kennedy may be known for his passion for national health insurance and other big issues, but he worked just as hard getting federal money for the city, state, hospitals, schools and community projects. I often wonder if the bright young people who ride the MBTA Silver Line to work in the Seaport each morning would even recognize Joe Moakley if he were sitting next to them on the car. Joe was singularly responsible for the construction of the Silver Line. He understood that accessible public transportation had to be provided if the Seaport was to be developed. The very same equivalency took place when the South West Corridor money was used to rebuild the Orange Line. That led directly to the gentrification and prosperity of Jamaica Plain. The Seaport is what it is today because modestly compensated administrative assistants can use their Charlie cards to get to and from their jobs in the fancy offices overlooking the harbor.

I must note the contribution made by Thomas M. Menino, Boston's first Italian-American mayor and the first mayor to win a fifth term. Tom Menino will be well regarded by history for very different reasons than Kevin White. He was spared the type of crises which plagued Boston during the White

years. But he also freed the city of the stink of corruption and brought stability to Boston city government for an unprecedented twenty years. Every
person who had been elected Mayor of Boston, going back to Maurice Tobin
in 1937 (except for the low key City Clerk John B. Hynes) had sought higher
office. Tobin had been Governor; Curley had been Governor and also run for
the Senate and served in Congress; Collins had run for the U. S. Senate after
toying with running for Governor; Kevin White had run for Governor and
almost been the Democratic nominee for Vice President; Ray Flynn had considered running for many offices and later ran for Congress, unsuccessfully,
after he had returned from the Vatican. Tom Menino was only interested in
being one thing—Mayor of Boston. This means that he had a better working
relationship with whoever was sitting as Governor than most of his prede-
cessors because the governors never saw him as competition. The late Dan
Rudsten, who was a State Senator from Roxbury, Dorchester and Mattapan,
and later a professor at Boston State College, wrote a rarely-read doctoral dis-
sertation on the relationship between the Mayor of Boston and the Governor,
of which I am always reminded when I think of how well Tom Menino has
interacted with whoever was sitting in the Governor's office, whether Republican or Democrat. His reliable steady leadership kept Boston on course.

Some mayors are members of a governing class, the sons of successful
men who groomed them for public office. Kevin White, for example, was
the son, grandson and son-in-law of men who served as Presidents of the
Boston City Council. Neither Ray Flynn nor Tom Menino came from such
backgrounds. Tom Menino was even more of an outsider because he spent
his entire life in a city dominated by the Irish. He also came from a small,
obscure neighborhood—Readville—not a political powerhouse. One could
make the case that this contributed to his extraordinary empathy for the poor,
the disadvantaged, and members of racial minority groups. That empathy
may be why the waters of Boston have stayed relatively calm for the past
twenty years. Tom decided to retire at the end of his fifth term in 2013. From
all evidence, his remarkable legacy of stability and steady leadership will
stand during our lifetime.

And finally, people made a difference. I came across a book called *Boston,
City on a Hill*, written by two Boston College professors, Andrew Buni and
Alan Rogers. It was sponsored by the Greater Boston Chamber of Commerce
and a number of local businesses in 1984. Those business leaders felt that
they had a stake in Boston. Since that time, because of sales, mergers and
consolidations, a startling number of those companies no longer exist or are
owned by out of towners. For example, The Boston Globe has been owned
by The New York Times and Jordan Marsh has become Macy's. In those
years business leaders like Norman Leventhal put their money, influence and

time on the line over and over again and they and the city prospered for the investment.

When white flight accelerated after Judge Garrity's busing order in the 1970s, the vacuum created by the loss of large white families was filled by new Bostonians who were better educated, often single and childless, sometimes gay, and invariably richer. Those folks have changed the city. While the overall city population is lower in 2010 than it was 50 years earlier, the population of certain areas, particularly downtown Boston and the South End has skyrocketed. These new residents raised the average for the per capita family income of the city substantially and transformed the Waterfront and other dreary tenement districts into luxurious and high end communities. If you ride the Green Line at 10 p.m., it feels like 10 a.m. with an amazing number of young, multi-ethnic riders. Indeed, riding the MBTA or walking down Boston streets often has the flavor of a mini-New York City on a more comfortable and manageable scale. It is an exciting change.

It is important to acknowledge that there are many elements and people who made up the "old" Boston who are still living in the neighborhoods. And this is a good thing. The stalwarts who stayed in place are, however, literally dying off. Every month Dolan's and Molloy's bury a few more members of the Greatest Generation. The elderly widows still living in West Roxbury and South Boston and Roslindale are living in houses that are now worth appreciably more than they were in the 1970s, when depressed housing values limited the options for the families who did move out of the city and pointed them to places like Brockton and Randolph, where houses were cheap and public services minimal.

Sadly, many of the "old" Bostonians live at an economic disadvantage in a society where brains count for far more than the brawn of the past. In Jamaica Plain, where we are raising our family, you can see that the delta between the haves and have-nots has increased quite dramatically in recent years. But it has changed over time. When I was driven to Boston Latin School as a boy, the journey went from Dorchester through what was then a Jewish ghetto in Mattapan, past cemeteries and open space, and then, after crossing that enormous bridge over Forest Hills, onto the Arborway and the Jamaicaway. I thought those houses on the Jamaicaway in Jamaica Plain, including the famous mansion with the shamrock shutters installed by James Michael Curley, belonged to the richest people in the world. Indeed, Jamaica Plain had once been the home of the gentry. After a period of decline, JP is now a neighborhood of affluence again.

The differences between old and new are stark: we own; they rent. We go to college; they do not. We do not serve in the military, but they do. We go out to eat at restaurants all the time; they do not. They have lots of kids;

we do not. Twenty years ago, there were four Catholic churches in Jamaica Plain; now there are two. There were four Catholic schools; now there are none. There is a perception gap between the haves and have-nots living in the same community that is almost comical. I call it "the aluminum siding conundrum." There are people, like my own parents, who worked hard to save enough money to put aluminum siding on their homes. Then there are people, like me and Teresa, who worked hard to save money to take the siding off our house on Burroughs Street and restore it to its original Victorian splendor.

For those left behind or unable to get a decent start on the track to upward mobility, it is disheartening to be left behind, and I worry about the people who do not get the same chances I was given as the grandson of an Italian barber. Part of this is selfish. I want Boston and the United States to benefit from the talent, energy and potential of every one, not just the lucky ones at the top. If every immigrant, every poor child and every person of color gets a fair shot, we all win. And I truly believe that economic diversity is as important as any other type of diversity in a city and contributes to the vibrancy and rich tapestry of urban living. Just think about the great ethnic restaurants of years ago, where you could get a soul satisfying platter of pasta and meatballs for a couple of bucks. The Italian cuisine now available in the North End is delicious, but it is not cheap.

Boston also increasingly became, once again, a favored spot for immigrants. The city has always been a welcoming place for newcomers. The BRA estimated that more than 151,000 foreign-born residents were living in Boston in 2008 and half of them emigrated during the previous decade. The diversity is extraordinary. Foreign-born residents add up to one-fourth of the city population and came from 100 different countries. A total of 29 percent came from the Caribbean; 24 percent from Asia; 17 percent from Europe; 10 percent from Central America; 9 percent from South America, and 9 percent from Africa.

The newcomers behave just like the Irish and Italian and Jewish immigrants of the 19th century; they congregate near their countrymen, work hard, and strive to create opportunity for their own children. East Boston, which was Italian-American when I ran for the City Council in 1971, is now predominantly Latino; Roslindale, which was always Irish and then Greek, now has Latinos and Haitians. Allston-Brighton is Chinese, Russian and Brazilian, and Dorchester is loaded with Haitians and Vietnamese. Dot Avenue has turned into one big pho shop! In Hyde Park, the predominant ethnicity of foreign born residents is Latino and Haitian.

In the public schools, almost half, a total of 44 percent, of the students either spoke a language other than English or another language in addition to English in 2004. When the local newspapers print photographs of the valedictorians from Boston public schools, a number of the best and brightest were born in a foreign country. I am happy to report that the attitude towards bilingual education has changed since my childhood, so these children are not forced to abandon their first language, as I was.

There has been a substantial shift in political power as well. Thanks to district representation, every neighborhood has a voice in city government. Back in 1968-1969, three of the nine City Councilors, Bill Foley, Gerry O'Leary and John E. Kerrigan, all lived in Ward 7, South Boston. Today a candidate like Ray Flynn, who came to fame as the sponsor of an anti-abortion law, simply could not run successfully for an at large position though he might be able to win the South Boston district seat. Throughout most of the city, he would be viewed as far too conservative to win. We saw this play out when South Boston Councilor Michael Flaherty ran against Mayor Tom Menino. When the first city councilors elected under the district representation system stood for reelection in 1985, I heartily endorsed the new system which I helped to create. It was working out as well as anyone could have expected. With the city divided into 65,000 to 70,000 person segments, the likelihood is a city councilor would show up at neighborhood meetings in every neighborhood. I wrote an opinion piece that noted "We probably have twice as many Puerto Ricans as Polish, more Vietnamese than Lithuanians, more Haitians than Sicilians. Racial and ethnic backgrounds, however, are only the easiest of statistics to calculate. So many Bostonians were born elsewhere within the United States and have decided to make this their home; the numbers exceed, I expect, anyone's imagination. There are more lifestyles in the city than most sociologists could have catalogued even a decade or two ago: at least a tenth of the city's population is gay and an openly gay man now sits on the City Council." If anything, the city is even more diverse now.

I found it almost comical that some people in the black community now want to return to city wide elections, reasoning that the larger percentage of black residents would lead to more black elected officials. This is short sighted. The urban ballet never stops and the future does not guarantee that the percentage of black residents will remain the same or even grow. In fact, the percentage of black residents of Boston has remained fairly stable even as the number of Asians and Latinos has grown.

The greater diversity of Boston has led to greater tolerance, particularly among the young. My daughters are virtually colorblind. They simply do not notice the race of their classmates or see sexual orientation as anything different from eye color. To see my children and their peers so free of the prejudices that burdened my own generation and those who came before me is a great relief and an unexpected pleasure.

Although I have reached the age when I am fast approaching eligibility for Medicare, I am far younger in my sixties than my parents or grandparents were at this age. This is not mere denial, although baby boomers are notorious for refusing to accept the indignities that age can bring. Yet age does bring perspective and, I hope, a certain amount of wisdom. I am more introspective now than I ever was as a hard charging youth. I wonder if the characteristics that brought me success in my professional life, discipline, stubbornness and impatience, may have also complicated my private life, although wondering about this may also be a function of being married to a very smart psychologist.

I am still a creature of habit, perhaps ever more so than I was when I was younger. I still rise at 5:30 a.m. most mornings. I play squash at 6:30, or otherwise find a way to work out. I do not take lengthy vacations, but I do try to find my way to Spring Training. I still favor blue and gray suits and striped ties. I prefer the 10 a.m. Mass at the Paulist Center when I am in Boston. I still use a Dictaphone and engage in robust correspondence, both written and electronic.

Getting older means it is necessary to make an accommodation with loss of all sorts. I have experienced the loss of my parents and many dear friends, some well known. Like so many others, I felt acutely the death of Ted Kennedy. He was a hero to me when I was young and eventually became a wonderful friend. He took me sailing one day from the Key Biscayne Yacht Club in 1989 and asked me to talk to his younger son, Patrick, who was just beginning his own political career at a tender age. He thought I might have some insights for him. I miss Joe Moakley and Chris Iannella every day. I feel fortunate that I had the opportunity to enjoy their guidance and friendship. They were remarkable men.

While many of my fellow baby boomers are living longer, not all survive to old age. I lost many other friends who were not as well known. When Teresa was on the seventh floor at Beth Israel Hospital on bed rest awaiting the birth of our triplets in 1997, my old dear friend Bobby Hanson was on the fourth floor in the final stages of his battle against cancer. I would visit both of them each time I went to the hospital. I was at Boys State when Bobby's wife, Elizabeth, called to say Bobby wanted to say goodbye to me. We had a long talk; it was not easy. By the time I next drove back into Boston and parked my car in the old BI parking garage, he was gone. Bobby died on June 27, 1997 at the age of 49. A year later, in September of 1998, Kirk O'Donnell, another wise and good friend, died suddenly while jogging at the age of 52. His wife Kathryn also died prematurely, as did Bo and Betty Holland, Bob Holland, Lowell Richards, Bill McDermott and Elaine Guiney. We all worked together at City Hall. I think of these premature deaths often and wonder about the inexplicable vagaries that give long life to some and deny it to others who might be far more deserving.

My good memory means that I retain a veritable encyclopedia of data in my head. Yet there are some moments that remain particularly vivid. A funeral service that truly symbolized the end of an era was the funeral of my former City Council colleague Dapper O'Neil. I was never fond of Dapper. He was crude, sometimes cruel, and always narrow and bigoted. He eventually outlived his time and spent his final years alone and helpless in a nursing home, which is a tragedy for anyone. The most astonishing collection of characters showed up at his funeral in West Roxbury after he died at the age of 87 at the end of 2007. Gormley's hosted the gathering, which was as colorful as Dapper had been. It was a bitterly cold Christmas Eve morning. A man with long hair pulled back in a ponytail called out the standard count used in boxing for this fallen fighter. When he called him out, a gong sounded loudly and the coffin lid was closed. The procession of mourners crossing the street to St. Theresa's for the funeral Mass included Santa Claus in full regalia. It was the strangest scene.

There are many lingering images that remain with me from my years in politics. I signed on to be co-chairman in Massachusetts for Sargent Shriver's presidential campaign in 1976. Sarge, the first director of the Peace Corps and the 1972 Democratic vice presidential candidate, was married to Eunice Kennedy, one of the nine children of Ambassador Joseph P. Kennedy, the sister of President Kennedy and a prominent activist for mentally disabled children. I spent a lot of time traveling with him throughout Massachusetts and New Hampshire. On the Sunday before the Massachusetts primary, on February 29, 1976, I accompanied Sarge, Eunice and Cesar Chavez, the legendary labor leader of the farm workers' movement, to Mass at St. Stephen's Church, the North End Catholic church where Rose Fitzgerald Kennedy, Eunice's mother, had been baptized many years earlier. After Mass, I walked down Hanover Street with them in the midst of a clutch of U. S. Secret Service agents assigned to protect Sarge, and a Chicano security force keeping an eye on the iconic Cesar, all the while chattering away in Italian trying to explain to the North End residents precisely who these three people were.

In the 1990s, I shared a client with former New York Mayor John Lindsay. In the course of our legal work, I suggested breakfast at the Ritz with another veteran mayor, Kevin White. Kevin had been out of office for slightly less than ten years, but had effectively disappeared from the public scene. Lindsay had been out of office for almost twenty years. It was fascinating to sit with those two aging urban lions. Lindsay opened by saying he had suffered a series of small strokes and warned that from time to time, he might miss a few words. Kevin allowed that he was now deaf in one ear. There was something endearing about them admitting to their physical frailties. When Lindsay asked Kevin why he had run for a third term given that third terms are almost always disastrous, Kevin said that he just did not know what else to do at the time. After he left office, Kevin went on to teach at Boston University, an appointment made by the late BU President John Silber, who also supplied him with an office, staff, car and driver. Much later, Kevin developed Alzheimer's disease and eventually forgot who he was or that he had been mayor. His death in 2012 brought him the credit he deserved for helping to create modern Boston. For the record, Kevin White proved to be an excellent teacher, just like Mike Dukakis, who taught at the Kennedy School and still teaches at Northeastern University. The poignancy of seeing Lindsay and White past their prime reminded me that all things do pass and fame and worldly things indeed are fleeting. As we learned in Latin class: sic transit gloria mundi.

Given the right combination of factors, cities and communities regenerate themselves. There are tragic cases where this does not happen. Detroit, for example, never recovered from the loss of auto jobs and racial riots. But Boston neighborhoods, almost Phoenix-like, burst back into life, after a period of decline and loss of population. When one group left, another came in. The same pattern can be seen in politics and in civil service. Just as the Boston Police Department generation hired to break the famous 1919 strike replaced the striking union members, a generation later the returning World War II veterans displaced them. Those veterans who happened to be heavily Irish, in turn were replaced by a generation of more varied ethnicity and color. Twenty-five years after the GI Generation giants like John Kennedy and Richard Nixon, returning World War II veterans, won their first elections to the U. S. House, a feisty generation of Watergate babies transformed public life again after the 1974 election. We are now seeing old friends like Barney Frank voluntarily stepping back and clearing the way for younger men and women in the U. S. House. For most, politics, like sports, is not a lifetime career. The exceptions, long standing successful politicians like Michigan's John Dingell, the Dean of the U. S. House who has served since 1955, are truly exceptions who defy time and survive in office until old age. But most of us fade away and often against our wishes.

I often think of the quote from Alfred Lord Tennyson in Ulysses: " I am a part of all that I have met." I have been truly blessed by the many people whom I have met over the course of the first six decades of my life. I like to think I learned something from each one. Many stay in touch. I still send out 5,000 letters each January, which now often feature a photograph of our three daughters. At my 60th birthday party, an event that doubled as a fundraiser and raised more than $300,000 for the benefit of Boys State and Girls State,

I said, "Some at the age of 60, are looking to slow down. Others retire. I am just warming up."

As I look back, I am acutely aware of how opportunity and education transformed my life. My own father could not speak a word of English until he arrived at the school house door at the age of six. Within decades, his son earned two degrees from Harvard. As my grandparents would say: only in America. Others who have followed and who will come to Boston in the future deserve the same chance to work hard, study and succeed.

The 12 years between my first and last campaigns for public office turned out to be a pivotal period in Boston history. As I worked on this book, I realized my personal story was a footnote to a bigger tale of Boston in transition. It was a time of wrenching change. Transitions are always difficult. Boston came out of that difficult time different but stronger, more diverse, more affluent and more progressive. Political leadership and government investment made during the 1970s did make a difference.

I do not yearn for the good old days, although I retain a deep and abiding respect for those who came before me. History does teach us a good deal, though it often takes the passage of time to fully appreciate the lessons. The courage of my grandfather, Lorenzo Alibrandi, still a boy at the age of 13, coming to a strange place where he could not even speak the language, still leaves me amazed and grateful. The urban ballet that Teddy White, that son of Dorchester, so eloquently described many years ago continues without pause in Boston. I hope to continue to enjoy the dance for many years to come.

Afterword

I am completing this memoir early in 2013: thirty years since I ran for Mayor and thirty-five years since I served as President of the Boston City Council. Today Boston is a dramatically different city, and America is a dramatically different country. I keep a well-thumbed version of Edwin O'Connor's classic novel, *The Last Hurrah*, on a shelf at home in Jamaica Plain. In that book, Mayor Skeffington speaks of the possible changes in his city: "For some time, something new has been on the horizon: namely, the Italians. But when they take over, that will be an entirely different story, and I, for one, won't be around to see it. I don't imagine," he said thoughtfully, "that it'll be too much fun anyway." Well, Boston had an Italian Mayor for 20 years, and the City did just fine. Believe it or not, when I ran in 1983, intelligent people still questioned whether a candidate of Italian descent could ever be elected Mayor of Boston.

In the same era, America has elected a black President, one raised, in part, outside the boundaries of the United States. His father was a student from Kenya. Our Governor is also a man of color, raised on the south side of Chicago in the most difficult of circumstances. The Republican candidate for President this past November, an old friend from Massachusetts, was a Mormon. The very fact that the 2012 election saw a black man and a Mormon contest for the Presidency is, in and of itself, an extraordinary commentary about the United States and one which none of us likely could have predicted 30 years ago.

This year, Boston will elect a new Mayor. I would contend that almost anyone of almost any background could be a viable candidate; there is no certainty as to what the next mayor will look like, or where his grandparents may have lived.

It is always dangerous to predict the future but the demographic trends in the city have exposed a political conundrum that will unquestionably affect the future of the city. While Boston is now ``majority minority'' in terms of population, the power in elections still lies with white voters. That is because many of the newcomers to Boston are immigrants who are not citizens and cannot vote. The path to citizenship still is sadly too long and winding for those who come from foreign lands in search of a better life. And, as I noted in this book, the white residents of Boston today are more likely to be affluent, single, liberal, and perhaps gay, with no children or few children. Children under the age of 18 make up just 17 percent of the city population, half the percentage of 1970. The average household size has decreased by nearly 25 percent in the last 50 years. The high cost of housing is discouraging to families with children who find more economical homes in the suburbs. A generation ago, an O'Hara from St. Gregory's Parish marrying a Sullivan from St. Brendan's was considered a ``mixed'' marriage. Today, a young educated white resident could live in a precinct where whites, blacks, Hispanics and Asians make up equal portions of the overall population and may be married to someone of the same gender.

However, these newcomers feel disconnected from municipal government. They vote for Governor, Senator and President, but rarely for Mayor. This is why precincts with elderly housing developments have a disproportionate impact on city elections. Those seniors rarely miss voting in any election. The residents young enough to be their grandchildren who grew up someplace else do not engage. Less than half of those who voted in the 2012 presidential election are likely to vote in the next mayoral election. I do not have a crystal ball but it is clear that the successful mayoral candidate of the future may be the one who can excite educated Bostonians in their 20's and 30's, the voters who turned out in huge numbers for Senate candidate Elizabeth Warren and Presidential candidate Barack Obama.

Another important question, as we look towards the future of the City, is will the history of the City be repeated? Will the imperial mayoralty of Kevin White, which brought about so much of the Boston we know today, return? Will we revert to the populist impulse, which helped to elect Ray Flynn as the anti-White 30 years ago? Or, will we opt for another "urban mechanic", such as Tom Menino who served an unprecedented five terms and remained popular with voters even as he decided to retire from public life. Public opinion polls in 2013 suggested voters still liked him but were ready for a change at the top. It's anyone's guess how that dynamic will play out. Many years ago, Walter Lippmann wrote, "The law of politics is the law of the pendulum." What he did not write, and what none of us can ever know, is how far the pendulum will swing in one direction and how quickly it might swing back.

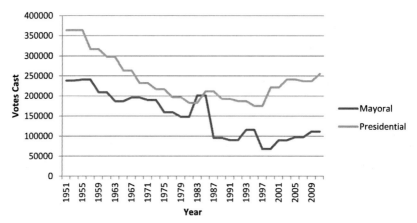

Voter Turnout in Boston Elections.

- Boston reached its population peak in 1950
- Boston's population, like many major cities, declined after 1950
- In recent decades, Boston's population has grown
- The 2010 Census marks the first time since 1970 that Boston's population has been over 600,000

Historic Trends in Boston Population.

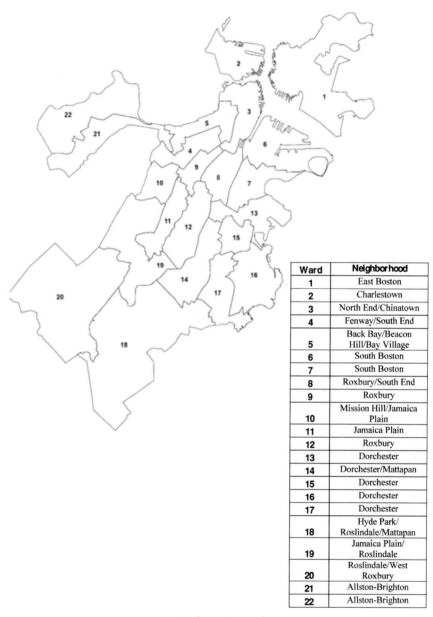

Ward	Neighborhood
1	East Boston
2	Charlestown
3	North End/Chinatown
4	Fenway/South End
5	Back Bay/Beacon Hill/Bay Village
6	South Boston
7	South Boston
8	Roxbury/South End
9	Roxbury
10	Mission Hill/Jamaica Plain
11	Jamaica Plain
12	Roxbury
13	Dorchester
14	Dorchester/Mattapan
15	Dorchester
16	Dorchester
17	Dorchester
18	Hyde Park/Roslindale/Mattapan
19	Jamaica Plain/Roslindale
20	Roslindale/West Roxbury
21	Allston-Brighton
22	Allston-Brighton

Map of Boston Wards.

Election Year	1971	1973	1975	1977	1979
Ward 1	4th	3rd	4th	4th	4th
Ward 2	16th	3rd	11th	12th	9th
Ward 3	5th	3rd	3rd	3rd	3rd
Ward 4	9th	3rd	3rd	2nd	3rd
Ward 5	3rd	1st	1st	2nd	2nd
Ward 6	15th	9th	11th	13th	12th
Ward 7	15th	7th	11th	12th	11th
Ward 8	16th	4th	4th	4th	4th
Ward 9	17th	3rd	3rd	3rd	4th
Ward 10	17th	7th	12th	4th	3rd
Ward 11	16th	4th	7th	6th	2nd
Ward 12	17th	2nd	3rd	3rd	4th
Ward 13	13th	2nd	9th	8th	3rd
Ward 14	17th	2nd	3rd	3rd	4th
Ward 15	13th	4th	11th	10th	5th
Ward 16	6th	3rd	9th	8th	4th
Ward 17	2nd	1st	1st	1st	1st
Ward 18	10th	4th	8th	7th	3rd
Ward 19	11th	4th	9th	7th	2nd
Ward 20	9th	5th	8th	6th	3rd
Ward 21	8th	2nd	3rd	3rd	1st
Ward 22	9th	2nd	6th	3rd	2nd

Larry DiCara's Rank among other candidates by City Council Election year and by Ward.

Related Web sites
The interested reader can find many relevant documents not easily reproduced in a book at the following web sites.

Historic City of Boston Election Commission reports at:
http://www.archive.org/stream/annualreportofbo1975bost#page/88/mode/2up

Current data on Boston Elections and registered voters can be found at the city of Boston Election Commission site:
http://www.cityofboston.gov/boardsandcommissions/elections.asp

The Boston Redevelopment Authority is a wealth of information on the demographics and diversity of Boston.
http://www.bostonredevelopmentauthority.org

The United States Census Bureau conducts a head count of the entire nation every ten years. Their web site has a great deal of comparative and historic data on urban population trends.
http://www.census.gov/population/www/documentation/twps0076/MAtab.pdf

Index

About the Authors

Lawrence S. DiCara is a Boston lawyer and civic leader who served on the Boston City Council for ten years, serving one year as Council President. He is a graduate of Boston Latin School, Harvard College, Suffolk University Law School and the John F. Kennedy School of Government at Harvard. In 1995, he was awarded an honorary doctorate by the University of Massachusetts for his service to the University and to the Commonwealth. DiCara is a partner at Nixon Peabody, a Global 100 law firm, where he specializes in real estate and community development, government relations, and public policy. He has served on the Democratic State Committee for more than 40 years and is sought after by the media and academics as a seasoned and knowledgeable commentator on urban politics. He has taught at the college and graduate school levels, and lectured across the country. He is a lifelong resident of Boston and now lives in the Jamaica Plain neighborhood with his wife Teresa Spillane, a psychologist, and their triplet daughters.

Chris Black is a professional writer and communications consultant. She worked as a newspaper reporter and television correspondent for more than 30 years and has known Larry since his days on the Boston City Council. She was a longtime political reporter for The Boston Globe and a White House and Congressional Correspondent for CNN. She is a native of Woburn, Massachusetts and honors graduate of Northeastern University. She lives in Washington, D.C. and Marion, Massachusetts with her husband, B. Jay Cooper.